# THE LOST VILLAGE

## IN SEARCH OF A FORGOTTEN RURAL ENGLAND

# RICHARD ASKWITH

D1392795

LARGE PRINT

Oxford

First published in Great Britain 2008
by
Ebury Press


Published in Large Print 2008 by ISIS Publishing Ltd.,
7 Centremead, Osney Mead, Oxford OX2 0ES
by arrangement with
Ebury

**British Library Cataloguing in Publication Data**
Askwith, Richard
  The lost village: in search of a forgotten rural
England. – Large print ed.
  1. Villages – England
  2. Country life – England
  3. Large type books
  4. England – Rural conditions
  5. England – Social life and customs
  I. Title
942'.009734

ISBN 978–0–7531–5685–8 (hb)
ISBN 978–0–7531–5686–5 (pb)


Printed and bound in Great Britain by
T. J. International Ltd., Padstow, Cornwall

*"The further one goes, the less one knows."*
Lao-tzu (6th century BC)

# CONTENTS

# Author's Note

This began as a book about modern village life and ended up as something rather different. I am glad that it did, because what I have ended up with — a collection of voices and stories from the English countryside — seems to me at least as valuable as what I was originally looking for. These are our countrymen and women, and their testimonies are worth listening to.

The book also describes a personal journey, physical and spiritual, in the course of which I learnt many things, including this: the English countryside is full of people — more than 9.5 million of them — who, for obvious reasons, know much more about their particular patches of the land, and their particular rural communities, than I could possibly know. Many are also remarkably well-informed about wider rural and historical issues. I feel presumptious pronouncing at all on so many matters about which I am relatively ignorant. The least I can do is acknowledge my debt to innumerable inhabitants of the English countryside, not just for the facts in this book but also for many of the ideas.

The following are not so much sources as books and archives that I have found particularly helpful. Some have more obvious relevance to *The Lost Village* than others. I warmly recommend them all . . . First, the three great 20th century portraits of individual villages:

*Akenfield* by Ronald Blythe, *The Common Stream* by Rowland Parker, *The Changing English Village* by MK Ashby. On wider issues: *The Death of Rural England* by Alun Howkins, *The World We Have Lost* by Peter Laslett, *The History of the Countryside* by Oliver Rackham, *The Making of the English Landscape* by WG Hoskins, *Country Matters* by Richard Mabey, *England in Particular* by Sue Clifford and Angela King, *Lore of the Land* by Jennifer Westwood and Dr Jacqueline Simpson, *The Villages of England* by Richard Muir, *The English Village* by Leigh Driver, *Commoners: Common Right, Enclosure and Social Change in England, 1700–1820* by JM Neeson.

On more specific or local matters: *Of Pigs and Paupers* by Sheila C Frewin, *The Last Englishman* by Byron Rogers, *Exmoor Village* by Hilary Binding and Brian Pearce, the Exmoor Archive, *Reflections* by Birdie Johnson, the BBC Voices project, *An Historical Walk Around Weston Longville* by Majorie Futter, *Poppyland* by Peter Stibbons and David Cleveland, *Potter Heigham* by Olga Sinclair, the Tolpuddle Martyrs Museum, *Dipping Into the Wells* by Angela Spencer-Harper, *One From the Plough* by Brendon Owen, *Dorset Man* and *Dorset Woman* by James Crowden, Carmela Semeraro and the Martson Vale Oral History Project, *Witton Park: Forever Paradise* by Ken Biggs, Keith Belton and Dale Daniel, *The Isle of Axholme Before Vermuyden* by Dr Joan Thirsk, *Storm Over Axholme* by Stephen R Garner. (This is just the tip of a huge iceberg of often astonishingly erudite works of local history to be found in English villages.

Such expertise is increasingly available online as well, as an internet search on almost any subject touched on in this book will demonstrate.)

My debts to the great English rural authors of previous generations will be self-evident. I am grateful to Faber & Faber Ltd and Farrar, Straus & Giroux LLC for permission to quote from "Going, Going" by Philip Larkin (1972; copyright 1988, 2003 by the Estate of Philip Larkin); and to Faber & Faber Ltd and Harcourt, Inc for permission to quote from "East Coker" by TS Eliot (copyright 1940 by TS Eliot and renewed 1968 by Esme Valerie Eliot). I am also more indebted than I can possibly say to the countless ordinary country people — some mentioned in this book by name and some not — who have shared their time and wisdom with me.

I should also thank Hannah Macdonald and Charlotte Cole at Ebury Press; Mari Roberts; Brie Burkeman; my sister, my wife and my children, for their patience and wise advice; and my fellow villagers, past and present, in both Northamptonshire and Hertfordshire.

The events described in this book were spread out over many months. My written account creates, inevitably, an impression of a simpler chronology. In general, my narrative is presented in the order in which the events occurred. In some places, for convenience, I have departed from strict chronology. In a few places I have disguised personal details that might identify those who would not wish to be identified.

But my main distortion has been to leave stuff out: masses of it — incidents, interviews, villages, whole counties . . . To anyone who is disappointed by omissions in what follows (especially those who were kind enough to help me in my researches), I can only apologise. Rural England and its stories are too big to be contained in a single book.

Richard Askwith

# CHAPTER ONE

# The dying tribe

We had been living abroad for a year. Never mind why. When we came home, our village seemed different. How? We weren't sure.

It wasn't a physical thing. Moreton Pinkney was still the same unremarkable scattering of brown stone Northamptonshire houses, neither pretty nor ugly, zigzagging along an undulating, rather-too-busy country road, with a couple of half-hearted greens and an old sandstone church that no one much went to.

Perhaps the road was busier. Perhaps the people were. I remember walking the length and breadth of the village one weekday morning and meeting no one — just cars hurrying past implacably.

Or perhaps it was us. Our time abroad had been spent in a little French village where children and pets played in the street and few people travelled further than the surrounding vineyards to work. We had grown used to an older, slower, more communal way of life. England jarred.

But there was something else, too. Our fellow villagers had, collectively, changed. Two well-loved older neighbours had moved away in our absence, and another had died; eight other houses — out of 94 — had changed hands in the space of 11 months (average price: £342,000) and five now had "For Sale" signs outside them. At this rate, the village would have an entirely new population within a decade.

That wasn't all. The pub had closed; the sub-post office was closing. The church was sharing its vicar with five other villages. (The school and the shop had closed years ago.) There was still, allegedly, a bus service, but it had grown so infrequent — and was so little used — that they had stopped bothering to stick up a timetable in the old wooden bus shelter.

I won't go on. Such changes had, as I'm sure you know, been taking place all over England.

None the less, these ones bothered me. Everywhere I looked there were bigger cars, new extensions and conversions, garages and conservatories, goals and climbing frames, satellite dishes and security gates — but no slow, bad-toothed, mud-spattered people standing and chatting. Several farmers had sold up and gone. One nearby farm — which hadn't even had electricity when I first visited it a decade or more ago — had become a state-of-the-art equestrian centre, staging prestigious events that attracted the horsey set from miles around — and not, as far as I could tell, farming at all.

"And what's wrong with that?" asked Clare (my wife).

I couldn't quite say.

★ ★ ★

Time passed. We hurried about our daily routines. The skies and hedgerows paled into autumn. From time to time we moaned — to ourselves and to any number of neighbours — about how busy we all seemed to be. From time to time we would meet and begin to get to know some new arrival to the village. From time to time we would pause at the end of our garden and drink in the evening light on the big rabbit-cropped pastures beyond it. Everything was as it used to be — except that something was different.

Then we went to church. It's years since this was something that many people in the village did on a regular basis. But this was Remembrance Sunday, when, for reasons few of us could put our fingers on, large numbers usually turn out. The small 12th-century church was comfortably full, with all sorts: old men with medals, middle-aged women with unaccustomed lipstick, children in hoodies, ex-soldiers in neatly pressed suits and ties, teenagers with sagging jaws and trousers. Every stratum of local life seemed to be represented.

When we moved outside for our two minutes' silence by the war memorial, I counted more than 70 people. What was it, I wondered, that made a community that was neither religious nor militaristic attach such importance to this occasion? There was no clue in the faces: just a generalised air of respect, for someone or something.

During the silence, my mind wandered. I thought initially about the young men named on the war memorial: Leonard Cross, John Osborne; Arthur

Prestidge, Walter Thomason. Who remembered their stories now? All I knew about them was that they died between 1915 and 1918, at the ages of, respectively, 20, 25, 21 and 20, two near the Somme, one at Gallipoli and one in what is now Iraq. What, I wondered, must it have felt like to stand here 80-odd years ago, with four families present whose sons had been freshly slaughtered? Pretty much the whole village — perhaps 400 people — would have stood here then. The English country silence would have sounded the same to them as to us. Yet how different it would have felt. Our sadness — at the passing of time, at lost innocence, at idiotic wars everywhere — was real but remote; theirs was catastrophically close.

A few birds sang. Trees, gold-leafed now, rustled. A bitter wind sliced us from the north; pride kept us from flinching.

I glanced up at the forest of contemplative faces. It bore little resemblance, I realised, to my mental picture of my fellow villagers. Some were strangers; others I knew only vaguely. There were old friends and neighbours as well, but a disturbing number of familiar faces were absent. Where, for example, was little Ken Poynton, bristling with dignity and medals, who always used to present a wreath at this ceremony? Where was Horace Merivale, who used to look after the garden up at the Manor, and who fought at Arnhem? The only men with medals today were from other villages. Where was George Stanton, the quiet farmer whose stooping figure, trudging indomitably across the fields in all weathers, had come to seem like part of the landscape?

4

Where was old Mrs Pratt, whose family memories of the village went back deep into the 19th century?

All dead, of course — as, on reflection, one would expect. The years speed past; the old die. But something had died with them.

Eighty years ago, when the villagers turned out to share the burden of bereavement, they were a *tribe*: the offspring of a network of interconnected families as rooted in the local soil as the trees and hedgerows. One family's son was another's nephew and another's cousin and yet another's prospective son-in-law. There were occasional migrations, in and out, but the majority remained where they were. Even 15 years ago — when I first moved here — that tribe was dominant. The village belonged, by common consent, to them; those of us who had moved in from elsewhere were intruders.

Now the old tribe had all but vanished. As far as I could see, there were only two people present, both widows, who had grown up in the village: Mrs Storer, the organist (and blacksmith's daughter), and Mrs Fisher, who used to live in The Grange. Neither lived in the village any more, though their roots often pulled them back. I could think of three or four other born-and-bred families who still lived in the village, but that was about it.

Did it matter? I wasn't sure. I had nothing against incomers: I was one myself. I knew how much non-natives contributed to village life. What did it matter if we didn't have "three generations in the graveyard"? Yet there was something about the abruptness of the indigenous villagers' vanishing that frightened me, like some medium-sized ecological catastrophe. Before long there really wouldn't be a single one left.

This thought then blended with some of the other concerns in my mental reservoir of generalised middle-aged anxiety: the plans I had read about in that morning's papers to roll out hundreds of thousands of new homes, not to mention roads and runways, across our region of rural England; the collapse of traditional farming; the darkening shadow of climate change. How precarious this all was: the crumbling stonework and crooked gravestones and old, weak-chested villagers. Change and decay, accelerating all around.

To my left, just behind the war memorial, were some other gravestones, leaning and time-worn. Lichen draped their tops in a bright camouflage of white, gold and green. I studied the inscriptions: "In loving memory of George Wright, who died November 21 1908, aged 78 — At rest". And, next door, "In [ . . . ] ory of Alice Wright, who departed this life on May 24 1904, aged 82. The g [ . . . ] of God is eternal [ . . . ] through Jesus [ . . . ] Lord". I wondered, briefly, if any of their descendants survived in the village — I had never knowingly met any. Then I began to wonder how and when, precisely, those missing numerals and letters had disappeared. Had they been dislodged by an especially violent gust of wind, or by a series of particularly big raindrops? Had some ravenous micro-organism taken a couple of bites too many? And how, if it came to that, had the next grave along achieved its current state — total illegibility?

6

Presumably, in such cases, infinitesimally tiny bits keep dropping off until one day so much has gone that the rest can't even be imagined, unless you remember what it originally said. There is never an identifiable moment at which the point of no return is reached — just many moments afterwards when you can say with certainty that the point of no return was passed long ago.

A huge lorry — Heygates Flour — crashed through the cold silence, rattling thunderously through the village. Simultaneously, the words of an old Philip Larkin poem began, for some reason, to rattle in my head:

> I thought it would last my time —
> The sense that, beyond the town,
> There would always be fields and farms,
> Where the village louts could climb
> Such trees as were not cut down . . .

How did it go? There was more, I knew, but I couldn't quite get a fix on it. Something else, and then:

> It seems, just now,
> To be happening so very fast . . .

something, something . . .

> For the first time I feel somehow
> That it isn't going to last . . .

A bugle blew (courtesy of the Royal British Legion). A bemedalled old man and a young boy whom I had never seen before walked up to lay wreaths at the base of the memorial; as they walked back, the old man put his hand on the boy's shoulder. I looked again at the watching faces and saw — I thought — tears on three. It was hard to be certain, because my own eyes had clouded.

There was so much to weep for: not just the bitterness of death, and the ebbing away of memory, and the hundreds of thousands of brave little soldiers who have grown up and still grow up to have their hearts and bodies broken in battle, but the fact that — 35 years after he wrote them — the truth of Larkin's words had suddenly struck me. It — this village — wasn't going to last.

Oh, the buildings would last; the fields and woods had a few more generations left in them yet. A handful of born-and-bred villagers would no doubt survive for a while. But the actual village — that miniature, self-contained eco-system in which past and present were all tangled up, and people, buildings and vegetation shared one reasonably coherent collective story — that village had passed away long ago.

This realisation (which some people might classify as bleeding obvious) almost winded me. I felt bereaved. I had lived in this village for just a decade and a half, but I had thought of myself as a villager — in a broader sense — for as long as I could remember. Earlier in my life, the village in question had been Green Tye, in a quiet backwater of Hertfordshire. I wasn't quite sentimental enough to think of myself as, in either case, a true member of the village in question. My parents were white-collar country people, and so was I. I spent most of my school holidays working and playing on various farms, but I was away and earning my living in distinctly non-agricultural ways as soon as I was old and educated enough to do so. More recently, I had often been away from Moreton Pinkney, for work and leisure. Yet through all my travels, and through all stages of my life, I had never lost the sense of having a village near the heart of my mental landscape: a fixed point of continuity, permanence and peace to which I could always return. No matter how rootless, frenetic and metropolitan my own existence, I told myself, the village and its people remained, just beyond the edge of my vision, planted solidly in familiar fields, as they had always been.

Or rather — because I had never consciously thought this through before — perhaps I had imagined something more than that. Perhaps I had assumed that, somewhere in the background of my life, there would always be, not just one village, but a whole network of many thousand villages, each with its own story and its own local families and its own unique landscape and memories and its own peculiar way of saying and doing things. In short, I had imagined rural England, and had blithely gone through life (eagerly embracing the modern wherever I found it) under the impression that it would always be there, like a great rock, with the past clinging to it like lichen.

Now, when I turned to look at it, it was gone.

We filed back into the cold church. As we did so, a few more lines of Larkin's poem came back to me, and echoed in my head as if I had never forgotten them, with the dull clarity of a muffled funeral bell:

> And that will be England gone,
> The shadows, the meadows, the lanes,
> The guildhalls, the carved choirs.
> There'll be books; it will linger on
> In galleries; but all that remains
> For us will be concrete and tyres.

Three decades later, that same train of thought had crashed into me.

# CHAPTER
# TWO

# A journey

I decided to go on a quest. Well, I called it a quest. My wife called it a midlife crisis.

It was a long time gestating. For months, my nostalgia had darkened. By the following autumn it was a melancholy obsession. Where other people saw the countryside, I saw a giant graveyard, haunted by the ghosts of a lost tribe that had once imagined that its lifestyle would last for ever. Where others saw rolling green fields, I saw the abandoned ridge-and-furrow corrugations of the dead. Where others saw villages — my own village, friends' villages, villages I just happened to be passing through — I saw the ruins of a collapsed civilisation, no more connected to modern life than the remains of Hadrian's Wall. Yes, there were people living in them. But they were a new breed, adapting the physical remains of rural England for the purposes of their new, post-agricultural society — in the same way that, in the fifth and sixth centuries, post-Roman Italians broke and baked the marbles of antiquity to make plaster for their pre-medieval huts.

And the question that kept nagging at me was: was that it? Was that really "England gone"? Or might there still be places where living remnants of the lost rural past survived — in the same way that some ancient Britons held out in England's wild places long after the Roman conquest?

There was only one way to find out.

One fine morning, without any clear idea of what I was doing, I set out in search of this (possibly imaginary) lost rural world. I had saved up a large chunk of annual leave from my job as a commuting journalist, so it wasn't entirely impractical (I thought) to spend a few weeks on the road. Just — as my daughter put it — a bit odd.

Attached to my quest was a vow: I would travel as people used to travel — in books, and perhaps also in reality — with a light, hopeful heart. Like most English people of my generation, I have spent much of my life in transit, usually grudgingly: rushing to work, dashing to the supermarket, ferrying children, sitting in traffic jams, racing to beat the bank-holiday crowds, polluting and congesting and endangering life. But I was also aware of another mode of journeying, from the same half-remembered, half-imaginary old England I was seeking. In that land, travellers would stride out bravely on summer mornings, heads filled not with the ticking of a clock but with breezes and birdsong, and be delighted to embrace whatever adventures befell them — floods, yokels, brigands, damsels, giants . . . the more the merrier.

So it would be with me, I decided, as I kissed my family goodbye and drove into the unknown.

Well, it was actually the known. I left on the little back lane to Weston, as I had done thousands of times before, and my elderly Nissan Micra seemed happy enough to proceed on autopilot as we creaked around familiar bends. None the less, I felt supercharged with adventure. The radio chattered about rail strikes and gridlock on the M25. Very well: I turned the radio off. I am, I said to myself, a free Englishman; I am in good health, in peacetime, happily married, gainfully employed, only moderately in debt. I am setting out to explore my favourite country. How else should I travel, except in hope?

I opened the window and breathed in the damp, fresh smell of English fields. The air was clean from a recent downpour, the sky glowed with a deep, warm blue; the hedgerows were spotted with blood-red hawthorn berries, rich as wet paint; the meadows were thick with bright green grass, with springy mud beneath. In short, it was just the sort of day I imagined as the backdrop to all those other glad, life-affirming journeys that were so tied up with my idea of England's past.

Which journeys? I don't think I really knew. My working vision of the rural past was — like most rural nostalgia — blurred around the edges and light on specifics. I suppose that, if pressed, I might have fallen back on English literature and muttered something about Laurie Lee, walking out "one midsummer morning" from his Gloucestershire cottage in 1934, or William Cobbett on his "rural rides" in the 1820s; Mr Pickwick setting out with "his notebook in his waistcoat, ready for the reception of any discoveries worthy of being noted down"; Bunyan's Christian, or Fielding's Tom Jones, or Malory's Sir Lancelot, or even Langland's Piers Plowman, rigging himself out "in shaggy woollen clothes" and setting out to "roam far and wide through the world, hoping to hear of marvels".

A more honest reply might have involved *The Wind in the Willows* or Tolkien's *The Hobbit*, and my immature yearning for the unthreatening adventures of childhood stories. More honest still: that I just had a vague, unsubstantiated hunch that the romance of the English countryside and the romance of the English journey were intertwined.

But there was at least one bona fide predecessor. Eighty years earlier, another English journalist embarked on a similar adventure, with, as he put it, "the road calling me out into England". On an April morning in 1926, Henry Vollam Morton, a 33-year-old feature-writer with the *Daily Express*, set out from London in a bull-nosed Morris on a self-imposed mission to find the England of his and others' imagination.

His premise was (for a while) famous: seriously ill in Palestine, he became homesick for a rural homeland of high-hedged lanes and wood smoke in autumnal village streets, where the setting sun "leaves a dull red bar low down in the west, and against it the elms grow blacker minute by minute". Returning to health and home, he realised that his nostalgic yearning was both illogical (he was a Londoner) and widely shared. English exiles, he reasoned, always see such rural idylls when they think of England — even if in reality they have little or no direct experience of them. Green fields and thatched roofs stand as a kind of emotional shorthand for the real land of our experience — because "the village and the English countryside are the germs of all we are". That was the England that the soldiers he had fought with in the Great War had imagined themselves to be fighting for, even if they had hardly seen it. And now — having hardly seen it himself — he was going to go out and see how much of that green and pleasant land really existed.

His account of his quest — published first as a series of articles and then in a book — made him famous and rich. *In Search of England* has sold more than a million copies and remains in print today. In a sense, this is odd. Morton was a nasty man: an anti-Semite and a snob who admired Nazi Germany and confessed to his diary that "I loathe the very word Democracy"; the cheerful charm of his writing only partially conceals his nastiness. There is a patronising edge to his treatment of the comedy yokels and blushing wenches he encounters on his travels, and you would never guess that, during much of his journey, the country was convulsed by the General Strike. At times it is hard to avoid the suspicion that he has simply made things up.

Yet his narrative has a momentum that makes it, for all its faults, irresistible. And there was a rightness to his premise that shone through his journalistic insincerities, and that still shines through them now. Even today, when 90 per cent of the UK population lives in towns and cities, and less than 2 per cent of the population works on the land, and one in 10 of us was born abroad, do many of us ever encounter the word "England" without at least momentarily imagining a soft, green, timeless landscape of village greens, old cottages and tangled hedgerows in which calm, solid country people coexist with a mist of gentle history?

If such an ideal is patently imaginary, that doesn't make it less potent. And I, at least, felt intoxicated by it as I set out to see if any of that England survived.

# CHAPTER
# THREE

# Into the woods

I soon sobered up. My initial meanderings took me through familiar villages such as Weston, Weedon Lois, Wappenham, Helmdon, Greatworth, Farthinghoe, Cottisford, Hethe, Hardwick and Stoke Lyne. Each had its charming cottages and pleasing views, but I could sense no trace of my imagined England in any of them.

I stopped now and then but my heart wasn't in it. Such passers-by as I could find were no stranger than I was. In a couple of cases they were people I already knew. No farmers leant enigmatically on five-bar gates; no old men gawped (as they did in Morton's day) at the arrival of a strange motorist. There was, in short, no rural wildness. Instead, each village seemed normal: dissected by the same wide grey road, with white lines and bollards and black-and-white "sharp bend" signs in sensible places. Every pavement was empty; each garden gate closed; each house-face expressionless; and the same chunky, multi-coloured necklace of parked cars was draped around everything. No doubt each had its secrets, but none commended itself as a gateway to adventure.

I took to the motorway — thinking to start again further from home — and was surprised to find that, as the river of vehicles bore me smoothly southwards, slices of the land I was seeking began to appear. This sounds bizarre, yet there they were: every few minutes, among the damp meadows and thick-hedged pastures that glinted green and silver on either side, I would catch a glimpse that provoked an overwhelming sense of looking into the rural past.

Typically, I would see a cluster of distant trees, dense as broccoli, on the crest of a hill, with a few old cottage roofs alongside and, rising above the leaves, an old stone church tower, its needle-sharp spire a still pinpoint of eternity. Variations included: an old farm glimpsed from the back, its sagging sheds and rusting machinery being eroded by nature and time in what their owner probably imagined was privacy; a cottage in a field, apparently deserted, with the front door and gate hanging open; a herd of cows being driven up a tiny mud-smeared lane; an overgrown riverside hut.

It doesn't sound magical in print. It was when seen from the corner of my eye. Try it next time you're on one of the bigger, straighter motorways. Instead of encountering villages at their point of interface with the road, you catch them from, as it were, backstage. Thus you bypass the usual clutter of overwrought 21st-century life and see instead an older, more peaceful land: a place of stillness and permanence and slow-growing vegetation, where every field and copse and cottage and shed has its own secret store of

memories, waiting for someone to unlock them. All I
had to do was find them.

I turned off somewhere south of Oxford — and
immediately felt myself tugged back into the turbulent
but numbing stream of the mechanised, unmysterious
present. Traffic jostled; rumbling lorries loomed and
belched. The roadsides bristled with lights, signs and
speed cameras attempting to keep the rush in check —
with little success. Each time I slowed down to consider
my surroundings, bad-tempered queues of cars formed
instantly on my tail, and I could think of nothing more
sensible to do than to keep driving, taking the line of
least resistance at each junction. I had little idea of
where I was, and the incessant instructions and
exhortations did little to enlighten me: "Ring road!"
they snapped. "Superstore!", "Country club!",
"Champagne happy hour!", "Polo!"; "Luxury cattery!";
"Exclusive Apartments!", "Two-way traffic!", "Watch
your speed!", "Take extra care — 172 casualties in
three years!", "Oxford Thames Four Pillars Hotel!",
"Oxford Science Park!", "Littlemore Park!", "European
School!", "Park and ride!", "Caravan and camping
site!", "Recycling and waste centre!", "City centre!",
"Garden centre!", "Slow!". It was like having a nagging
parent in the car.

Eventually, among some wooded hills near the bottom
of Oxfordshire, I stopped at a smart village of about
300 houses called Stoke Row, whose attractions
included a rusting metal structure, the size and shape
of a bandstand, around whose roof were inscribed the

words "His Highness the Maharajah of Benares". I am indebted to a nice old man called John Pitt for the information (no doubt familiar to many) that this structure conceals a well, whose creation was funded by the aforementioned Maharajah in the mid-19th century because he was so moved by the stories of the villagers' poverty that he had been told by the local squire's son, Edward Reade, when the latter was out in India. Reade had dwelt particularly on the lack of a clean water supply (villagers being "dependent for water retained in dirty ponds and deserted claypits", according to one letter, while "water used in cooking in one cottage was passed on to do the like office in others, urchins being cruelly thumped for furtive quenchings of thirst and washing days being indefinitely postponed").

"It goes 365ft deep, I think," said Mr Pitt, a small, smiling, white-haired man who was born in the village 76 years ago, "and it was all dug by hand. We used to get our water from it. We lived in that cottage there — it used to be two cottages then. My brother's pigeons used to get on the roof, so you can imagine what the water was like.

"But when the doctor used to come to the village, my mother used to let him use our front room as his surgery. She'd put out a jug of water from the well and he'd mix up his medicines with it. I often wonder if it was the medicine or the water that got the people better."

The Maharajah also funded the creation of a neighbouring cherry orchard, whose proceeds were to fund the employment of a well-warden, as well as a tiny, octagonal well-warden's cottage. The last well-warden was a Miss Turner, the local schoolmistress, who died in 1972. The lodge is now a private dwelling; little remains of the orchard, and the well is boarded over. Why? Mr Pitt rolled his bright blue eyes. "Health and safety, or whatever they call it."

The tale of the well intrigued me — the village's current prosperity can arguably be traced back to that far-sighted act of unilateral international aid — but I was no less interested in Mr Pitt himself. He had spent much of his life in the village — although for the past 30 years he had lived in the adjoining hamlet of Gallowstree Common — and was happy to share his memories of it. We spent some time driving round the area together, and he also gave me coffee in his house, which he had built himself.

He had, he explained, done well for himself, through years of hard work in the car-repair business, but his childhood had been a poor one. "We were extremely hard up," he said cheerfully. "It was hand-to-mouth, pretty well — especially when my father was ill and couldn't work. I remember once they held a whist drive for us, because we had so little. But I think most families in the village were pretty hard done by in those days.

"We didn't have water; we didn't have electric. We never had new clothes, and we certainly didn't have toys. I don't think we ever actually went hungry, though — you could always get food from the land, you see, and there was always rabbits. I used to go out with a mate on Sundays. He'd have the gun and I'd have the ferret — you could get three-and-six for a rabbit, if you gutted it, so it was worth doing.

"Everyone worked wherever they could. My dad was a journeyman decorator, but that only kept him going in the summer. In the winter I'd help him working on Mr Greenaway's thrashing machine. That was a dirty old job, if you were on the end where the chaff was coming out. Oh, terrible."

He chuckled, crinkling his face along well-worn laughter-lines. The memory seemed to warm him. "It was a happy childhood," he confirmed. "A lot of our day consisted of roaming in the woods. We'd be gone all day. Our parents never used to worry — they knew we'd be safe. The older children looked after the younger ones, and everyone knew everyone anyway. If there was ever a stranger about, the whole village would have known about it in 10 minutes.

"It's different today. It's changed out of recognition. There are still community activities — there's lots of things you can join — but it's not a community like we had when we were children. Nobody locked their doors then. But that's gone."

We drove in and out of a bewildering lattice of lanes, among tall, mysterious beech trees, as Mr Pitt pointed out old and new features. There were considerably more of the latter. "I reckon the housing here has trebled since I was a child. Look, those have all been built since I was growing up. And all those houses down there have all been built . . . That was a blacksmith's shop . . . That was a carpenter's shop — if someone died you'd see them making a coffin there . . . And a

22

lady lived here who used to make boiled sweets . . . That's new . . . So's that . . . My mother used to put her washing out on this piece of land here, but the guy who lived just there, Geoff Page, he kept goats, and the bloody goats used to eat the washing . . . That used to be a pond . . . There's another place been developed down there . . . And this" — a former mental asylum on the outskirts — "has all been converted to very, very posh flats, a million and a quarter."

No one could dispute the prosperity of the place: there were businesses operating under such headings as (to name just a few): architect, antiques restorer, classic cars, graphic design, kitchens, exhibition construction, photography, precision engineers, racing-engine reconditioning and marine-equipment supply. Had the Stoke Row of his childhood vanished? "Not exactly. But the world has changed a lot. I still feel part of the village: I wouldn't want to move. But most people there don't know me.

"The woods haven't changed so much, though," he added, as a threadbare lane took us back into the depths of the forest. For the first time in a long while, I felt that I was in a countryside older than myself. Cold light played mesmerically on the pale, upright trunks, which seemed to stretch indefinitely and identically in all directions; I could imagine getting badly lost here. "I'd never get lost in these woods — even in the dark," Mr Pitt declared. "And I wouldn't want a torch, either. I can still walk from here to Ipsden and only cross a couple of roads."

He showed me a clearing where the US army had had a camp in World War II. "Then after D-Day they put barbed wire all round it and put German prisoners here. They had guns all around. And then after the war people from Reading — people who'd been bombed out — began to come up here to squat. My father and I helped make the huts a bit nicer for them.

"I used to walk for miles in these woods as a child. Everyone did — a lot of people worked in them. There weren't even paths, but we knew it all backwards. I knew where all the tent-peg shops were."

Shops?

"Not real shops. They were like outdoor workshops — the places where the bodgers and people worked.

"It was the main industry then. Not just chair legs, but brushes — Star Brush in the village used to employ about 40 people — and pit props — I remember doing that with my father on Streetly Hill, sawing small fir trees to the right length. We'd cycle about two hours to get there. And then there was tent pegs, of course — they'd do that with a spoke shave, on a horse. Have you seen those horses that they sit on — they're like three-legged benches? Anyway, in the war they made several million tent pegs for the army. And rifle butts, obviously."

Those were good times — in the economic sense. But they weren't easy. "It was pretty cold. I remember that. The trees would be felled in the wintertime, you see. And you have to do it straight after they've been cut down, or it would get to be too hard, whereas the green wood turns easily with a pole lathe, and you can just put the chisel into it.

"So the bodgers and people would do their work in a 'shop', which would be made with three or four poles with some old galvanised as a roof, a bit of sackcloth hanging down, and then slowly you stacked the shavings of the wood from the work into a good wall all the way round to keep the winds and the cold out as much as possible.

"I used to look after Silas Saunders's shop," he said proudly. I don't think I looked as impressed as I should have done. "His chair legs were famous. I think he stopped making them in 1961. I must have been about 12, maybe 13, when I worked for him. I was only rolling the wood, of course, but it was very interesting to watch him. The wood was cut into lengths, and then it was rolled down to where we were working in the wood, near Herrold Farm, where my mother used to be in service before she married my father. And these would then be what they call 'bodged', using a wooden mallet — you'd split them into almost like a triangle, roughly, and then from that you would shape it up a bit with an axe, and then they would go on to a pole lathe. And then he would produce from that chair legs of various lengths, and then of course the spars between the chair legs, and then they were all stacked out in the open air to dry. And then we'd take them to Wycombe in a horse and cart to be finished.

"I'd clear the shavings up for him mainly, and look after his shop. I was still at school then, and I did it until I left, when I was 14. You couldn't make much money from it, but it was interesting work — the knack of it."

There are, apparently, 24 movements involved in making a tent peg. The best way to learn them is to do so as a child. And the best way of dealing with the blisters that frequently arise in their making is to pass a needle and thread through them, drawing off the liquid while leaving a largely intact layer of hardened skin.

The lane brought us back into the village. "Look," he said, "there's the Cherry Tree. That's where we had our 'codgers and bodgers' dinner last year. There's a group of us that get together every year. Not all of us have been bodgers, though, because people keep dying off, and each time they do we bring in someone new. It's very nice there, very good food. But it's very different from how it was. Pubs are all about food now, and not about just sitting and chatting. So you don't get the local characters, not like you used to.

"Many, many years ago when we used to go to the Cherry Tree, this old boy used to sit there, Bert Carter. He was a funny old boy. Used to smoke this little clay pipe — I remember he used to smoke it upside down if it rained. I used to take my dad's saw down to him, and he used to sharpen that for sixpence, on a Sunday morning. Anyway, he used to sit on one side of the fire, all snugged up. It was only a tiny fire and he'd sit there having a pint. And they said to him one night, 'Bert, you'll have to move.' He must have been well into his eighties. And they said: 'You'll have to move, Bert. The chimney's on fire.' He said: 'Not bloody likely.' He said: 'It's the best fire we've had here, and I ain't leaving.'

"Eventually they got him out. But the fire went on for three days — it got up in the timbers and under the floor, and they had a hell of a job to get it out.

"And this," he added, pausing outside another pub, "is where that actress got married — what's her name?" The Crooked Billet was, I discovered later, famous among connoisseurs of gastropubs, as well as being a popular film location: its white-walled, black-shuttered, low-beamed aspect suggests, rightly, a long history. Dick Turpin used to go out with the landlady's daughter. (Not the current one, obviously.) A more recent landlord was known for his habit of dozing in front of the fire, leaving customers to serve themselves from the barrels in the cellar and to leave the correct money on the kitchen table. But Mr Pitt was more interested in an earlier incumbent. "This was Silas Saunders's place. He used to keep his pole lathe there, and he'd use it there too." He also kept a horse that liked to wander out of its paddock and stick its head through the stable-style front door to be served beer.

"The food's good there, too," said Mr Pitt. "I suppose it is in most pubs these days. You have to go a long way to find a pub that doesn't do food. But this one's very upmarket. Kate Winslet — that's the name. She had her wedding here, in a marquee."

# CHAPTER
# FOUR

# High-fliers

I turned back up into Oxfordshire in search of the Cotswolds. It took a while to find them. On my way, I stopped at many villages, and bothered many innocent villagers, without ever feeling that I was quite on the right track yet. The prosperity dazzled me: the country clubs, the award-winning gastropubs, the delicatessens, the luxury boarding kennels, the car showrooms; the friendly entrepreneurs taking afternoon strolls and the ladies of leisure chatting in tea-rooms; and, in a different way, the ubiquitous signs of warning to other passers-by: "Private", "Keep out", "Beware of the dog", "No cold callers" and "This is a Neighbourhood Watch area".

Every now and then, I would have a brief encounter that suggested a wilder, more primitive countryside. In Nuneham Courtenay, for example (the original for Oliver Goldsmith's great poem of 18th-century rural dispossession, "The Deserted Village"), I stood outside a defunct motorcycle shop opposite a boarded-up pub — and just up the road from an ex-post office and a fire-damaged school — and spoke to an immense 70-year-old lorry-driver from Banbury who had grown up on the Oxfordshire-Northamptonshire borders. He had, he said, started out as a farm labourer. "I was driving a tractor when I was six. Never went to school. All through the summer, everyone would be out on the harvest. Driving tractor was the easiest bit, so that was my job. Never learnt to write nothing — I still can't."

He seemed quite proud of this, grinning toothlessly while the wind flapped his thin black hair over his tanned forehead. "But that's all gone long ago," he added. "Since combines came in, there wasn't the work."

He was still interested in old farming methods, but his real passion was old motorbikes, which he collected and restored in his retirement. "I always loved bikes," he explained, in a thick Oxfordshire burr. "I eloped to Gretna Green on one. I was 21 and my wife was 16. My parents never knew I was married until weeks later."

A little further north, in a field near Banbury, I met an 82-year-old tractor enthusiast with wind-reddened cheeks and watery eyes who lived on the western edge of the town and had been a farm labourer until 1951. "I went to a factory on £7 a week. It was a big rise, and it was the first time I was ever able to take a holiday." I know he was a tractor enthusiast because that was what he wanted to talk about: Fordsons, "Fergies", Marshalls; trailer ploughs, mounted ploughs; various engine designs and parts whose details, I'm afraid, were lost on me. But from time to time he let slip a memory of his early life in the fields.

"It was blooming hard work in them days," he said. "I used to carry two-hundredweight bags on my back — two and a half hundredweight for beans." This was hard to believe: he was stooped and thin and looked as though the wind might blow him over. "Of course, now you're not allowed to carry more than half a hundredweight — health and safety." A hundredweight, in case you were wondering, is about 50 kg. How was his back today, I wondered? "My back's fine. It's the rest of me that's the problem. That's why I've had to have two new knee joints."

Then he said: "I started with the horses, ploughing. If you did three-quarters of an acre in a day with horses you did well. I was only ever so young when I did that — I just left school. I only did it when the one what was in charge of the horses was sick. Well, these horses, they knew more about the job than what I did. They did, honestly, because when you turned up at the end, they know where to go back in better than what I did. Mind you," he added, "I didn't like walking behind horses when we see these tractors come out. I wanted a tractor."

On a busy junction just outside Bourton-on-the-Water, I stopped to inspect an old-fashioned gypsy caravan, where a handsome, weather-beaten woman was grooming a great piebald horse that every now and then flinched at the passing of a high-speed lorry.

Wasn't it getting a bit dangerous, I asked her, living like this, in the age of the 24-hour rural rush-hour? "It's not so bad, if you travel at the right times. I been here, there and everywhere, to be honest with you. But I keep to places I know actually, to be honest with you.

"I been doing this a long time," she added. "A good few many years. I live like this all the time."

She showed me the caravan, whose floor area was no bigger than a large double bed. "It's very old: 19-0-12 or something. My husband knows more about it. But it keeps us warm."

She earned most of their living by doing palm and tarot readings for passers-by. "No one ever learnt me. My mum used to do it and my nan used to do it, so it's been around me all my life. It's self-taught: everything I do is self-taught. No one ever learnt me anything." It was, she added, hard to get much business at this late time of year. "In the winter, I might get one, I might not get none. It's hard in the winter to earn a living. So what I do, I work hard in summer to earn a bit, to take my ease in the winter."

It seemed churlish not to let her do a reading for me. She "revealed" a few things that I suspect would be obvious to anyone who met me: "You don't enjoy your life enough"; "Sometimes you look into things too deep in your mind." Then she said: "I can say that you are going to be doing a lot of travelling. And I can say that this is going to be very positive for you.

"Yes," she concluded with satisfaction, "I can see a lot of travelling."

I did as she foretold, wandering for days along many nameless Oxfordshire and Gloucestershire lanes, heading where I could for higher, less populated ground and wondering often at the blue-and-green haze of Cotswold hills in all directions. Birds swooped playfully; hedgerows bristled; small trees cast occasional shadows. Everything else seemed dusted with traces of pale dry mud. The Cotswolds can't have looked much different to Laurie Lee. The only strange thing was that, though I rattled for miles among pastures and wheat-fields, I never saw a single farm worker. The fields were empty.

Every now and then, a grubby signpost would draw my attention to a nearby village with another evocative name: Westcote, Little Farringdon, Toddington, Winchcombe — yes, they all sounded familiar. More careful consideration reminded me that the resonance derived, in each case, from the village's links with the cult of celebrity. (Readers of *Heat* or *Hello!* will immediately recognise the four villages just mentioned as the country seats of, respectively, Kate Winslet and Sam Mendes, Kate Moss, Damien Hirst and Elizabeth Hurley.)

No matter how narrow and dishevelled the lanes I chose, a sense of metropolitan glamour pervaded them. Look, that was where the best-selling author lived; that was where that TV chef lived; that was where that famous newspaper editor lived; and wasn't that where Jeremy Clarkson lived? I was reminded of a phrase I had read recently in an article by another famous Cotswold-dweller, the Blur guitarist Alex James (who lives in Kingham). "Cotswold high-fliers", he had called them, approvingly. I could think of no reason not to share his approval; none the less, I didn't. I was looking for an older England.

On the outskirts of Guiting Power, I peered through a gap in a low stone wall at a rich, empty meadow and a tumbledown stone shed, half hidden in the long grass, with a big black hole in one side that might or might not have been an intentional doorway. I am pretty sure, but not certain, that this was the very cattle-shed that was subsequently sold at auction for £325,000 — real estate being so precious in these parts that even the most basic building has development potential. What struck me at the time was how profoundly uncommercial it all felt: the sleepy, deserted lane, the derelict shed, the scent of dew-freshened English fields, the bright singing of the birds. For a moment I felt an overpowering sense of a different countryside: an organic, ancient place where every life-story was enacted in the same living sea of natural sounds and smells — birds, insects, beasts, weather — whose ebb and flow imparted an unavoidable sense of being part of something bigger than oneself.

Later, I reflected on the fact that this field, too, had been empty; that the shed, which must once have had a purpose, had clearly been abandoned for years. Had the farmers just given up and gone?

A little way off, I found a farm. Well, a farm of sorts. On the one hand, Cotswold Farm Park was everything you would expect an authentic English farm to be, with traditional — and rare — breeds of sheep, cows, pigs, goats and chickens. On the other, it was itself an example of a new breed: the farm whose main *raison*

33

*d'être* isn't agricultural but educational. People visit it in order to learn about what farms used to be like. It was rather well done: you wouldn't normally get that close up to a Cotswold Lion — the shaggy-fringed, all-but-dreadlocked sheep whose luxuriant fleeces were the main source of the region's wealth (and of its grand churches and houses), from the Middle Ages onwards. But that didn't make it feel real. On the contrary, it was plainly part of the 21st-century leisure industry. There must have been 200 cars in the car park when I visited — maybe it was half-term in Gloucestershire? — and the paths were full of the same harassed-looking parents and ice-cream-stained children that you meet in any visitor attraction, urban or rural, with the same play area and picnic area and café and gift shop. "This is crap," said a fat boy of about seven or eight as I passed him on a path. I don't know what he was referring to. His father pretended not to hear.

"Step into living history", invited the Farm Park's publicity material, which also boasted that "we have supplied animals for David Attenborough Natural History programmes, as well as period dramas and feature films". The Park's owner was a television celebrity himself: Adam Henson, presenter of *Countryfile*. And good luck to him, I said to myself. But he, like me, was a member of the species *Homo media* — not the old, endangered *Homo rusticus*.

A few miles to the east I came to a long stone farmstead. A sign outside read "Daylesford Organic Farmshop: seasonal organic vegetables, organic meats, fine cheeses, artisan baked goods". I stopped. Daylesford is famous. Founded by the wife of bulldozer magnate Anthony Bamford in the early 1990s, it has been described as "the poshest shop in England". To others it is "the Harrods of the Cotswolds". We'd even heard of it in Northamptonshire.

I parked among polished convertibles with personalised number plates and walked into what felt like an exclusive country club. The site included not just a farm shop — a stunning high-roofed barn conversion with lots of pale wood and absurdly large numbers of absurdly good-looking staff in pale aprons — but at least three other barn conversions: one selling "luxury clothes and objects for the home", another selling "all things horticultural" and one devoted to yoga. There was also a Chinese Tea House, where shoppers were invited "to be revitalised as you sip freshly infused rare teas", which had "special medicinal properties for cleansing the system, and acting as anti-oxidants while they refresh you and delight your senses with their delicate fragrance", and a gleaming toilet block — marked "Loos" — in which you could happily have eaten your organic dinner.

I browsed for a while in the farm shop, among the balsamic vinaigrette, sesame dressing, sun-dried tomato pesto, apple-and-garlic jelly and butternut, sage and honey soup and eight different flavours of salt, hoping to spot a celebrity: Kate Moss and Elizabeth Hurley are often seen there, as is Alex James.

None of these were in evidence. But I did get a strong sense that the slim, expensively dressed cappuccino-drinkers in the farm-shop café were highish-fliers, at least. One young mother was telling another about a weekend trip to the south of France, while their toddlers gorged on organic pastries. A balding man with baggy jeans and a vaguely creative air was reading *GQ*. A middle-aged man with a goatee was telling a pretty young woman about his builders. "Nearly all the blokes doing up my house are wurzels," he explained. "It's quite hard to understand a lot of what they say."

I should perhaps have felt shocked by this remark, but I didn't. I was too busy thinking about glossy magazines, and, specifically, about celebrities. What is it, I wondered, that makes so many of us so hungry to learn about their lives? Presumably we feel that their world is in some sense more vivid than ours — more *real*; and that, by studying the minutiae of their individual dramas, we can get a flavour of what it would be like to inhabit that world.

The drawback is that Planet Celebrity tends, in practice, to be quite a dull place, in which most lives follow the same predictable zero-to-hero trajectory and all normal priorities are distorted by the non-negotiable imperatives of image-maintenance.

Yet the principle is sound. Find out about the lives of individuals — hear their stories and their voices — and you get a glimpse of their world. In which case, shouldn't I apply that principle to my own searching?

Until now, I had vaguely imagined that, in looking for a lost rural England, I was seeking a physical place: some settlement that had for some reason remained untouched by the social and technological revolutions of the past 50 years. Yet this was, clearly, an improbably long shot. But if I focused instead on individuals — on listening to specific voices and personal stories — I might yet find a gateway into the past.

I made a new resolution: as I travelled through England — not necessarily all in one go — I would concentrate on seeking out and interviewing the non-celebrities of the countryside. I wasn't sure what I could expect to learn from them; but I was sure that, if I listened to enough voices, something valuable would emerge.

On the edge of Kingham, a mile or so to the south, I found myself on a lane of stone cottages that petered out into a wide field of short green wheat, with empty slopes falling away beyond. The cottage adjoining it belonged to John Cooper: a 75-year-old ex-saddler who had lived in the village all his life. He invited me in for coffee.

"I'm quite happy here," he told me, small blue eyes smiling beneath thin white hair. "Never considered living anywhere else." The house was neat and comfortable and not remotely like the popular image of a dark, low-beamed rustic cottage. Nor, for that matter, did he resemble my crude stereotype of an ancient, earth-encrusted cottager — except possibly for the broad, brown forearms that bulged from his rolled-up checked shirt-sleeves. Yet there was something in the way he spoke — with warm, unhurried Oxfordshire vowels — that made me glad to have met him.

Was he born in the house? "I came here 50 years ago, when I married. Before that I was just down the other end of this lane, back that way. That's where I was bred and born. My father was bred and born here too, and his father before him."

Were they real old countrymen? "They both worked on the land. That's all the work there was in those days. But then later on my father had ill health, you see, so he worked mainly around the church. He was gassed in the trenches in France in the First World War, and for the rest of his life he had ill health. So it was a job to get work. He didn't get no pension or nothing. But the parson who was in the rectory in those days took pity on him and found him work as a gardener and church warden and anything else that needed doing round the church. He used to dig graves, stoke up the coke in the heater, ring the bells. He used to ring three bells at a time — one in each hand and a loop in the third for his foot.

"He never complained. But it meant that I always had to do a lot of manual work. We had three chain of allotment to look after, so I'd go and work on that after school. And during the latter part of my schooling we was always having to do things for the war effort. We used to spend a lot of time in the harvest fields, too. Of course, there was no spraying then, so your arms would be red-raw [from thistles] after shucking up the straw for a day. So really you was a bit hamstrung when it came to schooling. I'd have got a better education without any wars."

Did he not enjoy his childhood? "Oh, yes, I did. It was hard — all I ever knew was hard work. But you knew everybody, and you trusted everybody. We all went to school in the village. Everyone played together. There was a lot of us down there where we lived — they used to call the row of houses round the back Babbies' Alley, because everyone had such large families.

"We never had electricity, or sewers, not until way, way after the war. Down where I grew up there was one well to feed 12 houses for water — you used to queue up to get your water, especially on a Monday morning, when it was washing day, for your mother to do the washing. So it was always hard work. But we all used to play in the road. We'd spin a top, or when the man came from Chipping Norton to kill the pigs — everyone had a pig in their garden — he'd give us the bladder and we'd rinse it out and blow it up like a balloon. We were never bored."

It sounded a far cry from the sophisticated Kingham I had seen outside: a place of high-fliers and commuters (there were 113 cars parked at the station, a mile away), with spotless pavements and immaculate, moss-free stone walls. Upmarket local businesses included a tile-making company, a vineyard and a company renovating vintage cars; and, with a range of upmarket hostelries that sold fine art and fine wines (the Tollgate Inn) and offered facilities for helicopters and limousines (the Mill House Hotel), it was easy to see why well-heeled country-dwellers thought so highly of the place.

Had the old Kingham been like that? "There really weren't that many rich people: just the parson, obviously, and then the farmers, I suppose, four or five of them and maybe one or two gentry. But the majority was just ordinary sort of people, either working on the land or going into Chipping Norton for work, which is what I used to do." This involved a hilly four-and-a-half-mile cycle ride in each direction, whatever the weather. He remembered struggling through 6ft snowdrifts on several occasions — "but you were inclined to go, because if you didn't you wouldn't get paid."

And today? "Well, I think we only got two farmers now. The one down here doesn't employ anybody, and the one over there, he just has casual labour — and then obviously they get contract work, when they have combining or ploughing or drilling or hedge-cutting. So there isn't really anyone much working on the land. Most people, if they want to work, they've got to commute." Meanwhile, the price of property has soared. "My sons live in Chipping Norton. They'd love to live in Kingham, but they couldn't afford it.

"A lot's to do with these estate agents. They advertise in London and that, and the Londoners come down here to live, and they can afford more than the ordinary country person."

He didn't seem to mean any of this as a reproach to the present: he said many times how much he liked his fellow villagers, including the newcomers. But each time he spoke about the old days, his eyes and voice became a little more animated. "When I was little, there would have been about 30 or 40 children within about five years' distance of me. Everyone knew everyone. You trusted everyone. But there's only about 10 of us still here.

"Oh, there's still quite a healthy community here — people do muck in a bit. But a lot of it's gone. Years ago, everybody was bred and born, no one ever changed their jobs, you knew everyone personally, even in the neighbouring villages. Nowadays, you can say, 'Good afternoon,' to someone in the street and they'll look at you as if they're thinking, 'What's he talking to me for?' But we break most people in eventually."

He sighed into his empty mug. "There's a walking club in the village now. I go out with them as a sort of guide. We enjoy ourselves. But it was different back then. If you went for a walk, you'd take your catapult and you'd come back with a rabbit or something, because that was the way it was — whether you got your dinner or not. You'd never come back empty-handed."

We walked outside to gaze at the fields behind his house and stood there for a while, watching the wind brush over the winter wheat and the small white clouds tumble above the Cotswolds. "Stow-on-the-Wold is over there," he explained, pointing at one of three distant towns. "Moreton-in-Marsh is over there, and Chipping Norton over there. Of course, it's much more open than it used to be. All round these hedgerows used to be elm trees. But then we had that elm disease that killed them all. I never get tired of looking out here. But there's a lot of things," he added, "that we older villagers have known all our lives, about the countryside, that will die with us."

# CHAPTER
# FIVE

# Clutching at straw

I felt that I was beginning to get somewhere, but also that I had a long way to go, both metaphorically and — since I wanted to see as much of England as possible — literally. I hurried southwards, eventually slowing down in Hampshire, where I stopped a few miles from Andover to explore the thickly thatched streets of a village called Abbotts Ann.

You can't beat a thatched roof as a symbol of the character of rural England. Each one you see was made by a countryman, using not only traditional skills, passed down through the generations, but also traditional materials, grown by other countrymen from English soil. You don't see them anywhere else — they have been banned in towns and cities for centuries. (The new Globe Theatre in Southwark has the only thatched roof that London has seen since the Great Fire of 1666.) And if you live under one, as I did as a child, you realise that each one has its own subtle idiosyncrasies, as instantly recognisable as a loved one's hair. So I felt that I should at least pause here, as there were more thatched roofs than I had ever seen before in such a small space. In fact, this whole corner of northwest Hampshire could reasonably be described as thatch country: even some of the walls have thatched tops, and neighbouring villages such as Wherwell and Goodworth Clatford are famous both for their thatch and for their thatchers.

One of the latter had parked his pick-up truck at the end of what seemed to be Abbotts Ann's main street, outside a little cottage with a steep, low-eaved roof of dark, decaying thatch. His name was Paul Williams, and he was in his mid-forties. You might not have marked him down as a specimen of a dying rural race. With his blue jeans, blue sweatshirt and white baseball cap, he looked just like . . . well, just like any normal modern person. But the pinkness of his face suggested a life of outdoor work, and there was something about his steady gait and gaze that made me think of the calmness of a grazing beast.

"Just packing up for the day," he said. "But Em's still working out the back. Want to take a look?"

His hand, when I shook it, was swollen, hard and cracked. "We've just been on holiday for a couple of weeks," he explained, "so our hands have gone all soft, and now they're getting a bit cut up."

It didn't seem to have interfered with his work, which could be seen plainly on the roof just above us. The crisp new thatch gleamed blond against the old, like freshly applied highlights on dark hair, all trimmed as neatly as a best-turned-out pony.

He came from Goodworth Clatford, from a long line of master-thatchers. "My uncle did it, my grandad did it, my great-uncle — we thatched a lot of houses round

44

here. There used to be lots of thatchers round here who all knew each other, but I'm the only one left in our village — the last of the others retired a couple of years ago. A lot of them come up from Somerset now." He had begun his apprenticeship — with his uncle — as soon as he left school and had assumed that he would remain a thatcher all his working life. Now he wasn't so sure.

"It's nice work, if you can make ends meet. But everything's growing more expensive, and I think a lot of people are putting off getting their roofs done. It's all gone a bit quiet for us at the moment. Ominously quiet. We're rather waiting for the phone to ring. So we're glad to have this one to keep us going for a bit."

He locked the truck and led me through a rickety gate, through a ragged garden and up a rickety wooden ladder at the back of the house. "Do you know anything," he asked as we climbed, "about this new law that says the farmer can't burn my old thatch in his field?" I didn't. "It's the first I've heard of it," he continued. "Apparently it's only just come into force — something to do with Europe, I think. I don't know what I'm supposed to do with it instead. It seems mad."

We reached a low flat roof, where a longer ladder stretched right up the main slope of thatch. Halfway up this stood Emmeline Couch, Paul's partner (professional and personal), with a huge pile of yellow straw resting against the roof next to her. We stood and watched her for a while, as I attempted to follow what she was doing.

45

She took an armful of straw from the pile beside her; thrust it neatly alongside the thatch that was already in place; pinned it in place with a wooden yoke (in effect, a giant split pin); tapped and jostled the ends with her leggatt (a kind of corrugated wooden smoother), rather as an office worker might pat a pile of papers straight after photocopying them; pinned them into place with some split-hazel spars (that is, staples); then took the next armful of straw and began the cycle again. I think that's how it worked, but it was all a bit too fluid to follow precisely. She did it with a smooth, rhythmic grace that made it seem as though she wasn't really doing anything much — yet her sleight of hand was at times too quick to see.

"Is it difficult?" I asked.

"Not really," she said. "I'm just a slow learner."

Paul disagreed. "It is hard, until you've got the knack. You need to pick it up gradually. When I started, I wasn't even allowed on a roof for four years. I had to serve my apprenticeship. And that was 30 years ago."

"I've been doing this for six years," said Emmeline, whose long fair hair almost matched the new thatch. "You're meant to be able to do it after five."

I said that she seemed pretty good at it. "I'm much slower than he is," she said. "I can do most things, but once I get into the rhythm, I find I just start to daydream."

We watched a bit longer, in silence, as the afternoon ebbed away, and looked around us at the peaceful land below. It was easy to see how the daydreaming might take hold. Even at this modest height, we felt strangely detached from the world below. The angry traffic seemed too distant to remember, and my consciousness filled with the same warm breeze that I could see ruffling the clump of tall trees in the distance.

A small, clear chalk stream rippled innocently past the end of the little garden, with wide water-meadows beyond it, stretching northwards towards some sloping parkland. Far above, two buzzards circled; their occasional mews felt — preposterously — as though they had been uttered near by. I watched the brook for a while and thought I saw a fish jump.

"I've seen a couple of trout in it," said a voice behind me, and I realised that Emmeline had come down to join us. She was tall and rather beautiful, with a sleepy-looking face that had caught the sun, and the same slow, amiable way of speaking as Paul. "That's my problem," she added. "I tend to get distracted when I'm meant to be concentrating on thatching."

She was in her mid-twenties, and had got into thatching by accident — rather to the surprise of her parents, who also lived in Goodworth Clatford — when another labourer failed to turn up and Paul, her boyfriend, was desperate for help. "I found I really enjoyed it, so I stuck at it." Before that — I learnt later — she had been a cow-girl in Australia and a landscape gardener in Spain, as well as being a gifted pianist. You might not have guessed this last fact from her hands, which were, like Paul's, rough and raw.

We gathered up the remaining tools — mallet, shears, leggatt, kneepads, ladder — and gazed one last time at the afternoon fading over the meadow. Then we climbed back down to earth and they took the truck back to Goodworth Clatford.

Goodworth Clatford is a neat, prosperous village at the bottom of a wooded valley. Most of it is in a conservation area, with lots of well-kept thatch and ancient timbers, neatly clipped hedges and no street lighting, to prevent light pollution. The staff in the village store wear specially printed aprons and sell, among other things, Pimm's No. 1 and chive-and-garlic mayonnaise. There are two pubs, a school, a big church, a tennis club, a golf club, a bridge club, a quilters' club, a WI and a thriving Neighbourhood Watch.

Paul and Emmeline lived on its western edge, halfway up a long hill, on an ugly ex-council estate that was added to the village in the 1960s. Their rented flat was so small that for a moment I thought I was going into next-door's shed. But it was warm and welcoming inside, and we spent a pleasant hour chatting over coffee. Only the thatch catalogue on the coffee table — and the collection of tools and split-hazel spars near the back door — gave any suggestion that we weren't in the middle of a town.

"I've been in the village 44 years," explained Paul. "I went to school in the village, and I worked in the fields around it while I was still at school. It was different then: there was still all the old characters, and you looked up to them. You could learn from them, I suppose. I can still remember going out on a freezing morning and being taught by one old boy how to keep my hands warm. You'd break the ice on a water butt and put your hands in it for five minutes. After that they'd be warm all day."

He still enjoyed going out to work on a "nice frosty morning" but was less keen on the rain. "I've done more time than I want to working in the wet. You can't work when it's really bucketing down, but you can if it's just drizzling. And we do. You get a bit fed up with that. We never get ill, though — we're not allowed to. I suppose a lot of people would find that attitude a bit odd." He smiled — a bit sadly, I thought.

"I started work for my uncle as soon as I left school," he continued. "I just learnt as I went along, from the older ones. The work hasn't really changed — you had the sense that you were picking up where they left off. Now I just plod on and do what I've always done. But I don't know if anyone will be picking up from me. We've tried taking on a couple of 16-year-olds, but it's a waste of time. They're not interested. You say, 'Do you want to learn how to dress a roof?' and they say 'No.' I suppose they think what's the point, when they see how hard we work, and how little we earn."

Did he ever think the same? "No. But you do notice how other people are living. This village isn't the same place it used to be."

In what way?

"I don't know anybody in the village now. The people I was at school with have all moved on, and a different kind of person's come in. Most of the village used to work in the area — it used to be all working class. Now people treat you like you're all — you know . . . I get a bit fed up with it, to be honest."

"It's not that they're unfriendly," said Emmeline hurriedly. "We just don't see them. A lot of them are hardly here. Sometimes you think it seems a bit of a waste of a cottage."

"Everyone works in Andover," said Paul, "or London. Or they just come down for the weekend. And that's why we have to live in a flat." He seemed less at ease indoors than outside: not gloomy, exactly, but somehow frustrated.

"I think we both feel we'd quite like a change," said Emmeline, "because it's changed so much. Maybe we could go to another village, but I don't know where we could afford. But it's starting to feel a bit claustrophobic here. We'd love to have a cottage best."

"If we could afford one," said Paul. "Do you have any idea what a house costs round here?" I didn't, but subsequent research suggested that houses in the village regularly changed hands for sums well over £500,000, while even a two-bedroom maisonette a few doors down from Paul and Emmeline's would cost £285,000.

The village had changed physically, too. "Where all these houses are used to be all fields," said Paul. "There was just four or five houses on Barrow Hill. There's offices up the hill now, too, so there's a lot of lorries and vans and couriers going past. And they want to build out the back here as well — they're trying to get access rights at the moment."

Did they think their way of life was dying out? "Not really," said Paul. "People aren't going to stop needing their roofs re-thatched. A lot of these newcomers can afford it, which is one good thing, and of course they can get grants for listed buildings. But the whole countryside is changing. It's property prices that are the problem. Look at the place where we buy our straw: they can get more money from renting out a farm building than from actually farming. Sometimes I think I should just give it all up and become a builder. And then I think, No. This is what I've always done. I'm good at this.

"I'm happy enough," he said as I was leaving. "But I'll be sad if they build out the back there. I love looking out towards those woods. I see deer out there, buzzards — look, there's one up there now. We've had buzzards at the end of our garden for 10 years."

"A buzzard," said Emmeline. "That's what I'd like to come back as next time round. It doesn't look like a bad life to me."

# CHAPTER
# SIX

# The great migration

I looked in briefly at the Clatford Arms, where topics of conversation among the well-spoken clientele included world tennis rankings, the Prix de l'Arc de Triomphe and the intolerable fecklessness of everyone's student offspring; then I spent the night at a bed-and-breakfast some way off, whose well-spoken owner told me at some length about his disputes with his parish council and others about a planning issue, the details of which I couldn't quite grasp. "It's her that's behind it," he concluded, gesturing towards the house of an unnamed neighbour, and then made the sign of the cross. "She's evil — plain evil."

I left early and paused while the morning mist was still rising from the river at Longstock, a nearby village. A true connoisseur of villages would no doubt have been thrilled by its 41 listed buildings and the world-famous water garden in Longstock Park (which is part of a 3,750-acre estate owned by the John Lewis Partnership). Not being such a connoisseur — and no one else being about — I preferred simply to wander by the water's edge on a low lane behind the village.

The brown water flowed so gently it seemed almost still, inches below the edges of the cropped turf banks. A little further from the stream, pale reeds rustled around big bulrushes, with short coppiced trees standing enigmatically beyond. A small, round wooden fisherman's hut with a thatched roof squatted mysteriously on a turf island like a primitive Taj Mahal — so low in the smooth water that the hut might have been floating. Ducks and moorhens drifted by. The rest was stillness — of that profoundly natural kind that makes you imagine that you can hear sap rising. The land, in short, was at peace.

The odd thing was, there were, at the time, only three things I knew about Longstock, none of them peaceful. One: the local tribes were utterly wiped out by Romans after the invasion of AD43. Two: the Romans were comprehensively massacred in their turn by the Saxons in 367. Three: in 1016, the river at Longstock was a crucial location in the war between Cnut of Denmark and Edmund Ironside, and there was fierce fighting in the area. Indeed, somewhere near where I was standing, the Danes cut a 90m channel out from the banks of the Test, to create a fortified hiding place for their flat-bottomed longboats.

It was curious to stand here now, on such a gentle morning, and to wonder what it would have been like to have done so at any one of those murderous former times — to have breathed in the quiet of an English country morning knowing there was a good chance that that very day would see you sliced and mutilated to death by men whose own lives depended on killing you and who saw nothing wrong with doing so. Not so different, I supposed, to how it must feel to live in certain parts of Africa and the Middle East today. Yet somehow my habitual vision of the rural past — contrasted with the crowded, noisy, polluted 21st century — hadn't left much room for such chapters in England's story. Now, I felt sudden gratitude for the tameness of the rural present.

Shortly afterwards, it rained: gently at first, but eventually in one of those vast blankets of overwhelming downpour that have become a feature of today's English climate. I took refuge in Andover, in an ugly shopping mall that allowed me to spend all morning flitting from coffee bar to bookshop to public library without getting wet. My browsing — actual and virtual — proved surprisingly instructive.

Here are some of the things I learnt.

(1) More glossy magazines than ever before were being published that celebrated "country" lifestyles. These ranged from established titles such as *Country Life*, *Country Living* and *Country Homes & Interiors* to upmarket newcomers such as *Move to the Country*, *Country Home* and *Hampshire Life*, as well as any number of magazines devoted to horses, dogs, gardens and outdoor life. Some were aimed explicitly at Londoners. *Country Home*, for example, was being given away free to London's 70,000 most upmarket households.

(2) The bookshops bulged with accounts of "escapes" to the country, from the amusing (Brian

Viner's excellent *Tales of the Country*; Judy Rumbold's *Reasons Not To Move To The Country: One Woman's Calamitous Attempt to Live the Rural Dream*) to the practical (Richard Craze's *Out of Your Townie Mind: The Reality Behind the Dream of Country Living*, Carol Ekarius's *Hobby Farm: Living Your Rural Dream for Pleasure and Profit*, Willy Newlands's *Hobby Farm: Ideas for the New Countryside*, and dozens more). There were also countless newspaper and magazine columns in which journalists described how they had taken their lives in their hands and moved into the countryside, and the internet bristled with comparable websites and blogs.

(3) Television had been bitten by the same bug, with new or newish programmes then including *Build a New Life in the Country*, *Tales from the Country* (with Selina Scott) and *Restoration Village* (in which the un-rustically named Ptolemy Dean tried to identify "the perfect rural idyll"). There was even a new "multi-platform TV channel" starting up, Horse & Country TV.

(4) The local papers were thick with upmarket advertisements: not just for half-million-pound houses and extravagant cars, but also for a staggering number of what I would describe as insubstantial luxury services: beauty treatments, alternative therapies, party-organising, lifestyle consultancy and pet-grooming and so forth.

None of this was surprising, but the trends were striking in their volume. I counted the advertisements in two free directories of local services and found that fully 20 per cent were for those insubstantial extravagances, with most of the rest relating to home improvements.

I also found the trends puzzling. I'd been hearing for as long as I could remember that the rural economy was on its knees. I knew, for example, that farm incomes had fallen by 66 per cent in real terms in the past 30 years; that the number of people employed in agriculture had fallen by a third in 20 years; that some 70,000 jobs had been lost in farming in the past 10 years alone; and that up to 16,000 further jobs were reported to be endangered by the hunting ban, which had recently come into force. So where was all this money coming from?

I spent some time immersed in statistics, and emerged with some facts that startled me. For example: most people living in the English countryside are newcomers. Not "many": "most". Only 37.9 per cent of those living in the countryside at the time of the 2001 Census had been living in the countryside 30 years earlier: the rest either hadn't been born in 1971 or had been living in towns and cities.

And that was only the half of it. The proportion of born-and-bred countryside-dwellers will be even smaller today, because people are still migrating to the countryside at a rate of about 100,000 a year (that's net migration, when the countryside-to-town movers are subtracted from the town-to-countryside movers). By my crude calculation, by 2008 the proportion of born-and-breds will be down to about 37 per cent.

This rate of migration has been sustained fairly consistently for the past two decades and may well be accelerating. If that doesn't astonish you, it should. It's equivalent to a new person setting up home in the countryside roughly every five minutes — or, if you prefer, a 20-year period that has seen, on average, 45 new attempts to realise a rural dream in each square mile of rural England.

No wonder the lanes I had been exploring had felt overcrowded. If all of those 2 million newcomers had been housed in traditional "small" villages of, say, 1,000 people, then 2,000 new villages would have been needed to accommodate them. Instead, they've just sort of squeezed into existing villages and rural towns, using their urban wealth to make themselves comfortable.

Nor were they squeezing into empty countryside: England's rural population had already grown by about 2 million over the previous two decades. So that's 4 million newcomers in 40 years — equating to getting on for half the current adult rural population.

The last time migration took place on such a scale was during the early stirrings of the Industrial Revolution, between 1630 and 1750, when market forces and technological change drove 40 per cent of the rural population to abandon agrarian life. That was really when modern England began, and the pre-industrial age ended. Was a social revolution of similar consequence in progress now? And, if so, was it something to be welcomed or mourned?

The figures suggested that the great migration had brought great benefits with it. Today's country-dwellers are, for example, more likely than city-dwellers to have degrees. They live in bigger, more expensive houses (the average rural household has 5.9 rooms, compared with 5 in urban households, while in 2007 the average rural house cost some £246,000 and the average urban one £215,000). They are generally higher up the social scale: 32.3 per cent of England's rural population belongs to social classes 1 and 2 — compared with 22.6 per cent of the urban population. Some of these new countrymen and women are seriously rich, and have come to the countryside to enjoy the super-wealth they have earned in, for example, the City. The proportion of agricultural-land purchases that were made by such "lifestyle buyers" rose by 50 per cent in 2007, accounting for 28.8 per cent of all farmland purchases and causing land prices to rise by 27 per cent in 12 months — the fastest such increase for 30 years.

But most are simply comfortably off. They have longer life expectancy than the population as a whole, enjoy better health and are less exposed to crime. They are older, with an average age (in 2004) of 43.6, compared with 38 in cities. Young people (aged from 15 to 24) now account for only 15 per cent of the rural population — compared with 21 per cent 20 years ago.

Country-dwellers in general are less likely to be homeless, and their children are more likely to do well at school (59 per cent of rural schoolchildren achieve five or more GCSEs at grades A* to C, compared with 47 per cent of urban pupils). They may also be more enterprising, since there are many more businesses in rural areas — 415 per 10,000 people, compared with 379 per 10,000 in cities. And they spend more: in 2005, the average rural household spent £60 more per week than the average urban household.

It is hard to see why those to whom they refer should feel ashamed of these figures (although they are sometimes encouraged to). Even the subset of "new" country-dwellers can point to hard figures to show that they are net contributors to the countryside's prosperity. A study conducted a few years ago for the Countryside Agency (now Natural England) found that two-thirds of incomer household heads were economically active (while 23 per cent were retired); that, of the active ones, 21 per cent were self-employed. Just 12 per cent worked in agriculture, forestry or fishing; the rest worked mainly in services or sales (23 per cent), banking and insurance (14 per cent) or health and education (14 per cent). Some 67 per cent of them worked within 12½ miles of their home. The self-employed ones typically created 2.4 jobs each. About half (according to a different study) were under 44. And 30 per cent earned more than £25,000 a year (equivalent to well over £30,000 in 2008).

But there was also a counter-theme in the statistics that fitted uncomfortably with this portrait of middle-class affluence and enterprise. In 2004-5, average earnings in most rural districts were £17,400, compared with £23,300 in major urban districts; while in 2007 there were 928,000 people in the countryside — 32 per cent of all rural households — with an annual household income of less than £16,500. That put buying a house beyond the financial reach of the average earner in 72 per cent of rural wards. The price of the average rural house is 7.1 times the average local income, compared with 6.2 times in urban areas. Meanwhile, 15 per cent of the rural population cannot afford a car. And whereas about 23 per cent of housing nationwide is "social housing" of some kind or other, in rural areas the figure is 5 per cent.

Put the two sets of figures together and you get a paradox. On the one hand, a booming countryside buzzing with economic initiative and wealth. On the other, a countryside of poverty and struggle.

I was still wondering what to make of all this when I came across an out-of-date *Daily Telegraph* countryside supplement — packed with advertisements for conservatories, Rayburns, old rectories and off-road vehicles — that someone had abandoned in the library. The main article was by Clive Aslet, editor-at-large of *Country Life* magazine, praising an "urbane revolution" in rural England. It was upbeat and persuasive. After waxing lyrical about a countryside of pheasant-shooters and sloegin-drinkers, Aslet launched into a celebration of the social revolution in progress. Once, he wrote, the countryside was a "remote, unsophisticated" place, "with pubs that served only curled-up sandwiches and nowhere to buy an avocado"; today, by contrast, it had "caught the wave of rising expectations" and was "surfing on a board of Michelin-starred cooking and music festivals".

Far from deploring the metropolitanisation of rural England, Aslet welcomed the influx of former town-dwellers to the countryside and praised the "renaissance" they had created there: "City people bring with them jobs. They do up their houses, create gardens, need cleaners . . . It is in the interests of the countryside to have these dynamic people in their midst. Who works in agriculture any more?"

My heart sank. He was right. The countryside earns less from farming than from tourism. Soon it will be earning as much again from the crop of small new enterprises — mainly in the service industries — that has sprouted across it over the past two decades. Only a fool or a prince would argue that these "non-rural" activities — the pet-grooming and the party-planning and the waxed jackets and the aromatherapy — should be discouraged, or that a poor countryside is more desirable than a thriving one.

Yet there was a note of triumphalism in that *Daily Telegraph* article that chilled my blood. Yes, of course, we should celebrate prosperity and sophistication. But what about the culture that was being replaced? Was it all bad? Many of my happiest teenage hours were spent in grubby, half-dead pubs — where any given curly-edged sandwich might remain on display for weeks on end. Their half-deadness was the whole point. We used to . . . well, I can't entirely remember what we used to do in them, except that a lot of talking went on: not just among friends, but among old and young, wise and foolish, even, sometimes, rich and poor. Villages used to talk to themselves in such environments. It didn't bother us that the food was inedible: we didn't know any better. Whereas now everyone did.

My unease began to clarify. If Aslet was right, then all these books and articles and programmes I had been noticing were symptoms of something significant. A transformation of rural life was under way — was, indeed, largely accomplished. Most working countryside-dwellers (two thirds of them) now worked in towns and cities, and pretty much everyone had been exposed to the smoothing, cosmopolitanising influences of the electronic society — the new culture that all of us share. The old culture — dingy, unsophisticated, insular and economically moribund, but rooted in the past and the soil — had faded away; with each passing year, fewer traces would remain.

Not long afterwards, looking for something else on the internet, I stumbled across a Channel 5 blurb for an episode of *Build a New Life in the Country*, in which a couple called Glyn and Jan bought and attempted to convert a Derbyshire farmhouse. What I read shed unexpected light on my feelings.

"The farmhouse is totally uninhabitable," explained the programme summary. "It has wet rot; there is a drainage problem, and it needs damp-proofing. The interiors are just as bad and Glyn cannot believe that, until recently, someone was living there."

No, I thought: no, he probably can't. I don't suppose anyone could, these days. Yet someone was, even so. Not long ago, a family of human beings was living there: a subtly different kind of human being, for whom living in a damp, rotting farmhouse was just one of life's hardships, like rain when you're working in the fields or brambles across footpaths — or the occasional necessity for killing things — or stale sandwiches in pubs. Most of rural England used to be populated by such people. And that tribe is now in such decline — so swamped by sophisticated, high-earning incomers — that the new rural England finds their mindset all but incomprehensible.

# CHAPTER
# SEVEN

# The dispossessed

Much later, I arrived in Mottisfont, about 10 miles south of Andover, where National Trust visitors were ferreting about in their habitual pursuit of slices of "unspoilt" England. The village is famous for its abbey, which flourished — as a priory — for several centuries from 1201 onwards; fell into disrepute (the monks once persuaded the Pope to give them money because the village had been swept away by the sea — which is 12 miles away); was all but destroyed by the Black Death; recovered; grew rich; was seized by Henry VIII; and was given by him to a crony — a big-shot from Basingstoke — in exchange for Chelsea and Paddington. The crony and his descendants converted it into a stately home, which passed through various super-rich hands and became famous, by the mid-20th century, for its stylish interior and remarkable gardens, as well as for the beautiful people — Sydney and Beatrice Webb, George Bernard Shaw, Rex Whistler, Geoffrey Jellicoe — who frequented it. Finally, in 1957, it was given to the National Trust: not just the grand house, but 64 other properties as well — that is, almost the whole village, theoretically preserved for posterity in accordance with the wishes of its last owner.

It was a golden afternoon, with the vegetation still glinting from the earlier downpour, but there didn't seem to be any villagers about, just visitors, most of whom were in the rather waterlogged National Trust car park. They seemed tetchier than usual. ("Sarcasm I do not need," snapped a tight-jawed mother to a girl who cannot have been more than four. "That kind of behaviour is not acceptable." A few cars down, a moustached father screamed, "Just leave it alone!" to invisible miscreants within.)

I wandered briefly in the abbey gardens, among blue hyacinths and artful arrangements of limes and yews, marvelling at the exclusive paradise that previous generations had created there; then, as the afternoon grew warmer, I headed out for the village proper. It seemed a pleasant place: a well-tended block of old brick cottages, with plenty of thatched roofs and climbing plants. After looking in on a shabby church — 800 years old, apparently, with flint-and-rubble walls and rickety wooden belfry — I paced around the lanes on muddy verges, breathing in sweet evaporations as the re-emerging sun glinted from wet garden plants. A man in a giant tractor thundered past on a back road; he returned my wave but didn't slow down. Then quiet descended. I could almost imagine myself in the rural past — before the countryside acquired its near permanent soundtrack of traffic noise. Yet surely no village 80 years ago would have been quite as empty as this?

In a ragged paddock behind what had once been the post office, I inspected a pair of shabby little stables that sagged at the foot of a dangling hedgerow. As I approached, there was a sudden rustling from the one on the left. I looked over the lower door and saw a honey-coloured terrier bristling on what looked like the floor of a teenager's bedroom. A small, pasty-bodied, middle-aged man, clad only in what looked like a pair of suit trousers, was lying on some makeshift bedding in the corner, reading a Ruth Rendell book. The rest was scattered stuff — clothes, dog biscuits, beer bottles — and rough stable floor.

I said hello. He struggled up, pulled on a woollen sweater, stepped into some flip-flops and shuffled out to join me. He was tanned and unshaven, with thinning brown hair and sunglasses. His name, he said, was Andy; the dog was called Billy. The stable was, for the time being, their home.

We walked out towards the big hay-meadow that sloped down southwards towards Dunbridge: Andy limping, Billy bouncing and me asking questions. He was a born-and-bred villager. "I was born in that cottage there." He waved at a corner of thatch that poked over the trees from Church Lane on the far side of the field. "So was my father." His grandparents had lived there too. He had gone to the local school — "lovely little school" — played in the local fields, swum in the local rivers (the Dun and the Test) and worked, for a while, on two local pig farms. Then, in his early twenties, things went wrong.

"My father married someone else. We never knew our mother. So I lived here with my grandfather. Then he got old, and things got difficult for him here, so we moved to Romsey [the nearest town, about 5 miles away]. It was good for him, but it destroyed my life. I haven't sat still since."

It was hard to pin down the exact nature of the problem. There had been a failed marriage, and a certain amount of drinking, but not alcoholism: "I'll just have two or three pints and that's my lot." As for employment: "Ah: jobs. I've had so many jobs. Labouring mainly. Or driving. I got a licence. I just can't afford no wheels."

The real trouble, it seemed, was that he hated towns. "I like being out in open spaces. I can't stand being in a town. It's the being enclosed — sort of shut in sort of thing."

He was 47 now and, all things considered, seemed well preserved — although he had had a heart attack the previous year. He had travelled a bit, but for most of the past two decades had been trying to get a home in Mottisfont. "Even when I was travelling, I always had a photograph of the village with me. This is my home, and always will be." But he had never managed to get another fixed abode there. So, rather than live somewhere else, he'd lived rough instead, in various spots on the village fringes. "I've lived in the woods, I lived in a tent, I spent a year in one of the chalk pits by the main road, I lived in the bus shelter for a bit." He'd been in the stable for a couple of months, but was worried that the National Trust — who owned it —

were going to force him out. "They want me to move on. But I'm not going to move on no more.

"I wish they'd just leave me alone. It isn't as if I was a stranger and nobody knew me. I could understand that."

It wasn't obvious to me what harm he was doing. Most days, he walked over the fields with Billy to Dunbridge, took a train to Southampton and spent the day selling *The Big Issue*. There was also a day centre there where he could wash and get a meal. "It's nice to go in, in the morning, but it's even nicer to come home. This is my village.

"The councillors of the village [that is, the parish council], they've talked about me, 'cause I was in the bus shelter. But next to it on the agenda they put: 'No action taken.' So I thought, Well, that's fair play to you. Why can't the National Trust be like that?" Meanwhile, he said, the council were trying to rehouse him. "But it's not easy, 'cause I just can't go into a town. I just wouldn't settle.

"People say, why don't you sleep in Southampton? But it's too rough. You know, people actually carry knives and things. Here we're safe — we can go to bed where we want and don't have to walk about all night." Instead, he could settle down and — light permitting — escape into the world of books. "I love reading. I get a lot of books from charity shops. Thomas Hardy — I've read all his. I like Dickens, too, and Sebastian Faulks — I liked *Birdsong*. But Hardy: that's gorgeous stuff. I like to picture myself back at that time, I guess. It just seems beautiful, don't it?"

**68**

We stood on the crest of the hill while the sun sank and Billy scurried around in a pile of hay bales, hunting rats. Apart from his occasional yaps, the evening was peaceful. "The years just flash by so quick, don't they?" said Andy. "I don't know many people in the village any more. But I know all this. I could walk around here with my eyes closed." There was a family of foxes living near by that he liked to watch, and some buzzards in the woods and several woodpeckers. His favourite spot was down in the valley, to the south, on a stretch of river known as Spoilbank. "That was where we first swam as kids. It's lovely and peaceful there. But you can't swim there any more. You just get into trouble." He supplemented his diet with nuts and berries and, occasionally, apples, but he had given up catching rabbits a long time ago. "There's too much myxomatosis."

We strolled back towards the village, watching the hawthorn berries glow like tiny flames in the sinking sun. "I love nature," he said. "It's a wonderful thing. I'm just so gutted that mankind have destroyed it all. But it's too late, isn't it? For the children today, in 70 years' time . . . It's too late."

The last thing I asked him was: was he happy out here? "Happy? Yeah. Yeah. Weather don't frighten me, nothing like that. And the National Trust don't frighten me either."

He returned to his stable and his Ruth Rendell. "If the worst comes to the worst, I'll go back to the woods again. I don't mind, as long as I'm left alone. It's not going to go on for ever, is it?"

★  ★  ★

In the centre of the village, outside the church, I met a talkative, motherly villager in her late forties called Gillian Francis, who lived with two cats and a dog in a very rustic-looking cottage just opposite: thatched, high-chimneyed and hung with roses. She had just returned from work — as a podiatrist — and kindly gave me tea in a living room so low-beamed and higgledy-piggledy that I was worried about banging my head even when sitting down.

"These used to be poor houses," she said. "This central bit was stuck up in a hurry using ship's timbers. I don't know how many families used to be stuffed in. Mrs Russell did a lot of renovation in the 1930s — knocked down about 20 hovels, and some of the others weren't much better. In this one, you'd come in and step down on to an earth floor."

Mrs Russell — Mrs Gilbert Russell — was the last private owner of the abbey, and of the greater part of the village. She bequeathed both to the National Trust in 1957, although she continued to live in the abbey until 1972.

Gillian's father was Mrs Russell's butler, and used to live in a flat above the abbey coach-houses. Later, they moved to the cottage that Gillian now lived in. It was, said Gillian, a good place to grow up. "There was a lovely school, and there were children everywhere: at one point there were about 44 kids. We used to cycle all over the place. But my father's work was very poorly paid: he earned £6 a week. So it wasn't comfortable. I remember there was no heating. And I remember when I brought home my first wage-packet — I'd joined the

70

Wrens, in 1975 — my dad went out in the garden and seemed to be in a big sulk. My mum said: 'You've just earned twice what he does.'

"But it was a real village then," she said, glancing out of the little window at the wet garden. "There was a blacksmith, a grocer, a post office, a bakery; there was a wheelwright, down at Spearywell, and of course most people worked on the estate, or else at the quarries at Dunbridge, but they've closed now. And then of course all the fields had to be tilled and hoed and weeded. We used to work in the fields when we were kids, picking wild oats or picking poppies, and I remember how we'd all be out there with the bales at harvest as well. But none of that happens any more."

So the village hadn't been preserved in its pre-1957 form? "Not in terms of how people work, no. There isn't really any local work any more, or not for the likes of us. And of course we've lost the school, so you lose that immediate emotional attachment to the village that people have if their children are at the school. I don't know if there are any children here at all at the moment."

What about the children she grew up with? "Let's see . . . There's Alex. Philip. Andrew. I'm here. That's about it."

So who lives in all these houses? "A lot of the cottages are empty, and most of the rest are used for short-term lets to tourists and others or to National Trust workers. It's a shame. It would be so much better to see all these lovely houses lived in by real villagers."

It wasn't immediately obvious to me what the difference was between a "real" villager and the other kind of tenant. Gillian herself was articulate, educated and confident — with none of the narrowness of perspective that a sophisticated metropolitan type might expect to find in a countryperson. In what way was she more "real" than, say, a young, university-educated craftsperson from London who had come down to work for the National Trust? "It's partly a question of memory. Villages have pasts. A real villager remembers what so-and-so's grandad used to do, or where the wheelwright was, or who used to live in such-and-such a house. If you get rid of all the real villagers, a village loses touch with its past."

This led us into difficult territory. Gillian insisted that she and her fellow tenants in Mottisfont were big fans of the National Trust: "Without the National Trust we would probably all have sold up and left years ago, whereas instead you still have at least some old villagers. We're in favour of the Trust generally. We like what they do with cliffs and walks and bugs and things. And we like what they do with buildings and villages — except where it comes to the question of people."

The problem, it seemed, was that the National Trust considered itself bound to maximise its rental income, subject to certain constraints, in order to fund its conservation work. "So they don't put locals in the old houses. They let them to outsiders who'll spend money on doing them up, and then [for the next tenants] they put the rent up." They also put the rent up in unimproved cottages, such as Gillian's. Indeed, there had recently been reports of increases of between £50 and £400 a month right across the village — anything up to 68 per cent.

Nor was the issue confined to Mottisfont. There was, I would learn, a nationwide resistance movement against such increases, coordinated by an organisation called Tenants Associations of the National Trust (TANT), in which Gillian had for a while been active. There are dozens of villages around the country where the Trust owns dwellings with private tenants, and the same issues arise in most of them. Discussions with the Trust — some more constructive than others — had been taking place, and have continued since. The Trust insists that it has both a right and a legal obligation to make the best use of its assets to further the purposes for which it was established — and that those purposes expressly relate to the conservation of property.

As the property manager at Mottisfont told me over the telephone much later: "Our charitable status means that we have to charge market rents."

In Mottisfont, however, there is also the question of Mrs Russell's wishes. "She wanted it to be maintained as a living village," said Gillian. "A living village for the estate workers who lived there."

You could argue, of course, that putting National Trust workers in village cottages is compatible with Mrs Russell's wishes. Unfortunately, she isn't around to ask. And, as Gillian pointed out, Mrs Russell could never have imagined the realities of 21st-century life. "Nobody thought people would have cars, that everyone would own their home. She could never have envisaged a time when it wouldn't be an estate.

"Don't get me wrong," she added (several times). "We're all in favour of the National Trust, generally. And if they hadn't taken over in 1957 it would all be one big mess. We just want them to think about what they're doing. Apparently under the 1907 Act [which established the Trust], we're not a priority. We say that it's villagers like us who keep the village alive. If it wasn't for us, then apart from the National Trust car park there'd be nothing — there'd be no life . . . We may not have progressed as much as some people in terms of modern life — we don't have swimming pools or paved driveways — but there are a few of us left: real indigenous villagers.

"I don't think they can have done the costings — to work out the value of what we contribute — compared with an outsider who pays the market rent but is never there and can't even keep their garden looking nice."

Just dipping my toes in this subject convinced me of two things. First: that the arguments and counter-arguments could be extended indefinitely. And, second: that for those whose homes are at stake, it is an incredibly upsetting issue.

I heard several stories, from Mottisfont and beyond — not just from Gillian — of tenants driven to their wits' end by rent increases. Several involved evictions, one involved a suicide attempt. The property manager I spoke to insisted that everything was done "with a human face" and that "we would never evict someone just on one instance — it's got to be many, repeated aberrations". But there was no mistaking the note of desperation in Gillian's voice when she told me about her own experience. She had been living in her cottage for more than 15 years, after a brief period away from the village. It remained a distinctly substandard residence from the perspective of the well-paid Hampshire commuter. ("They couldn't let this one at the moment: it would need to be blitzed from top to bottom — look, it's got broken doors, every surface is uneven, there are all these nooks and crannies: it would be a nightmare.") But the location was desirable, and the potential was obvious. Suddenly: "They put my rent up by £100 to £575. I just gave up. It was physically impossible for me to find that sort of money. There weren't enough hours in the week to do enough extra work . . ." She paused and lowered her eyes. "I actually had the rope round my neck when I was found. If I'd tied the knot properly I wouldn't be here now."

It was dark outside. Not long afterwards, I said goodbye and moved on. Gillian's words rang in my ears as I drove — not just that last stark account of her own despair, but some earlier remarks, which in their own way were equally shocking: "If we were pygmies, or wore loincloths, or were gypsies, all the anthropologists would be up in arms. But because we look just the same as everyone else, no one cares what's happening to us. But it's the same thing — we're being ethnically cleansed."

I couldn't decide if she were being sensational — or just articulating my own thoughts. Obviously, there is a profound difference between, on the one hand, being forced from your village by gun-toting paramilitaries and, on the other, having your rent put up by the National Trust. I thought once again about the difference between a comfortable, modern land in peacetime and a raw, lawless land ripped by war. Then again: market forces can be pretty merciless, and villagers who are driven by these forces from communities where their families have lived for generations aren't just losing their homes: they are losing their pasts.

I resumed my travels, fretfully. Hampshire seemed crowded and bad-tempered: full of retail parks and business parks and new executive housing and, above all, cars, in Selborne, where Gilbert White, the 18th-century father of English naturalism, did his most famous work (despite strictly speaking being curate of my own village in Northamptonshire at the time), was all traffic. The narrow main street now carries 10,000 vehicles a day, including juggernauts, to increasing local distress. And although I talked briefly to the soon-to-be-ex-postmistress, and to a young ex-sailor who was selling woodcarvings next to the pub, it was impossible to pay proper attention to anything much beyond the merciless bellowing of vehicles and the bitter taste of exhaust.

With two pubs, a village shop, two museums, an art gallery, a craft centre, a gift shop, a Tea Parlour and a National Trust meadow, the village earns a large slice of its collective living from the heritage industry. Yet it was hard to feel any sense of the old rural England there.

Leaving, I drove up a tight side lane in search of what used to be the poorhouse (famously sacked by discontented farm workers in the agricultural riots that swept southern England in 1830). A big, muddy Land-Rover came in the opposite direction and, at the narrowest point, I found myself momentarily wedged, driver's-window to driver's-window, against a red-faced man of about 50 with a cloth cap and a waxed jacket. I asked him for directions. "Why don't you just fucking well back?" he said.

He was, I reflected later, probably a proper, born-and-bred countryman.

East Coker — a fastidiously groomed Somerset settlement of comfortable grey stone cottages, tastefully draped with roses and wisteria — was all money. I sat for a while in the Helyar Arms, where a few dozen suited, high-quiffed young executives from Yeovil were loudly enjoying the award-winning cuisine. Then, growing tired of an interminable discussion about the possible effect on property prices of some proposed new housing in the shrinking gap between East Coker and Yeovil, I wandered out into the cool, damp-aired twilight.

The village seemed deserted: the only signs of life were a man digging his garden outside one of the almshouses, and a short, plump woman striding purposefully down from the church towards him. She paused at his garden wall, produced a camera and photographed him, without a word, then strode on to her car and drove off. He glowered after her with such outrage that I couldn't bring myself to intrude into his life any further. Presumably he felt as many exotic species must feel, minding their own business in the wild only for David Attenborough to come along and, uninvited, observe them.

Instead, I walked on to the church, feeling faintly stupid to be "exploring" modern England at all. Then I stood in the churchyard and, as thousands must have done before me, listened to time passing. A plain gravestone commemorated 70 villagers who died from plague in 1645. There were birds and daffodils on the sloping parkland beyond; the still warm breeze carried a scent of old yew; a cow was munching somewhere; and the hypnotic words of T. S. Eliot's great poem of eternity, "East Coker", padded peacefully in my head:

> In order to arrive at what you do not know
> You must go by a way which is the way of ignorance.

At the side of a bumpy lane near Westhay, in the Somerset Levels, a curly-haired, gap-toothed woman with nicotine-stained hair and a muddy shell-suit was selling peat. Some was in bags, for gardeners, and some in neatly stacked, brick-sized turves for burning. Around us, the Avalon Marshes spread enigmatically into the distance: a low, scraggy, damp-smelling land sliced by dark ditches and rich with ancient memory. A mile or so away, a visitor centre marked the 6,000-year-old remains of a stilted wooden pathway built by the area's Neolithic inhabitants for getting across the marshes. Just beyond, birdwatchers and fishermen shared the overgrown banks of an old waterway with small, noiseless swans and myth-struck walkers from nearby Glastonbury. But it was the lumps of peat that interested me most.

"They've been digging peat here for thousands of years," said the woman, who looked to be in her fifties but had a much younger, gigglier way of speaking. "It was for fuel then, but now it's mainly for gardening. This was all extracted mechanically," she added. "But it used to be done by hand. That was really hard work: not only digging it, they've got to be putting it up to dry, put it in rows, then it's got to be picked up again. And they only had a pony and cart to deliver 'em." But that was long ago. "There was some had done it like that, but they've gone now -- died, really."

Many would have died young: long days of back-breaking work in the damp, only partially anaesthetised by cider, did little for the health. Their skills — an uncanny ability to dig in straight lines, for example — would have died with them, despite having evolved over hundreds of generations.

"Of course," said the woman, "the government don't want us to dig peat no more. Says it's the environment or something. But it's what makes the marshes what it is really, peat-digging. Without peat-digging there wouldn't be no wildlife."

She laughed derisively. "Most people here used to do it. Not so many now, but there's still a few around. My family's always done it. We only do it in a small way, though. Doesn't hurt anybody, really. But they think it does. Mind you, they'll have peat in from abroad — it's coming in on the ships all the time. How's that good for the environment?" She laughed again. "You work that out."

At Tollard Royal, in Wiltshire, I was scowled at by two separate blonde women on horses, either one of which (the women, not the horses) might have been Madonna, who lives in the stately home there and spent some years in dispute with villagers over footpath rights across her land. I couldn't see any villagers, let alone dissatisfied ones: the place seemed to consist exclusively of horses, paddocks, woodland and fences, as, now I thought about it, had quite a lot of the counties I had passed through to date. Apparently there are now 2.4 million recreational riders in the UK, keeping 900,000 horses and spending £4 billion a year on enjoying them — the very essence of rural life, some would say; or, if you are otherwise prejudiced, another example of the leisure revolution that is transforming the land. I hadn't given the question much thought before. Most of the people I know who work with horses are hard-working and poor. But now, seeing these huge tracts of manicured land, sterile as golf courses, I began to wonder if the cynics who moaned about "horsiculture" might not have a point.

At Shapwick, in Dorset, I climbed a wooded hilltop above Kingston Lacy — another National Trust estate — and, after talking to a family of tourists from Stevenage, found a wooden bench at the centre of Badbury Rings, the ancient earthworks that overlook the village. I sat and then lay on it, watching small white clouds gust wildly across a vast blue sky. It was about 10a.m. on, I think, a Thursday, and my head was full of confused thoughts. Was I engaged in a bona fide research project? Or had I gone slightly mad? I suspected the latter. A normal person would be in an office at a time like this, earning a living.

None the less, I lay there, watching the sky. Every now and then, black birds gusted past, flung by the wind like scraps of torn bin liner. I think they were crows. I hoped that at least one was a raven. Some believe that King Arthur had his finest hour on this hill, defeating the Saxons at the battle of Mount Badon around the end of the 5th century and so preserving Romano-British civilisation from barbarian invasion for another generation. His soul remains near by (believers add) in the form of a raven.

All highly unlikely, of course. (Such a battle was fought, but not necessarily by Arthur, and probably elsewhere; anyway, other believers insist that Arthur sleeps in Avalon — where the peat used to come from.) Yet it pleased me to lie there, thinking of that heroic stand against the seemingly irresistible advance of terror and darkness; and thinking, too, that men and women had been living out the dramas of their lives on and around this hill for 10,000 years. They too must have feared from time to time that the world as they knew it was about to be erased for ever. Yet the sky still hurtles past just as it did, and black birds are tossed above it, and the great plain that lies quietly below still fades to a blur as it approaches the English Channel.

My phone rang. It was my father, calling for a chat. I treasured such chats, although he had a knack of calling at the wrong time. He was 90 then, and had lived in the same corner of east Hertfordshire for 50 years; his current cottage was within half a mile of the hamlet where I grew up. He always expressed enthusiasm for anything I undertook, but you would never have caught him wasting time on a self-indulgent quest like this. He lived in a harder world: he grew up in the shadow of World War I, struggled to begin his working life in the Great Depression; fought in World War II; and for 60 years afterwards never stopped considering himself lucky to be alive, to have a job; to be living in a free country in peacetime. He still found it hard to believe that he could get free medical care on the NHS. For the past five years he had been alone, and, while his mind remained sharp, his body was fading. We talked of this and that, but the wind made it hard to hear, so we didn't speak for long.

Afterwards, however, descending the hill, I thought of him again, and also of Arthur. How simple life was for both of them; how comforting it would be to share their world-view. Yes, from time to time you might have to risk your life in battle, but the land you were defending remained the same. When peace eventually came, there was the same old England. Whereas now . . .

# CHAPTER EIGHT

# Old England

"Wouldn't it be better," said Clare, during one of my rare visits home, "just to concentrate on one place and really get to know it?"

She was right: even I could see that. My constant travelling was preventing me from learning all sorts of things about the places I visited. But I couldn't stop myself.

I had, I should add, already abandoned the idea of exploring the entire country in a single continuous journey, and was interspersing periods of exploration with periods at home and work (thus staving off bankruptcy and divorce). But I was continuing to travel as far, wide and often as circumstances permitted. And something about the nature of my search — a sense of something elusive just beyond the horizon, which perhaps had nothing to do with villages — kept propelling me further and faster, like a man searching too hastily for a lost document.

I noticed this when I went to Devon. I kept feeling that I hadn't quite reached the right place. From my car, the patchwork landscape seemed timeless. Yet each time I got out to inspect, the ancient mysteries receded.

I might meet a rural old-timer or two — and, indeed, had taken to actively seeking out rural old-timers by studying the local press, village websites and books of local history. But insights into the rural past eluded me. Everyone seemed to inhabit the same modern normality: the same supermarkets, the same high streets, the same fashions and phones. It all felt too close to home. No pubs went silent at the entrance of a stranger; shopkeepers and bed-and-breakfast owners were as middle-class as I was, and tended to admit, when questioned, that they had retired there from places such as Luton, Cambridge and Stoke-on-Trent. There were, perhaps, fewer commuters in the West Country, but there were just as many people who had no roots in the place; fewer celebrities, but more leisure-seekers. Wealth still stalked the land, just as it had in the Home Counties: it just did so less conspicuously, dressed as tourism.

On Exmoor, where one household space in 10 is a second or holiday home and the average house price is 14 times the average local annual income, I paused near Dunkery Beacon to admire the view. I would have needed a numb soul to have gazed over those soaring curves of hill and not felt warmed by inner sunlight. The huge slopes, brushed with straw-pale grass, seemed magnificently indifferent to human comers and goers, reminding me that, however pressing my own concerns now seemed, they were only the tiniest footnote in an infinitely bigger story.

Then I went down into Luccombe, a small, thatch-heavy village overhung with tall trees, where I chatted for a while with an old farmer in an old, messy farmyard. He was a small, tentative man, with thin white hair, leathery skin, big, quizzical eyes and a high, musical voice. He had lived in the village for 90 years; his family had been tenant farmers there for generations, after migrating from Bossington — 3 miles to the north — some time in the 19th century. His daughter, Roz, had taken over the tenancy now, but Bill Partridge, the farmer in question, still returned to the farm to help out most days. "I usually work from eight till five," he explained. "But I try not to do too much physically." He seemed pleased to have an excuse for a break.

"Mind you," he added, "the hard work's gone out of farming. We spent all winter putting up banks and making hedges and digging and shovelling earth down, and then early summer you were hoeing day after day. Hay-making was much harder: it was all done with picks and rakes and hand-work. Harvesting, you picked your sheaves up, making ricks; threshing — hard work again, and dirty and dusty work. And now it's all done by machinery. The bales, you hardly touch them now. But we were outdoors most of the time. Now you get stuck in a tractor or similar.

"I think you have to be more skilled now. You have to be able to maintain your tractor or your combine or your baler or whatever. Not that there wasn't skill in making a hedge or whatever, but it's a different kind of skill now. The art of making ricks and thatching ricks — that's all gone. And hedge-making, too ... The National Park tries to preserve it by teaching people how to make hedges, but nothing like as good as we used to do it."

Did he miss the old ways? "Village life has changed, but you've got to accept it — change is inevitable. Luccombe's still a friendly place. Everybody mucks in if the village hall wants money, or to raise money for the church. But I know more people in the cemetery than I do in the village."

I told him that the village, which is supposed to have a population of about 100, had seemed deserted when I walked through it, apart from a fierce dog and a Londoner staying in a holiday apartment. "That's how it is now," he said. "Did you see the car park by my house?" (He lives in a cottage in the centre of the village.) "It's absolutely empty by day — but it's full at night."

So where was everyone? "Well, there are people, because there are a lot of retired people here now, but not many people working. I think one or two of the younger people have businesses that they run from Luccombe, but most people go to Minehead or Porlock or wherever to work. There's no school here. Luccombe children go to school in Timberscombe first, when they're youngsters, and then they go to Minehead. And of course families are much smaller anyway. There must be an awful lot of homes in the village with only one person in."

There used to be four farms in Luccombe, which in 1944 employed eight people directly and several others indirectly. Now there were two, both manned only by the families that owned them — "although the other farm, he does employ one person permanently, although he has wider interests in other farms as well". The village had never had a pub — its former owners, the Acland family, wouldn't allow them. The role of the church was much diminished: like everywhere else, it now shared its priest with other villages. In Bill's childhood, there were three services to go to every Sunday, as well as choir practice.

Nor, according to Bill, was there much in the way of everyday communal recreation. "When I was young, they would play cricket in the summer or football in the winter, but that's lost now. There's no sport of any kind of the sort that everybody joins in."

Before the school closed, he added, "children would play games like Hare and Hounds, Fox and Hounds, Stag and Hounds in the playtimes or the evening. But since the school was closed and they go to town, that is lost, and they begin to lose their country interests. So when you get a bill before Parliament to banish hunting, had they still been at Luccombe, it would have seemed wrong to them, if you see what I mean, because it was a way of life, the way they'd grown up. But being in town, it probably didn't make much difference to them."

His own education was limited. "I think there was about 30 of us at the school, with two classes in one room. We had sand tables — you didn't waste paper, did you? — you did your sums or you wrote what you had to write — your letters, your figures — in the sand with your finger and then they just shook the sand and then you did it all over again. I don't know if they still use them anywhere but I doubt it. Anyway, I didn't go to school very much. I didn't have very good health when I was young. I spent some 16 months in a sanatorium and by the time I came home, I was over 14, and although it was intended that I should continue my education, one of my brothers unfortunately died of appendicitis and peritonitis, and that left a gap to be filled in the family, working. So my education ceased at that stage, such as it was."

The gap to be filled was essentially that left by his mother, who had died five years previously. "My father and brother were still living here, so I had to sort the meals out and get them ready, and look after the poultry and cows and the dairy part of it because we made cream in those days, and selling eggs and things, and shooting the rabbits, selling the rabbits, preparing chicken; that sort of thing."

This continued with little alteration until World War II. Bill went off to fight, feeling guilty at leaving the farm behind. By the time he came back, he was commissioned, married, lucky to be alive after a serious wound, and, in short, a quite different person. None the less, his old life resumed more or less unaltered. His father paid him, reluctantly, for his work; it would be another 20 years before he would allow him into a partnership. Bill might have questioned his lot more loudly had he not seen so many of his comrades killed in Normandy — and come back to find that four of his fellow villagers had lost their lives as well. "I felt guilty to be alive. So you didn't question anything."

From today's perspective he took a more critical view of that ostensibly idyllic past. "I think with hindsight maybe I could have been more assertive about my life." But, of course, those weren't assertive days, and self-fulfilment didn't really feature as an assumed purpose of an ordinary life. "You'd doff your cap in those days. I suppose people just had different values then."

And which was better? Then or now? "Well, we're all a bit further from nature, aren't we? Families were much more self-supporting in my youth. They maybe kept a pig down the bottom of the garden, they grew their own vegetables in the gardens, they snared the rabbits, they kept a few poultry so they'd got their eggs and when the hens were too old to lay eggs, they would kill, pluck and draw and boil and eat them — but not now. There are one or two people who still look after their gardens and grow vegetables, but not everybody as it used to be. Nobody keeps a pig now and I don't think that, other than possibly one person, anyone keeps poultry in the village. And very few people snare rabbits any more. The art of ferreting, catching rabbits, snaring rabbits — that's gone, too; whereas people were always snaring rabbits. That's how you lived.

"And then there was whortleberry-picking. That was a real event — you picked whortleberries and sold them for about 8 pence a quart and a man came and collected them. They probably went for dyeing. But nobody bothers to pick them now. People don't seem to enjoy nature so much.

"But you've got to look outward, haven't you? You've got to accept change; change is inevitable. For example, we grow our own grain and sell it [for animal feed], but we can actually buy wheat cheaper than we can produce it. We know that because we happened to run out once and we had to buy in about 16 ton, and it's cheaper to buy. Or milk, again: we used to milk cows for our own benefit, for our own milk and cream. Today it's never worth it, you couldn't afford to — it's cheaper to buy it."

Common sense suggested that this ought to be impossible, or at least unsustainable. But common sense has little to do with modern economics. No wonder, I reflected, that 20 per cent of the nation's farms were, according to recent reports, running at a loss.

But Bill Partridge seemed remarkably sanguine about the process. "Things get lost," he said, "because they cease to be valuable — like producing your own vegetables, or keeping your own poultry. Now you go to work, you earn a big salary and you drop in at the supermarket. It's much simpler."

A few miles further west, I wandered down into the village of Parracombe — a bleak, steep settlement of about 130 stone homes jammed on the edges of narrow, high-banked lanes — and, after some exploration, had tea with three charming old ladies in an ancient farmhouse on a cobbled slope. All three were local, although only our hostess, Ada Tucker, lived in the village. Pam Wyatt — who had dropped in with her sister, Barbara — was from the next village but one, Barbrook.

Barbara, a widow, had spent much of her life near Tiverton, just south of Exmoor, but she too had grown up on the moor, at Heasley Mill; the other two had never left this locality. Ada spent the first 37 years of her life at West Ilkerton, about 3 miles away as the stag flees, but had now been in Parracombe for 45 years.

"I haven't been very far," said Ada, who was small and neat and oddly childlike. "I never been to London. I been to Exeter, though."

We sat at a broad wooden table, in a low-ceilinged parlour with old photographs and religious texts on the wall. Outside, the afternoon was sticky with impending storm. Indoors it was cool and clean. It felt still here, even with four people talking and munching at the elaborate tea that Ada — who had not been expecting any of us — had insisted on serving.

Between mouthfuls, we talked about farming: how hard it was to make a living from it; how different it was these days; the forms that had to be filled in. "I'd hate it now," said Ada, who is retired, softly. "Some farmers now, they work at their farm, but all they're interested in is subsidies. I used to love my animals — I'd cry when we sent lambs to be sold. But some people, they have hundreds of sheep, because the more they have the more subsidy they get. Well, they can't look after 'em and those sheep got to manage themselves. What lived lived and what didn't didn't, but the farmer would still get his subsidy for 'em. But they that farmed proper and kept what the farm would carry in the way of stock, they only has so much. They didn't get so much as these that keep hundreds out over the moors. But I shouldn't be saying about other people, should I? . . . Pam's always worked hard," she added. "She's a proper farmer."

"I had to work hard all me life," said Pam, quickly, "and I'm still working." There was a sharp, feral quality to her accent, as if she generally talked outdoors in the wind; which, given that she farms 103 acres single-handed, seemed reasonably likely. Did she make a good living? "I don't know."

Her lined brown face made me think of the rusting beech hedges with which parts of Exmoor are scoured.

"It don't pay to work on a farm now," said Barbara, who was, or at least looked, the youngest of the three. "My son ain't so keen on the farm now. He's out making sheds 'cause there ain't nothing in the farms." The others nodded.

"I don't think the young ones are interested to know anything about animals," Barbara continued. She used to do bed-and-breakfast on her farm when her husband was alive. "But I wouldn't want to do it now. People expect it to be like a hotel."

Ada's mother used to take guests, too: many farms did. But that was a more naïve age, and there was a much more personal relationship then between visitors and visited. One family, from Liverpool, used to come every summer and were firm friends. They once took Ada to a hotel in Barnstaple as a treat. "I stayed there one night — just for something for me. In my whole life," she added, "I've only slept that one night off the farm. I was born on one farm, and then after father died and we came here I've lived on this one."

"People would be glad to see a farm then," said Barbara. "Families used to come and children used to run around all over the place. By the time I finished, not a single child was interested in what went on in the farm."

This didn't surprise me. Study after study has shown that startling numbers of young Britons are oblivious both to the general workings of agriculture and to the connection between agriculture and food. I had recently read of a survey that showed that 11 per cent of eight-year-olds didn't know where either pork chops or cheese came from, while 2 per cent of urban children thought that eggs came from cows. Ada, Pam and Barbara faced the opposite difficulty: that of imagining the world without the agricultural context in which they had discovered it as children.

Ada and Pam both left school early to help on the family farm, staying at home, while others were marrying, to support their weakening parents, and finally taking over the whole enterprise when their respective fathers died.

Pam used to ride to school in North Molton on a pony — about 10 miles each way. Ada used to walk to school — in Barbrook, a mile away from her then home — "but then I had an illness and I was home I should think for a long, long time. I enjoyed it before then, but then when I went back, they'd got a supply teacher there and she wasn't no help, because you see I'd lost all my teaching while I was ill. Mother tried to help me but her hadn't enough time. But the supply teacher wouldn't help me . . . I suppose I shouldn't be saying about people, should I?"

Ada left school at 14, by which time she had already been doing farm work for half her life. "I first milked cows when I wasn't very old — about seven or eight. And I farmed all me life. I loved me farming — it was lovely." She had a happy, lively face, and rarely seemed wearied by her 83 years. I couldn't help thinking, however, that she seemed very slight and delicate for someone who has spent a lifetime on back-breaking outdoor work. "Oh, I never done the real hard work, not heaving up anything that was heavy. Well, I was only short. Different people would come down and help carrying corn and things like that, and it was horse and cart back then that carried them."

Pam, who was nearly a decade younger, still did nearly everything herself, including driving a lorry when necessary. "But I get in a contractor for shearing." Like Ada, she had learnt to milk around the time she learnt to read. She was good at it, and once milked 28 cows by herself. Ada remembered being good at stacking sheaves on to the cart. "There was a bad corner on the top, and if they hadn't done 'em right, some of the sheaves would fall off, there. The men would be a bit annoyed if theirs fell off and mine didn't."

Both had mixed farms, sheep and cattle. Ada's was 235 acres: "It was a big farm in they days — not today." But the work had never ground her down. "We loved the animals back then," she said again. "We was really fond of them. I used to like me sheep and me cows — the cows that I milked, it was by hand to start with and then me father had a milking machine. That milk then was warm milk, it never went through a cooler, not back in they days. It tasted beautiful. I was good at making butter. I'm very lucky, I got cold hands. I could make enough butter in the summer to last right through the winter."

Social life, for all three, was limited: partly because of their physical isolation but also because there was so much less free time. Ada had boyfriends sometimes, but the needs of her own family, and of the farm, came first. I got the impression that she would have felt guilty if she had gone off and married. But she had sometimes gone to dances or whist drives in Challacombe or Simonsbath, which she reached — across the moor — by pony. She could still remember the magic of one particular journey home, from a dance right over in Hawkridge, on the other side of the moor. "I can't remember if it was a full moon or not, but we rode back again after midnight, and once we got down past Challacombe, it's open common there, there's no fences, and it was very foggy by then. And Father had said don't you pull the rein; let that pony go where she wants to go. So I did that, and it looked like the pony's went wrong, but I didn't pull the rein, and at last we come up to the gate that goes across the main road. I didn't worry after that, because I knew she'd come home all right."

It was, everyone agreed, a very different world today; all seemed to feel that the younger generation were missing out on something.

"All they talk about, you hear 'em youngsters sitting there all day, all they talk about is tractors and machinery," said Pam. "They got to go out and they get on a tractor and they press buttons and they don't know what work is."

"I don't suppose, if they didn't have subsidies out here, they wouldn't make a living, would 'em?" said Barbara.

"It don't pay to work on farm now, do it?" said Pam. "Times have changed."

The only thing that hasn't changed, I thought, is the farmer's timeless gift of complaining. Then Barbara let slip, almost casually: "I was married to a farmer coming up 30 years, and my husband died through depression in farming. Took his own life."

The room seemed to grow colder. Everyone looked sympathetic, without having anything very comforting to say. "Well, everything was changing, wasn't it," explained Barbara. "BSE was around at that time. He didn't have the BSE but the facts of having to sell all their cattle because it was coming, it cracked him up. Suddenly there was no income coming in, and that's when he left the milking . . . Everything was changing. It's one of those things, and other farmers have done the same."

That was putting it mildly. A survey in 2003 suggested that British farmers were twice as likely to contemplate suicide as the rest of the general public.

When the BSE crisis gave way to the foot-and-mouth crisis, farmers were killing themselves at a rate of one a week. All sorts of reasons — apart from the obvious economic pressures — have been suggested for this. They include the facts that today's farmers work in much greater isolation than previous generations; that today's more transitory and fragmented rural communities provide less emotional support than farmers enjoyed in the past; that, as Barbara said, everything was changing — a process that most living creatures find stressful.

It was interesting, in this context, that Pam and Barbara had dropped in to, in effect, see that Ada was all right — "keeping an eye on me", as Ada put it. There have been Tuckers in these parts since time immemorial — "My father's lot were at Parracombe, my mother's were from Brendon, but both lots have been there a long time. I don't know where they was before, neither one of 'em." Now, however, she found it hard to keep pace with her village's changing population. "I got lovely neighbours, and ever such nice people at the end of the lane out. And there's others I know in a way but I can't remember their names. There used to be plenty worked locally then but now they've got to go to Barnstaple or different places, and the farmers don't employ so many. I don't know many — they's all strangers really."

I felt oddly reluctant to leave: it seemed wrong, or at least unnatural, that such a gentle English countrywoman should be left alone to grow old among strangers. But Ada seemed more cheerful than her words implied, and

I wondered where she got her strength from. "You've got to carry on," she explained; then added: "I like me religion. I believe a lot in me religion. But I don't go to church much. If I go to church, you see, I can't hear the lady very well. She's very nice but I can't follow it."

I pushed on westwards, suddenly confused as to what was so precious about the old rural hardships. What was so awful about country life today? If ordinary people could now buy food rather than make it, and travel large distances easily, and live and work where they chose, make their individual destinies rather than be subsumed into the story of their immediate community — well, what was wrong with that?

The landscape soon distracted me: the low, slanting trees on my right, swept back by decades of sea breeze, and, on my left, the golden-brown moor, smudged in places by the shadows of oceanic clouds. To the south-east, I thought I could make out the bare, boggy, stream-scoured plateau known as the Chains. Tiny settlements gleamed peacefully in the distance, as if beyond the reach of history; on one far hilltop a scattering of black-and-white cows was illuminated with miraculous clarity. I thought of the young Ada Tucker, full of hope, crossing the moor with her pony by moonlight, and the land for some reason began to seem to me like a vast, benign parent, in the folds of whose hills untold millions of largely innocent dramas and adventures had been acted out. *England*, I thought to myself: I'm not quite sure what I mean by the word, but it might be what I'm looking for.

Before long, a sign to the seaside village of Georgeham reminded me that I was in Henry Williamson territory. Williamson's most famous book, *Tarka the Otter*, is set just west of Exmoor, but his later work — notably the *A Chronicle of Ancient Sunlight* sequence — drew inspiration from the moor itself, especially from the Chains. He himself was originally from south London, but he spent the last 30 years of his life in Georgeham, and a sense of the place infuses his semi-mystical brand of English ruralism.

Then I thought: *ruralism* — of course. That's the word for what I'm doing.

Which it wasn't, but it did describe the attitude that was driving me on — which was what I meant.

Then another thought shook me: I couldn't — could I? — be in Henry Williamson territory in another sense as well? Ruralism — a yearning for the healing power of English nature and the wholesome simplicities of life on the land — was big in the years between the wars. Williamson was just one of a group that also included Edmund Blunden, H.J. Massingham, Adrian Bell and Rolf Gardiner. Some of these (such as Blunden) are still admired as writers; others (such as Gardiner) as precursors of the Green movement. But the reputation of the movement as a whole suffered badly from the sympathy some of its members displayed towards Nazi Germany, where a similar longing for the purity of "soil and blood" had been conscripted to a more sinister cause. Williamson was one of the most obvious offenders, joining Oswald Mosley's Fascist party and being interned during World War II; but there were others, notably Gardiner.

And the thought that worried me now was: wasn't there an obvious link between ruralism and the extreme right? Weren't the attitudes of rural nostalgia — a distaste for decadent urban modernism, a resentment of outsiders and a fuzzy-edged longing for an ideal of traditional "Englishness" — a bit close for comfort to the attitudes of, say, the British National Party? Didn't H.V. Morton have Nazi sympathies? And where did that leave me?

I wasn't sure how to answer. I knew that I had never felt the least sympathy for far-right politics, or the least hostility towards any racial group, or anything but contempt for political programmes involving strong, authoritarian states or parties. I didn't believe — and don't believe — that a pure-blooded English race exists: it is a simple matter of historical and scientific fact that it doesn't. I know that I have Scottish, Welsh and Irish blood as well as that of people from Yorkshire, Lincolnshire and Birmingham; and that there are probably other strains further back in the mix. (It's reckoned that one white Briton in six has at least one non-white forebear.) I have friends who aren't white and friends who aren't English and if I were looking for a political label with which to define myself I would call myself a liberal. In short, I couldn't be more certain that I'm not a Nazi — closet, subconscious or anything else.

None the less, I felt uncomfortable at the thought that I was exploring unsavoury themes. I thought of Bill

Partridge and the price he and countless other ordinary village boys had paid to defeat Nazism, and, indeed, of my father — who like Bill began the war as a private, ended it as an officer and stared death in the face fighting in Normandy. The thought that his son was paddling in fascist waters would appal him.

But what could I do? Unable to resolve the worry, I bundled it hastily to the back of my mind and accelerated towards the setting sun.

# CHAPTER
# NINE

# Sea change

Near Boscastle, on the coast road to Tresparrett, seagulls circled the square stone tower of the old church of St Juliot. Behind them an empty, early-morning sky shone like polished armour. A blackbird, whistling, hopped between the slanting gravestones, as if he were enjoying the warmth that the uneven turf seemed to have retained from the previous day. I stood near him, inhaling the timeless scent of damp Cornish hillside, and considered the thought that Thomas Hardy worked here in the 1870s, in his younger days as an architect. He fell in love with the rector's sister-in-law, Emma Gifford, while restoring the tower. Was it fanciful to think that I could feel in the air some of their innocent joy, in the uncomplicated spring of their lives? Perhaps. Or perhaps the real folly would have been to visit such a place and imagine oneself to be standing only in the present.

My reverie was broken by the arrival of a large, red-faced hiker who, having sat down with a thump on to a gravestone to remove and adjust a boot, interrupted the process to answer her mobile — on which she then held a loud and astonishingly long conversation about a property sale.

Eventually I despaired of her ever finishing and walked back to my car. On the way, I stopped for a last glance back at the tower, jutting solidly from the band of thin trees beside it. As I did so, I was struck — unexpectedly but vividly — by another view, on a distant hillside, where a long piece of farm machinery was scurrying back and forth over a field, like a red-and-silver insect. I don't know what it was or what it was doing, but it jogged from my memory the thought that it was while he was here that Hardy claimed to have observed the agricultural scene that formed the basis, more than 40 years later, of his great poem of rural permanence, "In Time of 'The Breaking of Nations'":

> Only a man harrowing clods
> In a slow silent walk
> With an old horse that stumbles and nods
> Half asleep as they stalk.
>
> Only thin smoke without flame
> From the heaps of couch-grass;
> Yet this will go onward the same
> Though Dynasties pass . . .

I've always loved those lines. And yet, I realised now, how wrong he was. Nothing goes onward the same now. The permanence has evaporated from the land.

★ ★ ★

About four hours later, on Cornwall's opposite coast, I swear I saw the very same tourist, sitting on a stone wall at the side of the narrow road that leads down into the famous fishing village of Polperro. She still had the phone to her ear, although both feet were now booted. She seemed to be struggling with her signal.

A river of French teenagers emerging from the coach park distracted me from the idea of finding out more about her, and I followed the stream of people down the steep, winding road to the harbour.

"*Il n'y a pas de boutiques,*" complained one of them. "*Elles sont fermées.*" This seemed a spectacularly unperceptive assessment. Shops line the lane that winds down to the sea like shells on a souvenir necklace: gift shops, food shops, clothes shops, art and craft shops, even a Pisky Shop, all open and all jostling for village-space with several chapels, a church, a post office, six pubs, getting on for a dozen restaurants and cafés, about the same number of bed-and-breakfasts and at least 45 cottages available for holiday lets.

A scent of salt and fishy water led me past the Chip Ahoy chip shop, a craftsmen's centre and a fudge shop to a tiny harbour. Half a dozen worn-out little boats slept on the cold, dark sea that lapped against its grimy stone walls. Salt-bleached wooden ladders led up from the water to the quay, where a few tourists were huddled among the ropes and lifebelts in hope of boat trips. A damp wind brushed across grey rocks from the great and dangerous sea beyond.

An old sailor called Bill Cohen ("I'm a newcomer — I've only lived here since 1949") directed me to the

Blue Anchor pub, where, he said, I might find the harbour master, Chris Curtis.

He was right. Once my eyes had adjusted to the darkness, I found a small bar containing, among others, a little old man in a far corner reading the *Racing Post*, an enormous bearded man in a puffy anorak, a young, earringed barman and a bespectacled, baseball-capped man in his early sixties who was supporting himself next to the bar using a combination of a barstool and a pair of crutches.

"I got a new knee," said the man with the crutches. "It's my first day out." He was indeed Chris Curtis, he conceded; then he continued: "A lot of us get them now — us older ones. All that pulling in the nets. Most fishermen's knees go, and we all get arthritis in the end. In the old days you were never dry."

He had been fishing from Polperro for most of his life — apart from a two-year spell as a chauffeur in west London in the 1960s — and came, he said, from a long line of Polperro fishermen. "It used to be harder for them, of course. My great-great-great-grandfather spent nine years in a French prison. He used to fish off the Channel Islands, and then one day he went as far as the French mainland and was arrested as a spy. Nine years he spent there. But then he came back and had nine children."

Everyone laughed. The big man in the anorak was called Andrew and was looking after Chris's boat for him while he convalesced. He wasn't planning to go out that day unless he heard reports that the fishing was good — "There's an east wind forecast, and we don't like rolling any more."

Was Andrew local? "I don't think I qualify yet. It's only my 21st year here."

"He's working on it," said Chris.

"Once you get your tombstone, then you're accepted," said Andrew.

It was hard to be certain that he was joking. The question of incomers seemed to make both men tense. "People come in from the outside," said Chris, "and, after a bit, you become the outsider."

He swigged some coffee. "I should say — what? — 70 per cent of the village is holiday lets. When I was a boy it was 100 per cent local. Well, there was a few people here what had come here to retire, but that was it. Now there's much fewer locals."

"Fewer local locals," interjected Andrew.

Chris didn't smile. They take their suspicion of outsiders seriously in Polperro. Perhaps this is understandable. Until the 1920s, Polperro didn't even have a proper road leading to it. Villagers and smugglers left and returned by sea; the rest of the world wasn't really wanted anyway. In the 18th and 19th centuries, when high excise duties made smuggling as lucrative as today's drug trade, the village was a self-contained kingdom-within-a-kingdom, with its own currency — issued by the notorious Zephaniah Job — and, in effect, its own laws. The village prospered materially. Whether or not it was a pleasant place to live is hard to say from this distance. But the smugglers' myth has done much to sustain the local economy since; the drawback being that, today, myth is about the only thing that does sustain it.

"I think half the battle is, you've got people coming in here, it's always people who want to make money," Chris explained after a few moments' thought. He gestured out towards the harbour. "I rent that net-loft over there: I pay about £100 a year for it. How many have come up to me and say, 'What a lovely house that would make'? But I say: why does it have to make a house? It's already a lovely net-loft. I quite like doing my nets up there. It's only a loft, but I don't want a settee and a kitchen. I want to sit and mend my nets and look out the window. What is wrong with that? Why must it be change all the time? Why can't it be the very thing that they come down for in the first place? But they won't see it."

We all nodded. "Why do they always see the potential in things?" Chris continued. "What's wrong with how things are already?"

"Like that lady who came to Looe," said Andrew, "and said this would be a lovely place, if only the fishing boats and yachts would take their masts down and stop spoiling her view up the river." He mimicked a posh voice: "'Can't you make them go out at seven in the morning and not five in the morning? They wake me up.'"

The discussion turned to a wealthy newcomer who had begun a transport service for tourists which they felt had done nothing for the village's character. "He goes under the guise of, 'Well, I'm employing four people,'" said Chris. "So what? Why's he got to do it? Why's he got to come here and upset people?"

He nodded at the barman. "Rob here come here from Worcestershire and he's slotted in, and they're all locals now, locals in no time, because they've embraced the place. They ain't tried to change anything but they fitted in with it."

"There's two sorts of people," said Rob. "There's those who come here and appreciate what's here and enjoys it, or there are those who don't experience local life. There was a lady moved down from London and she was complaining about the noise of the fish cart."

"But, you see, it just makes us make more noise really," said Chris, proudly. "I said to one lad, I said, 'Be quiet with them boxes.' 'Why?' I said, 'You'll wake everybody up.' 'So?' he said. 'There's nobody local lives here.' So that's the attitude of it, unfortunately."

Although he still fished regularly, Chris now spent a large chunk of his time on land. As harbour master, he was one of 15 trustees who managed the affairs of the harbour on a voluntary basis — looking after its upkeep, controlling the coming and going of ships, closing the storm-gates, and so on. "We do it for free, and then there's also the Friends of the Harbour who do charity work, and they raise money for the upkeep of the harbour, and that keeps the industry going. Years ago, when the fish was there, there was 50-odd fishing boats. Now there's basically 15 boats fish out of here. But it's still an important part of the village, when you consider the families who rely on the income that those men bring in."

Fishing is also an important part of the village's "brand" and, as such, crucial for the tourist industry. The Polperro Fishermen's Choir (founded in 1923) is a major attraction, although, said Chris, "There's no fishermen in it now."

He was never involved in it himself. "The village always had quite a strong chapel side and quite a strong pub side. I was more on the pub side. But if you used to come down here on a summer evening, they'd practise there before they went to sea, in their leather boots and all their gear for the sea, practically every night. It was lovely."

"The sad thing," said Andrew, "is that not many youngsters are coming into it. Fishing."

"Our fishing fleet is just going to contract from now on," said Chris. "Everything's going, except tourism. The old shops have gone, the grocer, a couple of butchers, two banks . . . The only bit of good news we've just been given is that when you get to 60, you can travel anywhere you like in Cornwall on a bus for free. The bad news is, you have to find a bus first."

Had progress not improved anything? "I suppose so. Fishing is all computerised now. I've just had a new radar put on — you can pinpoint your position within 6ft to 9ft, you can plot your course anywhere you want to. Trouble is, though, that's opened the ground to everybody else too, so no longer can you have your own little favourite spot."

"It's got a lot more comfortable, too," said Andrew. "You've got better bunks, TV, you can keep yourself dry."

"Fishing weren't easy then," said Chris, "although you could catch anything you wanted, and go where you wanted. You didn't have to fill out a form or anything else. You've got to have all these licences now, and safety certificates and this certificate and that certificate. Years ago we used to go to sea with no life jacket, no life raft and a bloody old lead pump, and I can't remember any boat sinking then. If you got a leak you patched it up with a bit of tar and a few nails. Nowadays, boats go down willy-nilly."

A gust of wind rattled the window, and I was glad to be inside. "We didn't earn a great deal," said Chris. "But you didn't need that much. The older fishermen, they all had these little allotments where they grew all the vegetables they'd need in the winter, and they had these pilchards they'd salted, and they'd go up the hills and they'd cut wood for their fires, so they really needed very little money to live on. So they knew that they could eat, and if they felt like racing each other one day instead of fishing, they would. The thing about fishing now is that it's big money. Not just big money fishing, but they owe big money. A lot of them have got not just rent to pay, mortgages to pay, they've got boats to pay for. Once a chap's got a loan for a boat, that could be £100,000, and then they want a house and, well, some of them are in for half a million. A lot of them are in deep, so they've got to go, even in bad weather."

"And that's why so many boats go down," said Andrew.

**110**

"Oh, yes," said Chris. "It is a dangerous bloody occupation, no doubt about it. Always has been. But it was a community then: people enjoyed life.

"Mind you, we weren't rich. We could eat, but putting clothes on your back was another thing. I remember very well, when I was a boy . . . Cardboard don't last very long in the bottoms of shoes, I can tell you that. And I think I must have been about 13 before I realised that you could wipe your arse on specially made paper. We'd always just had newspaper cut into little bits. And when we moved to our bungalow — this was one of the council houses on top of the hill — I used to have two baths a day — I couldn't get over the fact that we actually had a bath in the house, with hot water. Yeah, and a flush. I couldn't get over it."

His reverie was interrupted by the buzz of a text arriving on Andrew's phone: "Fish down the bay." Chris was suddenly animated again, briefing Andrew like a football manager sending on a substitute. "You've got the green trawl and the fine nets . . . They'll have lemons [lemon sole] down there . . . Go all the way down to Falmouth." Then a thought struck him: "Do a trip! Falmouth for the night? A few beers? That does away with all your problems."

Andrew liked this idea. "The thing is," he explained, "from Brixham to Newlyn, everyone knows everybody, and generally they're good sorts. The younger ones get to know the older ones. Because it's a dangerous job, you get that camaraderie, where you help each other. You can always rely on anybody."

"The good thing about making a trip of it is that usually you meet up with old friends," said Chris, "and then there becomes a lovely sort of feel about it. There was one I did last year, and I walked into a bar and it was like there was everybody from my past that I'd ever known, and it was all 'I thought you was dead' and 'I thought you was dead as well'. And the beer started to flow."

He looked sad, as though pondering life's brevity. "The shame is," he continued, "that no one appreciates what's there until it's gone. It's a pity," he added after a pause, "that the Smuggling and Fishing Museum's not open at the moment. You'd find some interesting things there. It's over there, in the Warren, where the pilchard factories used to be."

The Warren? Why was it called that? "I think they used to farm rabbits there, hundreds of years ago."

"I can't believe you just said that," said Andrew, with what seemed like genuine alarm.

"Sorry," said Chris. "I meant small furry animals with long ears."

"We may have all the latest electronic equipment," said Andrew, "but we take our superstitions seriously. It's very bad luck to say that word." I laughed, searching uncertainly for a note of irony in his voice. He said nothing, but hurried out rather grimly into the damp east wind, in pursuit of lemon sole.

# CHAPTER
# TEN

# The wild west

I headed in the general direction of Bodmin Moor — where Chris had suggested that "old Cornishmen" might still be found — and listened to a local radio station as I drove. They were discussing a recent article written by the Bishop of Truro, who seemed to have ruffled a few feathers by claiming that Cornwall was facing a "rural crisis", because of a particularly unhealthy combination of high house prices and low wages for traditional agricultural jobs. This seemed quite plausible to me. The price of a house in Cornwall quadrupled between 1996 and 2006 (from £53,000 to £195,000, according to a survey by the Halifax), while the county's population had already increased by a third between 1971 and 2001. Meanwhile, the average (median) salary in 2005 was £19,000, some £4,000 below the UK average. The result, according to the bishop, was that "it is virtually impossible for many people who have been born and bred in Cornwall to bring up their children in the communities which have formed them". He made the point that "Cornwall is as it is because of the pattern of life that has developed over centuries. All that is now changing quickly and inexorably." All the more reason, I thought, to track down the wild men of Bodmin as soon as possible.

An hour or so later, I stopped on the moor, in the middle of a sweet-smelling brown-gold sea of rough, dusty turf and broken-topped gorse bushes that looked like the remains of a forest blasted away by war. Confused by the worn, rough-edged lanes and tracks that criss-crossed it in all directions, I consulted my AA atlas and was alarmed to notice that Cornwall was covered in red spots. Closer inspection revealed that these were symbols for local tourist attractions, the names of which were in tiny type beside them: Tamar Otter Sanctuary, Trethorne Leisure Farm, Dobwalls Adventure Park, Colliford Lake Park, Jamaica Inn (now officially known as "Jamaica Inn Featuring Daphne du Maurier's At Jamaica Inn Museum"), Moorswater, Porfell Animal Land, Royal Cornwall, Wheal Martyn Heritage Centre, Automobilia, Carnglaze Caverns, Monkey Sanctuary, Argal & College Water Park, World in Miniature, Poldark Mine, Merlin's Magic Land, Seal Sanctuary, Model Village, the Lost Gardens of Heligan, the Eden Project . . . To name them all would fill the whole page. It made me wonder how the Cornish would feed themselves if the hated tourists went away.

A vague sense of breathing around me made me look up from my ponderings. Six dusty ponies, mostly brown, some splashed with dirty cream, had gathered around me, noiselessly. I could smell the closest through my open window.

I got out, and, for a few minutes, we examined one another in mute, benign incomprehension. No breeze blew; there was, for once, no drone of traffic: just silence radiating from the warm gorse and the snapped bits of tree around us. The whole wilderness had a pre-human quality. Here, at least (I reflected), was some English permanence: a landscape more enduring than the wealth and power of men. For all I knew, the forebears of my current warm-breathed, quietly munching companions had been living off this turf since the dawn of civilisation. But where were their human equivalents?

A few miles later, halfway up the side of a steep, wooded valley, I stopped in Warleggan. There wasn't much to it: just a zigzag of lane with a few garden gates, a red letterbox set into a wall, a red phonebox, and a rough track scratched off below the church. There was no one about in the lane. If you didn't know better you'd be through the village and out the other side before you even noticed that it was there.

But I did know better — so I paused to look in the squat grey church. It was plain, white and unremarkable inside, but there was an old photograph just by the door, showing a few black-clad figures at a funeral. Among them, his face too blurred to see clearly, was the village's most notorious former inhabitant: the Reverend Frederick Densham, "rector of Warleggan, 1931–1951", according to the caption.

You may have heard his tale. He was 61 when he came to the village and almost immediately fell out with it. Accounts differ as to why. Some say that his style was too flamboyant — he painted the church in colours so garish that the Bishop of Truro made him

**115**

paint them over. Others say that he alienated some farmers by allowing his puppies to worry their sheep. Whichever the truth, by 1933 a petition had been sent to the bishop asking for him to be removed. He wasn't — the bishop dismissed five separate complaints against him. So the villagers began to boycott his services.

Before long, he was regularly preaching to an empty church. Undaunted, he started filling the pews with cardboard cut-outs: initially of previous rectors and then of ordinary villagers. And then — which is the truly remarkable bit — the impasse continued, for nearly two decades. Week after week, year after year, his sermons fell unheard on cardboard ears, while his parishioners muttered their sullen hostility from out of earshot. "No wind. No rain. No congregation," he wrote in his diary. If he hadn't been odd before, it would have been hard not to become so.

On the opposite side of the lane, a little way up the hill, I met an old carpenter who remembered him. "I used to do a lot of jobs for him and all, you see," said Cyril Keast, a cheerful 83-year-old with pink cheeks, a long neck and a soft, melodic voice. "He was very straight to deal with, a very straight man in business. Every so often he were eccentric, but old man weren't silly. We're not going to have him run down."

"He wouldn't hurt nobody," said Cyril's wife, Barbara, after Cyril had taken me into their house. "I used to work at the post office. He used to come in every Sunday and buy stamps, but he'd never leave the money, and he'd bring it in on Monday, when I'd be gone, and he'd always leave the right money. Here, you sit," she added, producing a teapot from nowhere, "and you shall have one of my buns."

I wondered why the rector had been so unpopular. Had it been just another case of a comfortable, educated clergyman failing to bond with a less privileged congregation? Or did it illustrate a dark underside of village life: the tendency of close-knit rural communities to make outsiders unwelcome and to nurse local grudges unforgivingly for years?

"Old man [Densham] was before his time," argued Cyril. "He used to come to the Methodist chapel, sit in the back seat and take notes. He got the Methodist minister to read a lesson [in church]. Well, the church people wouldn't have that back then. So he ended up going to church for 20 years with no one there."

"Daphne du Maurier, she wrote about him," said Barbara (apparently in reference to a passing mention in her *Vanishing Cornwall*). "But it was all lies," she added, handing me a giant rock cake. She blinked indignantly through large, owl-like glasses. "We lived with him. But this is years ago now."

"He was always very reverend at a funeral," said Cyril, who used to make coffins and assist at funerals when required. "I won't say his surplice was that clean, but the old man would go over to the grave at the last and take his hat off, and say his last few words.

"Well, the churchwarden, who hadn't been to church for years, died. So: funeral. He had to come to church then, didn't he? I said to Densham, 'Several around today, sir.' 'Yes, Cyril: but we get 'em at the end, don't we? We get 'em in the end, Cyril.' "

When the Reverend Densham died, it was several days before he was found. "They came here to see if they could see smoke coming from his chimney, and they couldn't," said Cyril, "so they broke in there and they found him dead in the stairs, you know. And he was carried away like an animal, in a truck, and his feet were showing out the back of the truck."

Their house was still a carpenter's shop then. Cyril and Barbara moved in 50 years ago but had been there for a couple of decades before they transformed it into the comfortably furnished home, shining with family photographs, that it is today. "For 20 years it was one-and-a-half down and one-and-a-half up. We lived in this piece, with a piece across there, and the landlord lived next door."

Cyril had been in the village all his life — "I were born out there, just out by the barns there" — and his family had been on the moor for at least 500 years, mainly as farm labourers. "We never amounted to much." Yet he, it turned out, was almost a local celebrity, having featured more than once in local media features about Cornish tradition. "Oh, yays, yays, yares," he said, almost as if he were showing off the richness of his accent. "The BBC's been here recording our voices — 'cause we speak how we always did, ye see."

"We had a writer from Germany come here once," said Barbara, returning with a magazine cutting from one of several forays to her collection of memorabilia.

118

"Look, this is a German book, this is, and this is what he wrote about Warleggan. It's in German."

"But when you come to our names, that's not translated, is it," said Cyril.

"No, the names is the same."

Barbara came from Mount, where her father had been postman and she, following her mother's death, had been England's youngest postmistress. "She was 15, and you was supposed to be 16, but they had no alternative but to swear her in," said Cyril proudly. "There had to be a post office."

There doesn't now. "Everything's closed in Mount now," said Barbara. "There used to be three butchers' shops, a pub, a petrol station, a carpenter's, a reading room. A blacksmith would shoe horses on Friday. There was a school, too, that I went to, but that closed 50 years ago. Now there's nothing. It's very sad."

There used to be a tin mine near by, too, employing up to 70 people in its heyday. "My father worked down in the tin mine," said Cyril. "It was a hard life, underground. I remember him coming home streaming wet, yes. But he lived to a good old age.

"Oh, yes, age." He rocked his head and smiled enigmatically. "He was a tough bloke," he continued. "They were a big family — very poor. They couldn't afford to buy meat, but they kept a herd of goats that lived on the moor. My father told me that when they really wanted some meat they'd take a pony and run a goat down and kill it. But as the boys got older and went to the mine to work, they were bringing home more money, so they could buy meat and different

**119**

things, so they never bothered with the goats, and we think that the goats went over Brown Willy or something like that, and they never bothered with them no more. So we've lost a herd of goats. Sometimes I think I should go out and try and look for them."

The family's prosperity was limited and short-lived. "When my father finished at the mine, he only had a smallholding. It weren't a living, so he used to go round collecting butter and eggs from the farms, and then he'd drive to Doublebois station on Saturday morning and take the train to Plymouth with his eggs and butter and rabbits. But when rationing came he packed it in, because you were only allowed a quarter of a pound of butter.

"I never had new clothes. Brother was bigger than I, so everything I had was second-hand. But we were happy with what we had. Didn't know what 'bored' meant."

Cyril learnt his carpenter's trade in Bodmin: "I cycled 9 miles each way, for 5 shilling [25p] a week. Then local people at Mount, I think they offered me 10 or 12 shilling to come back there. But that was doing a different thing. That was agricultural machinery: wheels, carts and all that, you know — making wheels, wagon wheels and cartwheels and carts and all this — yes, wooden ones — shafts and all that for horses, back then.

"But that died away out because people got more modern," he continued, swaying slightly, as if reciting some ancient legend. "We used to go round repairing. We worked at every farm or house that was in the area.

120

When anybody died, we'd make a coffin for 'em. If they wanted a new window, you'd go and make one. But nowadays they don't do it — they go and buy one, don't they?"

"It's all altered now," said Barbara, topping up the tea.

"Yes, all altered now," said Cyril. "Years ago, you see, well, there was the same families, around the farms an' all, for years — Willses, Warnes, Keasts, Alfords, Wardens. And in the village itself, people who worked for farmers, generally. Our landlord worked for a big farmer, ploughing. He'd walk so many miles a day, ploughing with horses, yes, back then, yes, walk to work, get his horses and take them, and do all the farm work with horses, oh, yes, yes. He's gone now, oh, yes. But it was the same farmers and people around for years. There were wonderful old families — they'd do anything for anybody. Good as gold. But the old ones just died off, you see, and people came down from up country."

"The people next door are local," said Barbara. "All the rest have come in. We and John" — their son, who lives a few doors away — "and the Hills are the only ones that are Cornish."

How did the new villagers earn their livings?

"Let me see," said Barbara. "Our neighbour's husband does forestry, fencing, trees. Jeanette teaches in St Austell: it's dark when she comes home. There's a holiday cottage next door. There's one who goes to Plymouth every day, working at the airports. One's on the dustcarts at Bodmin. There's one who works on submarines — he was in the Falklands. The people in the Rookery goes to London. One goes to a garage at Bodmin. There's a bloke used to work for the *Daily Telegraph* — he's retired now. Some of them do join in and some don't."

"Some we do know and some we don't know," echoed Cyril. "We distribute this parish magazine, and some of them I think it don't mind if I put it in the letterbox or the dustbin, because they don't mix with us."

"You miss the ones that have gone on," said Barbara. "We forget a lot. You think, oh, so-and-so will know that. But they're gone."

A few weeks before, they had buried one of the village's best-loved old characters, Cyril's brother Tor. "My brother was a bit older than me, and he passed away. He was old-fashioned, you know: he was out on the moors with his few animals all his life. For his funeral, we didn't have trestles under the coffin: we had two bales of hay. It made a bit of a mess on the red carpet, but we had to have it — he carried hay all his life.

"He had a wonderful life," continued Cyril. "No worries. He had his animals and his farm, and that was all. Until he had his fall, he'd never slept away or lived anywhere else. He'd never been further than Plymouth.

"He never made much out of farming. He'd feed his animals too much. But for his funeral, the church was full. All the people we know were there. Yes, old farmers come from all around for Tor Keast's funeral. Church was full. It was the old generation."

122

Cyril was still looking after Tor's cattle, in tandem with his son, although the farmhouse had been let out. "That's where I just come from — checking on cattle. Got to keep an eye on things for brother. It was all he had.

"He was alone most of the time, but he knew everything that was going on. He used to have big phone bills. I'd go out there and he'd tell me things. I don't know how he knew it all, but since he's been gone I've had to find out for myself. But that was his life."

Later on, Cyril's son, John, a chartered surveyor in his mid-fifties, took me up to Tor's house and out through its rough farmyard on to the moor above, where he showed me some old stone cairns that he thought might be ancient representations of the distant tors on the skyline, notably the great pyramid of Brown Willy. We sat on a rock in the wind, trying to imagine the mindset of the moor's first human inhabitants, and how mysterious and unreachably distant that skyline must have seemed to them. It was hard to make the necessary leap: the defining assumption of the 21st-century mental landscape is that there is nowhere that cannot be reached reasonably quickly.

John worked mainly in Lostwithiel — about 10 miles away — but also travelled widely. Looking after his uncle's cattle was quite an extra burden, but he seemed to carry it gladly. "I go up before work and feed them, and then my dad goes up in the afternoon. We don't make any money from it: it's a cost. We should sell it really," he added, indicating the farm. "But I can't bear the thought of someone else having it."

Back in the village, he took me on a little path below the church and pointed out some strange, overgrown shapes in what used to be the rectory garden. Closer inspection revealed them to be the rotting remains of a children's playground: a sand pit, a paddling pool, a roundabout. "Densham built it. He hoped the village children would play in it. And when he wrote that he wanted his ashes to be scattered in 'the garden of remembrance', that was what he meant." But only a few villagers, who weren't asked, knew that the garden in question was the one the lonely vicar had created in the vicarage; so the ashes were scattered in the Garden of Remembrance in Plymouth instead.

I spent the night near by, at a more upmarket bed-and-breakfast than I had intended, which was owned by the explorer and author Robin Hanbury-Tenison, who in 1969 co-founded the charity Survival International. Survival campaigns on behalf of indigenous tribal peoples around the world, with the general aim of allowing them to preserve their own ancestral lands and distinctive cultures in the face of various forces of modernisation and homogenisation. We were soon discussing my quest. I asked him if he saw any overlap between Survival's concerns and my own worries about the death of the distinctive culture of rural England. It would have been odd if he hadn't: he also helped set up the Countryside Alliance, of which he was chief executive from 1997 to 1998. Yet he seemed reluctant to say so explicitly. "Yes," he said (apparently making the field-sportsman's habitual assumption that rural culture is synonymous with field sports), "you could make a case that killing animals for fun is part of our traditional rural culture, in the same way that halal slaughter is part of Muslim culture. But as to the degree of threat . . ." He began to talk about recent arguments in court — during a legal challenge to the 2004 Hunting Act — in which the question of whether "immigrants have more protection in law than native-born English people" had arisen. "But," he added, "it's probably not a good idea to make too much of that, because it's the sort of thing some people might make mischief with." I knew what he meant. We left it at that.

Later that night, I gazed out of my rattling window at the moonlit clouds that were tumbling across the cold moor and thought uneasily again about ruralism and right-wing politics. Was it wrong to value England's rural traditions? Was anyone who felt uncomfortable about the homogenisation of cultures a racist? Of course not. Yet there was something about ruralism that troubled me. Perhaps it was a sense that there was something ungenerous, in a world bursting at the seams with suffering and injustice, about the "I'm all right, Jack" conservatism represented by some supporters of the Countryside Alliance. Or perhaps I was thinking about Warleggan's rejection of Frederick Densham, and the general unthinking hostility to outsiders that I kept sensing just below many rural surfaces.

I couldn't decide. But I felt that I needed to be on my guard against something.

★   ★   ★

The next morning, I went north to the tiny village of Temple, where I visited the little 12th-century church of St Catherine's. I was surprised not to find tourists there: the site was once owned by the Knights Templar, who seem to draw them in these days; the place was also notorious once as a kind of Gretna Green of the south-west, where (between the Reformation and 1753) marriages could legally be performed without banns or licence.

But there was no one there, and I heard only the mewing of a buzzard as I wandered among the graves. I found the particular tomb I was looking for near the top of the slope, slightly lopsided, carved in the shape of an urn and inscribed: "Charles Lambert, Rector of Warleggan and Vicar of Temple, who fell asleep on the moor after service on January 19th 1901, aged 43 years".

Cyril Keast had told me about Lambert the previous day. According to Cyril, "This church [at Warleggan] used to go with the church at Temple across the moor, and the parson used to walk across the moors of an afternoon. He was a big fat feller, liked his drink. But he used to stop on the way at a farm where they couldn't afford to buy clothes to go to school, and he'd draw some problem or question on the kitchen floor, and then when he come back he'd see how the little girl had done. She told me later he'd learnt them more than they learnt at school. Then when he got back here he'd like to have a drink, and then sometimes he didn't show up for the service in the evening. So if he didn't show up the congregation would just sing a hymn and say a prayer and go home. One evening he didn't turn up. So they sang a hymn and said a prayer and went home. He was found on the Wednesday morning, dead on the moor, and his little terrier dog was still by his side."

I don't know who chose his resting place, but it couldn't have been more obvious what they had in mind. The tomb was angled to face out directly towards Bodmin Moor, which slept in the distance like a calm brown sea. It was hard not to feel a sense of peace here. Yet it was also hard, as I retraced my steps to the car, to dispel a darker thought: so that was two Warleggan rectors who lay dead for several days before they were found; just as Tor Keast — who was much loved — lay undiscovered for 16 hours after the fall that ended his active life. Daphne du Maurier described Warleggan as "the loneliest place in Cornwall". Perhaps she was failing to appreciate the romance of inaccessibility. Or perhaps she was right.

I headed back down towards Warleggan and, before I got there, stopped in what I can only describe as the middle of nowhere to visit one of Bodmin's oldest farming families: the Willses. "Wonderful old folks," Cyril had said. "Clive Wills, Ken Wills — you know, if someone had a cow in trouble, they'd help them. Good as gold."

There were about a dozen buildings to choose from in the muddy, messy yard: stone huts and corrugated sheds and a couple of big metallic barns, interspersed with various trees and rusting items of farm machinery. I tried a door in the building that looked most occupied and found myself in a front room so small it might have been a caravan.

Ken Wills, who greeted me, was a slight, upright old man in mucky overalls and wellingtons, with a quilted body warmer on top and a tweed hat. His skin was brown, stretched and leathery, like a turtle's, but his blue eyes were clear and bright, and there was the kind of strikingly well-preserved handsomeness to his face that one sometimes sees in old film stars.

We sat down and chatted, initially about how long the family had lived there. "Been here a fair while," he said. "I'm 83 end of this month, and I was born here. My mother was born here. Farm been in the family for over 200 years." The family had probably been on the moor a good deal longer.

He sat erect and still on the ancient sofa, as if rooted in it. I sat on the only other chair, by a formica-topped table on the opposite side of the room. Our knees were almost touching. An old flypaper, dark with flies, hung down between us. An ancient television sat on an ancient radio, near an ancient stove, and paperwork and odds and ends took up most of the other space. There were socks stuffed along the top of the sofa.

His only son, Clive, did most of the farming now, but Ken helped out as well. "Oh, yes," he said brightly. "I keep going. I en't gonna give up. And I do a bit of gardening and hedging and stuff like that. That all keep me able like, keep fit."

It was, of course, a rather different kind of farming. "Years ago we used to cut hay with horses, and carry it with wagons. Then we got to horse and sweep [i.e.,

**128**

hay-sweep], then tractor and sweep, then we got to the baler, then got the big square baler . . . And then now I suppose it's all combines. It's all gone up.

"We only had tractors from 1946. He wouldn't have anything to do with them to start with, my uncle. That's the way, with old people. I'd say, look, we ought to do so-and-so. He'd say, we managed without it before: what you want it now for?"

His father died when he was nine. "He had creeping paralysis — he was bad for years; he couldn't work. But he was partners with his brothers. You might say my uncle reared me. He wasn't married — that's why my mother was here looking after him. Then afterwards, me and sister stopped here and looked after uncle, till she got married and left. Then we had 18 months here on our own before we got a housekeeper [Ruby, who became Ken's wife]. But we lived all right."

He flashed a brilliant, defiant smile that made me think, for some reason, of some photographs I had recently seen of earthquake victims in Pakistan: the tired faces worn almost expressionless by hardship, the eyes miraculously bright and expressive by contrast.

Had his life been hard? "Oh, yes, yes. But we was brought up to it.

"We never had telephone or electric — we was always trying to get it. Had to go with what they called hurricane lanterns, years ago — the wind would blow them out. After, we had the oil lamps. Well, then the Tilleys come in, that was a fine thing — they give a lot more light. But electric's a fine thing. Got to go with it.

"That stove weren't there back in them days, and this was a peat fire, and we cooked in what you'd probably call down in the ashes. We cut our own peat, down the end of the farm. But all that's gone now, all under water." (Colliford Reservoir, an embankment construction that impounds water from the river St Neot, was completed in 1983.) "They took away all our peat rights. We couldn't say nothin' — no one knew we. They just stepped in and said I'm putting a dam there."

Childhood, like many traditional rural childhoods, had been short. "From schoolchildren right up, soon as you were old enough you'd milk cows, or you'd go to fields and bring 'em in. I'd have to walk down to St Neot to get bread when we'd get snowed in.

"But we used to skive off sometimes, play with the other children that grew up around here. We had to make our own fun. We used to get together, two or three of us, and we used to go out on common and set it on fire and all the likes of that. We didn't go all that long away, but we would run wild like."

Where were those children now? "All disappeared. When I was going to school in St Neot, I knew everyone that was there, just about. Well, now you go down there, there's only four or five you know. All strangers who've come there. I don't know 'em.

"There was a time round here," he added, "when it was just about all relations. All round the moors, they were all our neighbours, just about all relations. We helped one another out — what one don't have, other may have."

130

We were joined briefly by Clive, who was in the middle of calving. A strongly built 43-year-old with short, curly hair and a big, crooked-toothed smile that made his weather-beaten face look like an old prize-fighter's, he seemed harassed. "We had a cow that was bad," he explained, "so that hindered us this morning. So everything's a couple of hours behind, and you can never gain back that time that you lost like."

I asked him how the farm was doing. "Put it this way: about 15 years ago our bank manager come out and looked at it, and he thought it was just ideal for him like, just to do a bit of hobby farming." He didn't buy it, but, said Clive: "That's what they think of a small farm like this — just a hobby kind of thing now. It's 100 acres all told like, all fields. We've got beef and sheep. But you've got to have about 300, 400 good acres to make a living."

"Houses is makin' some money now more than cows," said Ken. "If this house come on the market someone may buy it for their house, and sell ground off, then they'd have this house for nothing. They could buy the whole farm for what they'd give 'em for a house in these towns, turn they barns into chalets. We'd be pounds in pocket."

A farm near by that Ken's brother once rented — and nearly bought for £2,000 in 1952 — had just been sold for £900,000. "It's all been divided up," said Clive. "There's a farmhouse and three or four fields and a couple of holiday lets. But that's the way it is. You get someone from London that's got a house up there, then they can buy a place down here and it's pocket money to them.

"The trouble is," he added, "people move in the area, because they want it because it's unique. Then they want to change it to how they had it up country. And that spoils it for what they came here in the first place for.

"What puts me out," he continued, "is some people can't understand how Ken speaks. I don't notice anything, you see — he speaks proper. But you see some people, they nod their heads, and you know that they can't understand him, but they're just nodding their heads — and thinking he's stupid. But he speaks English. It's just that people who come from up country, they can't understand his dialect. They have this stereotype of language."

Presumably any rich incomers crass enough to sneer at the Willses for their accents would also despise them for their relative poverty. I asked Clive how the family managed to make ends meet.

"Well, we keep our pennies tight and stuff like that. It depends how much luxuries you want. I mean, if you want your DVD and everything else like that, you aren't going to make a living like, are you? If you had that money, you could spend it. But if you don't . . . We manage. But you're working all the time." And with that he hurried back to calving.

I suggested to Ken that he was lucky to have a son, living with him and supporting him. "Oh, yes," he said proudly. Then, after a pause: "He en't married though. Farm may have to go I expect." He seemed, for the first time, a little gloomy. "But you got to travel around if you want to meet people." Which, obviously, would be difficult.

Did he miss the old days? "I miss the horses. Yes, I do: I miss they. I'd dearly love to have a pair now. And the people I suppose — old people have gone and new comed in."

Did he see much of them? Did he go out much? "No. I'm happy home."

What about church, or chapel, or anything like that?

"No, not very often. I had a Jehovah's Witness here other day — he calls every now and again. Well, the old chap tells me that Christ is comin' to the ground, and all we non-Christians will disappear like that. So I told him, I said, it won't make no difference to me — I'm 82. I've already had my life. He didn't know what to say to me then."

He grinned. "But I tell you," he added, "I en't going to give up as long as I can go." And he hobbled out into the windy yard to help with the calving.

# CHAPTER
# ELEVEN

# Roots

I went home for a while.

"Is that it then?" said Clare, when I showed no signs of setting off again.

"Of course not," I said. But I had, for the time being, run out of steam. I was tired of being away from home, tired of driving. And I had been growing doubtful about the value of my quest.

Specifically: I was worried that there was something deeply complacent about the premise behind my travels: the idea that the passing of the "old rural ways" was something to be mourned. Even a cursory study of English social history suggests that the true story of our countryside over the past 1,000 years or so is largely a squalid one of poverty, disease, exploitation and ignorance. Who outside the comfortable metropolitan classes would view the past with such lazy sentimentality? Surely any genuine members of a lost rural "tribe" would have rejoiced at the coming of modernity? Who was I to suggest that they were wrong?

I picked up the neglected threads of my real life and, without going quite so far as to declare that I had abandoned my quest, said no more about it.

But the social revolution that had prompted it in the first place showed no signs of dying down. Instead, cosmopolitan modernity continued to erupt over the countryside, overwhelmingly, until I found it impossible to ignore.

Every media mention of the countryside showed the same trends: the flight from the cities, the decline of the old rural labouring classes, the soaring price of rural property. As the world's financiers and moguls increasingly converged on London as a congenial environment for the super-rich, so their cash had been spurting out into the Home Counties. The Royal Institution of Chartered Surveyors reported that rural land prices were rising at their fastest-ever rate — up 18 per cent in one six-month period alone. Other reports suggested that would-be smallholders were being priced out of the market by "hobby farmers" and "horsiculture". A leading social forecasting group, the Future Foundation, announced that a whole new breed of "urban farmers" was colonising the "glamour belt" around the M25, buying up agricultural holdings for leisure purposes; and that 22 per cent of city-dwellers aspired to join them. Even the traditional farming lobby was starting to admit that, for farmers, things could be worse — even if they couldn't make money from their land by producing food from it, at least they could do so by selling it. Yet it was equally clear that there were losers as well as winners in this process. The agricultural workforce had shrunk below 250,000. The number of agricultural businesses going bust increased by 27 per cent in a single year. And a report by the

Young Foundation claimed to have detected a sharp increase in rural homelessness: 700,000 rural children were living in poverty, it stated. "The countryside is becoming posher but poorer," declared one of the report's authors.

The months hurried faster, and I felt a sense of melancholic restlessness returning. Maybe, I reflected, there had been a germ of sense in my wanderings. None the less, I was reluctant to resume them.

For a start, I had a living to earn — which is difficult to do if you are driving vast distances around rural England each week in vague search of a semi-mythical lost past.

I had also realised — belatedly — that driving vast distances around rural England has severe limitations as a mode of research: the more villages I visited, the more superficial my inquiries became. I would have been better off staying at home and spending more time with the dwindling number of "real" country people I already knew.

Unfortunately, even that was proving increasingly difficult. Over in Hertfordshire, my father's health was collapsing. The details don't matter now, although they did then. (Millions must be familiar with the basic sequence: the fall in the night, the refusal to use his personal alarm because "I didn't want to bother anyone", the mild pneumonia, the complications in hospital, the slow, relentless failing of the flesh . . . ) The relevant points in this context are simply these: that (despite a heroic sister who bore most of the burden) I found myself having to spend increasing amounts of time in and around his home rather than mine; and that — since failing health in a 90-year-old generally points only to one outcome — my recurrent sense that an old England was slipping away took on renewed poignancy and urgency.

Life was, as I said before, much simpler for my father. It was also harder. He never knew any comforts that he hadn't struggled for. But in one respect he was privileged: he drew strength, inexhaustibly, from the little patch of rural England in which he lived. He loved his village and never lost his enthusiasm for pottering around it, watching the fields and the people evolve as the seasons passed. (I say "it". He lived at different times in two villages, Green Tye — strictly speaking a hamlet — and Perry Green. But since they adjoined one another, and had scarcely 400 inhabitants between them, they were to most intents and purposes the same village. I spent most of my childhood in Green Tye; he spent most of his retirement in Perry Green.) It's a cliché to talk about roots, yet no one who knew him would dispute that he had roots in the land around him; just as he had roots in a wider ideal of Englishness. Many people would laugh at that ideal today: as he saw it, real Englishmen weren't cool or sexy or fashionable (as most of us now aspire to be), but were instead — if they hadn't been corrupted by urban luxury — quietly admirable: strong, modest countrymen more comfortable outdoors than in the drawing room, with qualities of fortitude and selfless reliability that tended to emerge in crises. In his world, the English were the good guys, because they had done the right thing in the war; and the UK was a good nation because, for all our faults, we had a unique and immutable respect for law and liberty.

I had often argued with him about his world-view, which I felt was simplistic to the point of self-deception. Now I could only mourn its fading. Who thinks of the English as good guys today? Who looks to us as a democratic role model? How many English heroes are modest, solid and quietly courageous?

One evening, after a day spent visiting my father in hospital and working from his home, I went for a walk through Green Tye and noticed how much the village had changed: how much prettier — or neater — it was than in the overgrown days of my youth. Everything had been touched with money: a clothes boutique in what used to be the village shop, a new, not-remotely sagging bench on the not-remotely shaggy green, wooden bollards with reflectors on the drive to the White Horse, the thatched fringe of Tumbledown Dick's trimmed into a neat bob, two red sports cars outside the Prince of Wales, extravagant topiary by what used to be the Fulfords' house, a complex of giant, state-of-the-art greenhouses at the tomato farm, some smart iron railings outside Grudds Farmhouse, a symmetrically paved driveway at Uffords, a conservatory, several climbing frames, a trampoline. I suppose you would call them mod cons. And, everywhere, chunky, expensive cars guarded them, blocking driveways and gateways like hi-tech dogs. Thriving, I thought to myself; thriving, but a completely different village.

I crossed back into Perry Green, past the little churchyard on the corner. A more familiar sense of the villages' soul began to tug at me: first the ancient, resinous, bittersweet scent of the three dark yews that sprouted from the lumpy turf among the worn gravestones; then the realisation that I was now looking at something profoundly natural: living trees drawing life from the rotting remains of generations of human beings who had, in turn, drawn life from this same quiet earth. Why, perhaps even I had drawn life from it; except that, if I had, I had long since been uprooted — only a top-of-the-range stockbroker could buy a house round here these days.

I felt suddenly resentful of the rich newcomers; then, immediately, berated myself for snobbery, or racism, or some such prejudice. Why shouldn't outsiders who had done well for themselves have a share in the village? Was it their fault that I had moved away? In what possible sense was it my village rather than theirs? (And, if I was strictly honest, I had spent much of my youth itching to get away to some town or city where life was a little less boring . . . )

None the less, my body ached with loss. Perhaps, I had finally realised, deep down, that it might only be a matter of months before nothing remained of my father — or of my childhood — but a grave in this very place.

I found myself once again making little expeditions: not far or frequently, but from time to time, taking brief diversions from other journeys, glancing down familiar lanes, revisiting the villages of my childhood.

**139**

I don't think I learnt much: I had other things on my mind. But it was therapeutic to potter from village to village, trying to find the scenes of long-lost events, or work out who used to live in which house, and promising myself that, as soon as my father was better, I would go over the past with him in detail, matching his memories against mine.

Many of my excursions were motivated by curiosity of the most idle kind: either personal (where was that pub where we spent so many teenage Saturdays after pretending that we were going to watch the hunt?) or gratuitous (does Ugley really have an "Ugley Women's Institute" sign, or was that just a myth?). Anything I learnt from them was random and superficial. What struck me about Barley was not its Norman church or its famous Tudor Town House but the fact that there was a thriving charity based there, supporting a poor village in Rajasthan. What I took away from Abbots Langley was not any lasting sense of its architecture or character but the unnecessary information that a 12th-century villager, Nicholas Breakspear, became the only English Pope — Pope Adrian IV — in 1154, only to choke to death on a fly five years later. And what I took away from the apparently uninhabited Bambers Green was the image of people sitting in their cars in improvised lay-bys in the oak-lined lane leading into it, waiting (one of them told me) to pick people up from flights at Stansted Airport. (I subsequently learnt that the village really was largely uninhabited, with dozens of its picturesque cottages and farmhouses having been bought up by BAA with a view to wiping it from the map to make room for the airport's expansion.)

These small, superficial excursions had two lasting effects on me. They rekindled my interest in exploring rural England. And they reminded me of the curious but incontestable fact that *every village has a story.* Even the smallest settlement has its own little back-story — the reason it ended up the way it is; the local tragedies and mysteries; the points of pride and shame. Some have several, but every village has at least one — even if not everyone who lives there knows it.

Returning from one journey, I picked up a hitchhiker. It was late, on a wet, black night; I might have run him over if he hadn't been wearing a fluorescent waterproof jacket. Raindrops bounced from it like shards of glass in my headlights. It turned out that my cross-country route went right through his village, 6 or 7 miles away. He smelt of the pub from which he was walking home — he was already 3 miles into his journey.

"I have got a car," he explained. "But they took away my licence. It was eight years ago. I passed out when I was driving a tractor. They said I had fits. But I didn't. I never had one since. But now my parents won't let me have the car back."

He was a big man, whose large, wet frame made the front of my car seem even smaller than usual. Steam rose from his matted black hair, and from the corner of my eye I could make out a pale, rubbery face dotted with pimples and raindrops.

"They're holding me back," he complained, baring his family affairs with an abandon that makes me reluctant to mention details that might identify him, "because how can I work if I can't drive? It really upsets me. I haven't had a proper job for eight years now. How can I? I can't get anywhere."

He had grown up, and spent the first decade or so of his working life, on a grand estate near by that I had passed earlier. "My father ran the stables. He's retired now. I worked there too. Just general labouring mostly: driving a tractor, working on the estate, farm work. It was a good place then, although it's got a new owner now. I was working there when I had my accident — what they said was a fit.

"The last job I did there was laying a hedge. It's still there — a long one. You can see it on the lane when you drive past. Beech. I enjoyed that — it was satisfying. It was a good hedge. I liked to look at it when I went back.

"I like that kind of work. Outdoors. It's all I know how to do. I don't know what sort of job I could do now. There's not much labouring around. But I'd like to work. It's really frustrating just being on benefits."

He was living now with a woman some years older than him. "I'd like my own place, but I could never afford it. The trouble is, you need a car. I can't even get work, let alone enough for a home. I've got a bicycle, but that's no good in the rain. And you'd think twice on these roads anyway. But the buses are a joke."

I would have questioned him further, but we had reached his village and he was anxious to get home as soon as possible. (He would, he said, "be getting an earful".)

Instead, early the next morning I drove over to the big estate he had described, and walked alongside what I assume was "his" hedge. It was a golden morning, and yellowhammers were darting in and out of the frail brown leaves. A few rabbits hopped casually for shelter beneath it as I approached. On the far side, expensive-looking horses grazed in twos and threes; their lush paddocks seemed sterile compared with this living eco-system. I could imagine how satisfying it must feel to have created something like this, even if you didn't own it. Then again: who did own it? The owner of the estate? The previous generations who shaped the landscape that sustained it? The public? The creatures that lived in it? The very idea that a piece of the fabric of the countryside could be privately owned seemed suddenly absurd.

But the one person who plainly didn't have a stake in it was the person who created it.

I thought again about lost tribes and severed roots. And I thought, too, about the fact that it is not just villages that have their stories. Each piece of the landscape does as well.

# CHAPTER
# TWELVE

# The cottage
# in the woods

One day, emboldened by a previous phone-call, I drove to the edge of Wormingford, in Essex, where I bounced and creaked down a steep, rutted, overgrown track that led, alarmingly, down a darkly wooded hill. I abandoned the car by a hand-painted sign announcing "MUD — turn here" and continued on foot deeper into the woods. I had almost despaired of finding human habitation when I began to notice flowers among the trees and, in due course, a garden, with a cottage sunk in its midst.

I knocked on the door, and was greeted by an old, jolly man with a hint of wildness in his big eyes — just the kind of man whom adventurers are supposed to meet in tumbledown cottages in the middle of the woods. But this cottage wasn't really tumbling down: just low and dark-beamed, and the old man, for all the twinkle in his eye, was no marginalised eccentric. On the contrary, Ronald Blythe might reasonably be considered the Grand Old Man of traditional English rural life. He was 83 when I saw him, but is admired

144

worldwide for the masterpiece he wrote 40 years earlier: *Akenfield*.

If the themes I have been discussing interest you, and you haven't read *Akenfield*, I urge you to put this book aside — throw it away, if you like — and read *Akenfield* instead. It is a meticulous and lyrical study of a Suffolk village in the mid-1960s, cast largely in the form of first-person interviews with 49 of its 300-odd villagers. It is also one of the very few successful attempts of which I am aware to capture alive on paper the collective "story" of a rural community. Blythe had lived in the village for most of his life, and his family had worked on the Suffolk soil for generations. Some of his interviewees had memories going back to the 1880s; the indirect memories, passed down from parents and grandparents, went back considerably further. Perhaps as a result, his rendering of the disparate testimonies of his interviewees is powerfully harmonious: they speak in their own voices, but with a perspective that is also Blythe's and, ultimately, the village's.

Even then, there was much social change afoot, notably in the rise of high-productivity, low-manpower agriculture. But plenty of deep rural tradition survived. You can sense the weight of the heavy Suffolk soil and the ache of the "mindless knife-bearing wind" as you encounter villager after villager whose most important working relationship is with the landscape or animals around them. You read of long, dark evenings in remote cottages and old people who, according to the district nurse, did not seem fearful of death — "They had all worked so hard and so long, I suppose there was a kind

145

of comfort in it." There is much talk of the frightening poverty of the agricultural depressions surrounding the two World Wars, when, as one old worker puts it, "I learnt never to answer a word. I lived when other men could do what they liked with me." One farm worker remembers joining the Army in 1914 and gaining a stone in weight in four months: "They said it was the food but it was really because for the first time in my life there had been no strenuous work." Another talks of killing blackbirds on Christmas morning in order to get a festive meal. And there are memories of an even older Akenfield, in which death-knells were still tolled from the village church ("three times three for a man and three times two for a woman"), bees had to be informed when their keeper died, and farm workers would strike a "harvest bargain" with the farmer before they would get the harvest in. This was a village where ploughmen "talked softly to their teams all day long and you could see the horses listening" and, at harvest-time, "20 men and boys scythed the corn and sang as they went".

Little remained of those older days, even then. An old farrier told Blythe: "The old people have gone and have taken a lot of the truth out of the world with them." But there was still a network of live links to the past, through the children and grandchildren who remembered. And most of the villagers he spoke to still lived and worked in a close relationship with the land around them: not only understanding how individual fields and hedgerows had evolved as they had but also knowing (like the ploughman who worked alone for seven days a week but didn't feel lonely — "not ever, at all") the movements and foibles of the wild creatures with whom they shared them, right down to the location of each linnet or kingfisher's nest.

Blythe's great achievement was to preserve all that and communicate it to the modern world. He wrote down the village's "story", not in the sense of a single, defining anecdote or myth, but as a whole collection of interwoven threads, from interconnected groups and generations, which together made a miniature epic. Without him, a whole lot more truth would have been taken out of the world.

He had written or edited at least 25 subsequent works — many of them on the shelves of the low-beamed, book-lined room in which we sat and talked — but *Akenfield* remained the one everyone wanted to talk about. You would have thought that this might irritate him. If it did, he was too polite to show it.

Could he have written such a book today?

"No. The old traditional village life has almost gone, and so swiftly, and has been replaced by 21st-century technology and comforts which are much the same nationwide, whether one lives in the town or the country. Everybody now has television, everybody has fitted carpets, everybody more or less has a computer, everybody has foreign holidays. None of this really existed when I was writing *Akenfield*. It is quite amazing to someone like myself, who as a boy saw the old harvests, and the old poverty — the good and the bad, all more or less vanished."

He smiled a lot, from beneath a mane of white hair that made me think of some kind of Chinese dog. His cottage — which he was bequeathed by the painter John Nash — is so remote that you could imagine its single occupant feeling isolated. Yet he seemed contented, sometimes participating vigorously in village life — he is, among other things, a lay reader — and sometimes revelling in his solitude. Like several Akenfield villagers, he seemed to have a relationship with his surroundings that meant that, even when unaccompanied, he was never entirely alone.

He moved from Akenfield — or Charsfield, to give it its real name — 30 years ago. Wormingford, 25 miles to the south-west, is nearer his birthplace (Acton, in Suffolk). But he was still in regular touch with his former village, and felt that both it and Wormingford had much in common.

"It's a different world, wherever you are. People move about so much — often they have to, because of work. They move in, and then someone else moves on. So bit by bit villages lose their links with the past.

"And they lose their links with the land as well. Fifty or 60 years ago you'd have looked out of the window and you'd have seen people doing all sorts of work, wouldn't you? This is a very agricultural place, but not one farm is now being farmed by the farmer: it's all out to contract. I shouldn't think there are half a dozen people working on the land here.

"The landscape is beautiful here but most people aren't connected with it. It doesn't belong to them, and, because it's now controlled to a degree, they can't do what they like with it. So it isn't theirs.

"I like Wormingford. It's a friendly place — have you been to the flower festival? But how distinctive is it compared with other villages? I don't know.

"There are lots of new people who are very good for the village, lots of very nice commuters, who do good things. But there are also people who live here and don't want to join in, or maybe they can't — they live in houses and they go to supermarkets and they commute, either to the big towns round here or to London. So a lot of people don't know who many of their fellow villagers are, which once upon a time would have been unthinkable."

That's a shame, I said. He looked quizzical. "Up to a point. But life has changed very much for the better. When I was young, the poverty in village life was appalling. People died earlier. They had all kinds of illnesses caused by heavy work, and that sort of thing. The houses were wet, they had no electricity, the lavatories were all outside, there wasn't enough food. So, no, it hasn't changed for the worse."

He paused, and gazed meditatively at the wall. Then he added: "Yet even so, although it's a ridiculous thing to say, you do get the feeling that people were somehow more content."

Might that be because, whatever else they lacked, they had a sense of a permanent, scarcely changing backdrop to their lives? "Possibly. There was certainly a lot less contact with other communities, other worlds. Unless you were a very brave soul, or very imaginative, you tended to be just stuck where you were. So the place you lived in necessarily played an important part in your life.

"But, of course, people have always wanted to get away. That's why, as soon as bicycles were invented, everybody got a bike — suddenly life had a 30-mile radius. Now people go to football matches in Istanbul. But that's very exciting, isn't it? A neighbour's son here married a Thai girl — I think that's marvellous. And of course people can do what they like now. In the old days, fear of local gossip was ferocious. But the reverse of that is that you don't know much about people. You've no idea where people come from. In a way, people aren't interested: they've no time, and, anyway, they can get all that from the soaps."

We talked through several cups of tea and touched on many subjects but kept returning to the same theme: the evaporation of rural permanence. "The other thing," he observed at one point, "is that the generations have less to do with each other now. I don't know when people first began to be segregated according to age, but young and old used to be together to a much greater degree. Right through history, the tradition was that the old were informers of the young — they might hold secrets that could be passed on to the young. In lots of ancient societies, the old are venerated because they know secrets that the young don't know. I don't think the old have much to pass on now. A lot of what they know is perfectly useless . . ."

Again, he smiled. Then he added (echoing Larkin): "It's all happened in a very short space of time, really."

I told him about my recurrent urges to scour the countryside in search of old rural voices. To my surprise, he seemed excited by the thought. "A quest. That's a very good idea." And a look of enhanced animation came into his already animated face, as if he fancied the idea of undertaking such a quest himself.

"Of course, it would be very hard to find what you were looking for," he reflected. "A lot of villagers now are just like people in any other village — people with cars who shop in supermarkets. They all watch the same television programmes; they all have certain kinds of holidays. Consumerism is identical for the whole of Britain.

"I'm sure you'd find a lot of craft things — people carefully doing things in the old ways. But then that's not necessarily the same thing, is it?"

The silences grew longer; yet it seemed that our conversation had grown more interesting to him. "Yes, you must do it. It's true, everywhere is the same: every village is comfortable and well kept, with the same kind of people living there. But at the same time, if you keep your eyes open, you'll see other things too. Behind most people's daily preoccupations — the mortgages, the shopping — often there's a profundity. The difficult thing is finding it."

Finally, after another pause, he said: "I don't think there's anything you can do to make things appear for you. But I'm sure there are still many traces of the past that you can find. You just have to be patient, and be in the right place, and notice things."

# CHAPTER THIRTEEN

# Wood and iron

One day, inspired anew, I tried to retrace a journey we often did in my childhood: across Essex from Green Tye to Suffolk, where my aunt and uncle farmed pigs in Polstead. How wild the countryside had seemed then — a windswept ocean of rolling wilderness through which roads wound and climbed precariously. I had never felt entirely confident that we would get home again. Yet how bland it seemed now: tamed by decades of road widening and white lines and road signs and safety signs and expanding towns and improving cars. Before I knew it I had overshot and was in Dedham Vale, which I knew both as Constable Country and as Witch Country. It was from Manningtree — claimed by some to be England's largest village and by others to be its smallest town — that Matthew Hopkins, the Witchfinder General, conducted his reign of terror from 1644–6: 19 local "witches" were hanged at his instigation, with another four dying in prison.

I saw no signs of any attempt to cash in on this last strand of local heritage with a witch theme park, but there was a steady stream of visitors to Flatford Mill, which is owned by the National Trust and leased to the

Field Studies Council. Sadly, the mill made famous by Constable was no longer operating — reportedly because the floodgates did not comply with modern health and safety standards.

I retraced my steps towards Nayland, whose little houses seemed worn down by time, with low-hanging roofs and miniature timbers in their pastel walls. There was a "heritage farm" attached to the Anchor Inn, while somewhere near by a company called Bunting & Sons was in the process of creating a Constable theme park, which by the time you read this may well be up and running and achieving its stated aim of attracting 750,000 visitors a year. If it is, it will have been over the dead body of the Nayland with Wissington Conservation Society. A few miles to the north-east, meanwhile, in Great Blakenham, planning permission had just been given for a £320-million indoor winter-sports centre.

Polstead was a bit of a shock. I'd remembered a wild, ragged place, smelling of pigs, with an overgrown orchard where my uncle used to set traps for bullfinches. What I found was an intimidatingly neat village of big, immaculate houses with big, expensive cars outside them. Only the wide brown pond felt familiar, with its hypnotic pattern of reflected foliage, old brickwork and cloud-blotched sky. But I could still remember Polstead's story, which is better known than most. In 1827, Maria Marten, the mole-catcher's daughter, was lured to the Red Barn by her rich lover, William Corder (a pig-farmer's son), believing, as did her parents, that he was going to take her to Ipswich to marry her. He wasn't. Her decomposed body was found 11 months later, buried in a sack at the bottom of a grain storage bin in the barn. Ten thousand people saw Corder hanged in Bury St Edmunds in 1828. An account of the murder, bound in his skin, can be seen in Bury's museum today.

I was sure I remembered my uncle showing me round the barn, but there didn't seem to be any sign of it — not even a Red Barn Conversion. (Subsequent inquiries suggested that it had either burnt down in 1842 or been dismantled and reassembled near Manchester in 1975.) But I did find, in an overgrown lane on the edge of the village, a low thatched cottage called Maria Marten's Cottage; and, among some wooden sheds next to it, a farmer's son called Dylan Pym.

He was a stocky, cheerful man, 41 years old, with intelligent blue eyes and the unmistakable air of being more at home outdoors than in. He had matted hair, stubble, an earring in one ear and a pencil behind the other, a faded rugby shirt with holes in it, grubby, sagging trousers with torn pockets and flies at half-mast, and old loafers with frayed laces.

I met him in a yard that contained, among other things, some cushions, a rusty barbecue, a cardboard box full of crumpled pieces of newspaper, several chickens dozing in the dust, some rope, various dustbins, a big flower pot full of weeds, a bicycle, a metal bucket, many other enormous weeds and a big brown goose that seemed to be finding it hard to keep its eyes open. But the air of chaotic dereliction was deceptive. Inside the sheds, Dylan made things out of wood.

He was making a garden bench when I met him, bending pieces of oak into uniform curves by the traditional method of steam-bending. This involves placing the wood — a plank about ¾ in thick, in this instance — in a coffin-like wooden box that is filled with steam by one of those giant kettle devices you get in village halls. After 15 minutes or so, the wood is soft enough to be placed against a curved wooden "former" — essentially a mould, or one half of a mould, created for that particular job — and pulled around it until it follows the precise curve required. It is then fixed in this position and left for anything up to a year to dry out. "And then it just stays in that curve. But it's important that the wood you use is completely straight to start with" — without any of the stresses that might pull it in one direction or the other.

He took me to an upstairs room that contained some of the pieces he was proudest of. These included some classic tables and chairs, but the ones that excited him were some unconventional pieces whose exuberance reminded me of the architecture of Gaudi: a sideboard with bulging sides, a tall, concave cabinet, an asymmetric sideboard that slanted and curved like an ocean wave. "I sell a lot of basic chairs and tables and sideboards — especially to people who've just bought a property and are trying to make it all nice. But you can get several thousand for these bigger things, if someone wants them. If I could just sell a few more like this then everything would be a lot easier."

He was proud to use traditional materials and methods — also including hand-cut peg and dovetail joints — but his aspiration, clearly, was to push back the frontiers of his craft; in short, to be an artist.

"A lot of furniture-makers these days treat it as a science — you know, they wear white coats, they're working on squares and corners, everything has to be exactly measured. I'm working on the organic of it. This is something you have to use your hands for.

"It's all made of local wood," he added proudly, "mostly from within a 10-mile radius. There's a sawmill just up the road. We plant a lot of trees here — walnut, cherry, lime, oak — up to 200 a year. They won't be ready in my time, but someone else will work with them, I hope, in 50 or 60 or 80 years' time, so I want them to be straight.

"The best oak country is just up the road from here, where the soil's richer. I made a sideboard recently. I saw the tree — fallen down — a couple of miles away, and the sawmill's just 3 miles away, so it was trunk to furniture in 3 miles. I like that."

There was something very natural about the whole process, from the sweet scent of steamed wood — a bit like mulled wine — to the quietly humming beehives on the far side of the field, which provide the beeswax with which the finished furniture will one day be waxed. Presumably, I suggested, doing work like this must help him feel connected with his roots?

"Not really. It's an old technique, but I'm the first person in my family to do it. My parents are just smallholders — there's about 22 acres here. They don't do as much as they used to — they're both in their seventies — but they've still got about 30 Suffolk sheep, as well as lots of chickens, some geese, bees, and of course there's a massive vegetable garden, as you can see."

Dylan had lived in the village all his life. After leaving school with no qualifications — "I couldn't even read the questions in the exams" — he spent a decade or so working on the smallholding: "I worked with the sheep mostly, but I'd help with everything. There's lots of work here. I lived in a caravan up in the woods."

About 15 years ago, having saved up some money to buy a motorcycle, he decided on the spur of the moment to spend it on a course in furniture-making instead. Now furniture was his main source of income.

"You don't make a lot, but I've been very lucky. The only trouble is, I always want to try new things — like this cupboard, which curves in two directions — but the things that sell best are just straightforward tables and chairs. So I try to keep a balance. But I want to keep testing myself — otherwise what's the point of living?

"But the good thing is that we've got this place, so you don't always have that pressure to find rent. You just have to keep your costs right down and do everything yourself. And of course you pay in other ways — I'm always having to help with this and that, making hay or shearing sheep or whatever. But I don't mind that."

He lived, with his wife and two sons, in a bungalow up in the village — "It's a terrible bungalow really, with

**157**

the gable end nearly coming off, but at least I managed to buy it before the prices got silly. I don't know what I'd do now. But that's the way it is. You can't choose where you come from."

The village, he said, had changed a lot in his lifetime. "There's loads more traffic. And a lot more rich people. Hardly anyone farms now — it's all just the big boys, isn't it? No one works on the land really, any more. A few farmers' sons, but that's about all. The others go to the towns. The pub used to be full of farmers and farm workers, drinking their cans of Double Diamond — you know, old boys. Now there are lots more holiday people coming through. It's still a nice pub — they've got one of my sideboards. But it's not the same." He used to enjoy going up there for a sing-song, playing the banjo in a three-part combo with his son and a friend — "but of course now you get problems with these music licences."

"Quite a lot of new buildings have gone up in my lifetime," he added, "and they're never the kind of places local people could afford. They're always great big ½-million-pound ones. The school closed years ago, and a lot of children end up going to public school now.

"The other thing, which is a pity, is that there's so few places left for the kids to play. There's always been a lot of pheasant shooting in East Anglia, but it's shocking how much there is today. So of course they want to keep everyone off the land.

"My dad doesn't mind who comes and wanders round. It's a pity that some landowners don't think like that any more. There's a new bloke up the road who's fenced his in with barbed wire, keep-off-my-land signs, the lot.

"But I just wander where I please, and when people see who it is, they don't mind. They just say, oh, there's old Dylan, he won't do any harm."

And he went back into his shed.

One day, just outside Stowmarket, I saw what looked like a pair of large whalebones standing in an arch astride the brown stream that drifts through Rattlesden. Village legend offers several exotic explanations for their presence: that, for example, a whale found its way 30 miles up the river Gipping from the sea before getting stuck. I was lucky enough to meet Lee Patterson — a regular at the nearby Five Bells pub — who not only knew the true story but was also responsible for putting the things there. "They're actually made of oak. There used to be some real whalebones, but they'd been there for centuries, and they rotted away. We tried to get some real ones, but they're a little bit rare now. So I carved them out of oak."

But why were the originals there?

"Because Rattlesden was a big centre for cargo coming in from the sea. The big boats would offload their cargo into barges at Ipswich, and they'd sail up the river to Rattlesden, which was where they'd turn around. They brought all the stone there to build the abbey in Bury St Edmunds. And all the whalebone used to come up here as well — for doing all these things for the women's dresses and all of that stuff. So someone must have put up two of them across the river then. It seemed a pity to lose them. Little things like that are important in a village."

He had done a pretty convincing job of the new pair. Yet he wasn't a woodcarver by trade. "I work with old buildings. I do lime-plastering, timber-framing, flintwork, pargeting. I build oak-framed houses finished with lime plaster. Basically I can build a 16th-century cottage, apart from doing the thatching, using all these traditional crafts."

Pargeting? "It's a form of decorative wet-plastering. You see a lot of it round here: when there's a pattern on the side of a half-timbered house. I did quite a lot of them."

I imagined a long line of pargeters, passing their secrets from father to son in the same cottage. In fact, Lee was relatively new to both the trade and the village. "I started life as a gamekeeper, which I loved, but that sort of stopped about 20 years ago. So I gradually got into this." As for home: "I was brought up in Hargrave, on the other side of Bury St Edmunds, and even though I had a fantastic time there as a child, out in the countryside doing all the things that I loved, it's been dying. I slowly watched the school go, the shop go, the pub go, and it is now a dead, desperate place to live. My parents still live there and I don't even like going back any more. It's had the heart ripped out of it. Rattlesden's a much more vibrant place to live."

It turned out that Lee — a slight, energetic-looking man in his mid-fifties — was, if anything, more worried than I was about the fading of rural traditions, and was busily teaching himself as many old crafts as he could before it was too late. "Each time you learn something, it's like you've become a guardian for it in some way. It's a precious thing to have. You really feel you should give it to someone else at the end of the day.

"I've got a child — Grace: she's six — and I just want to teach her everything about the countryside that I've learnt. But it's disappearing so rapidly. It's so sad, because it's disappearing before your eyes — it really is."

His latest enthusiasm was learning to be a blacksmith, helped by another Five Bells regular, Graham Chaplin. Graham lived in the neighbouring village of Great Finborough, where his forebears (several of them blacksmiths) had lived for at least 400 years; his forge, where he, Lee and I spent much of an afternoon chatting, was closer to another neighbouring village, Buxhall.

"I prefer drinking in Rattlesden," said Graham, a big, ruddy man with thinning ginger hair and bushy ginger sideburns and eyebrows. "At least there's a bit of a community. Buxhall's more for older people who just want a quiet life. And Great Finborough's a dormitory village really. I can be there and I don't know hardly anyone there now: they're away in the morning at 7a.m. to catch the train to London and when they come home they shut the bloody door — you don't see them. I used to know everybody and what their fathers did and what their mothers did and all that. You don't any more."

He said all this with a grin on his face, as though he enjoyed his grumbling. "You walk out in our village at 8p.m. on a summer evening," he added, "and there won't be anybody. Just cars going past. No chat over the gate, no finding out how Mrs So-and-so is or does she want any firewood or any of that. All that stuff has gone. I blame television, because it means people can lock themselves safely in their homes at night, which I'm sure is what the government wants."

His forge was a big, old, barnlike building on the edge of a farm, with a furnace at one end and assorted tools and chunks of iron hung on the walls. Someone had chalked "Our policy is to plan ahead" on the hood over the furnace, while a "No smoking" sign (obligatory for a workplace) was just about visible behind the open door. It might have been a little gloomy for some tastes, as a workplace, but to Graham it was close to heaven. "I love doing this. Sometimes I can't believe that I'm actually getting paid for it. It's like making mud pies. There's no stress, no anger — the world can go racing by, and other people can do what the hell they want."

He made some tea, dug out some wooden stools and sat down to talk about the past. Like Lee, he was pursuing his traditional craft through conscious choice. "My father had a little agricultural-engineering works here in the village, where I played about a bit, as you would. You know, you smack bolts about and make them into funny shapes and split them. And I learnt from an old farrier-blacksmith in the village called Stanley Forster. I used to wander around and turn up at his forge and watch, and he'd say: 'Come in and

162

pump the horn, boy.' Lovely old boy; they called him the gentle giant. So you tend to pick it up, and you think this is all right, I can have some fun with this. And you make yourself a fire at home and you learn very early that when you burn yourself it hurts — a lot — and you get holes in your clothes and all that bollocks before you get an apron. So I built myself a metal shed — it had to be metal and not wood so I couldn't burn it down. I blew it up a couple of times, mind. Oh, there's some lovely stories I could tell you — I just can't remember them.

"But the trouble was, it's really not an ideal way to make a living, especially not back then. So for 23 years I also did engineering. But I built a forge in my garage and every night after work I'd work in it. I found it so relaxing: the time just disappears. The next thing you know — blimey, it's three o'clock in the morning. She used to complain for a bit" — he nodded homewards — "but she got used to it. Then in 1993 I gave up the engineering, and that's what I'm doing here now. I earn a lot less, but I've worked out that it's not what you earn that matters — it's what you haven't got to spend. I'm not jealous of all those people with big cars and big houses and whatever. They're jealous of me. Because when I'm working, it sweeps over you, and you can't think of anything else."

"I'm the same," said Lee. "You've got to really want to work in traditional crafts, because it's not always that easy to make a good living out of it. But if you do — well, when it's time to go home, you don't want to stop."

Graham relit his pipe. "I get people in here saying, 'You lucky bastard, you can make all this stuff and it can be there for ever.' And then you think, Christ, yes, it will be. I'm not making this for tomorrow: this is going to be here for hundreds of years."

I had already seen the elaborate, metal village sign he had made for Buxhall. A number of other villages boasted such signs, he told me; one of which, a 4ft-high angel he made for Blythburgh for the millennium, became quite famous in these parts. I could also see what looked like the beginnings of a suit of armour stood up in the middle of the workshop. This was his latest work in progress: an extraordinarily ambitious statue — for a rich incomer client — of a young woman balancing, naked, on a wheel. "The more I do this, the more I've pursued the artistic side of blacksmithing," he explained. "I still do the basic things: brackets and gates and fire-grates and things like that. But it's the artistic side that interests me. If you don't stretch yourself, you'll never know what you could have done.

"The trouble is, to try and indicate to somebody what the finished item will look like is so damn difficult. If you could, then they could understand the amount of work and wouldn't take in their breath like this when you suggest a figure which would make it worth your while doing it . . . You think you're going to be all right, but then it just swallows time, because there's so much work involved." He was thinking of exhibiting some of his other artworks in London, but wasn't sure if he could afford the transport costs. Meanwhile, he seemed happy to continue exploring the

164

limits of his craft. "Basically, being a blacksmith hasn't changed in thousands of years. It's just bashing a piece of metal. But that doesn't stop people being fascinated by it."

"It's amazing how interested people are," said Lee, whose own claims to immortality included a spectacular pargeted "Green Man" on a nearby farmhouse. "If you had three guys working on houses in the same road, and I was lime-plastering and putting the traditional lathes back on one house, and the other two were doing the ordinary sand-and-cement slap it on and run, people wouldn't leave me alone. They always come and stop and they're always really interested in what you're doing. It's like, 'I've never seen that before. Why are you using the materials you're using? Why are you doing it that way?' Or flintwork. I can never get anything done when I'm working on a flint wall, because people are constantly stopping and want to know what you're doing, how you're doing it. People are fascinated. You're never, ever short of someone to talk to when you've got a traditional craft.

"Did you know," he added, "they actually now make flints in a block — they set them in blocks and just build with blocks?"

"No," said Graham, appalled.

"I even saw in Stowmarket last summer," Lee continued, "they were building a big estate there, and they were actually putting chimneys on the roofs with a crane that had been built from metal and then faced off with fake bricks, and they were placing them on the tops of roofs. I couldn't believe it. And that actually drives me on to do things in a traditional way. I don't like false things — I like real things. Real crafts, real skills."

We wandered over to the furnace, where Graham resumed work on the next section of his young woman. The hot coals glowed like the inside of a volcano, but he worked and chatted with the insouciance of a television chef, grasping the shaped metal sheet with his gloved left hand and the thin-handled hammer with his ungloved right one. Every 30 seconds or so, the area he wanted to shape would become red hot, and he would move it over to the anvil to hammer. It was hard to believe that such happy-go-lucky heating and bashing could produce anything but the most crude results, yet he seemed to know exactly what he was doing.

"You can see how long this is going to take," he said, his face beginning to glow with the effort. He wore a leather apron and a cloth cap, and it was clear that he would soon be very hot indeed. It didn't seem to bother him. "I've been doing this bit all day," he said, waving the half-formed torso-front in the air, "and I've still got a long way to go. The body needs to be slightly twisted, you see, so I've got to get the stomach in and the waist in. So I'm just beating the hell out of that . . .

"The problem I'm creating for myself here is that I want this to be like the Greek statues, where they formed them to perfection, and this beautiful carved marble is completely smooth. I'm trying to get that in metal. In any blacksmith's eyes it's almost bloody silly to try, but I'm hopefully going to get close to it."

He was, I noticed, wearing both a belt and braces. Presumably it's pretty catastrophic for a blacksmith if his trousers fall down. I was also struck by the thinness of his hammer's wooden handle. "That's nothing," he said, pausing to hold a thumb and finger scarcely an inch apart. "I've seen some that are this thin — worn away with use. But because they've got the balance and the bounce right, it doesn't break. Like the old blacksmith said: 'Handle's worn away. Hand hasn't.' It's all a matter of balance."

He bashed on happily. It was hard to decide if what I was watching was a trace of the lost rural past or just the timeless phenomenon of a human being absorbed by the creative process. Graham, in any case, wasn't sure that the past was all it was cracked up to be. Previous blacksmiths in his family would, he reckoned, have had a pretty miserable time. "They'd be getting out of their bed at 5.30 in the bloody morning in the middle of winter, going to work, no heat, no lights. Especially in the forge they would have the bloody doors wide open so they could see what they were doing first thing in the morning and then light the ruddy fire, and this is wintertime as well. They had to work until it got light and the only heat they'd got was on the forge, so if somebody was up the other end it'd be freezing. And then they'd have to walk 6 miles home in the rain — didn't have nylons and polythenes then, it was just clothing — when they got home, what had they got? A little tiny fire, steaming everything so you could go to work the next day, and that was 12 hours a bloody day regular, wasn't it, six days a sodding week, and on a Sunday you were almost forced to go to church because the squire required it."

But Lee was convinced that the past and its relics were "a precious thing to have" and that more should be done to protect them. "I cherish doing that kind of work. It feels like a miracle sometimes — to be touching history. I remember when we rehung a bell at Bradfield St Clare church and being up there working on it, and hundreds of years ago they'd hacked all the popish figures off the bells during the Reformation, and every single stroke that that guy had made with the chisel, in anger, to hack them off, was still there and still as sharp as the day he'd done it. And there's me sitting in front of this huge, great tenor bell thinking, what an honour . . . I remember looking at those marks and thinking, he was left-handed. And before you know it, a picture has started to build in your mind. It's just history sitting right there in front of you. But you've got to have a special way of looking at it — to think: if it could speak, the things it could tell you . . ."

He paused. Then he said: "I sometimes feel I was born in the wrong age. I don't want to be always rushing to get more of everything. I just want a simple life."

"You're right," said Graham. "A simple life. What's wrong with that?"

# CHAPTER
# FOURTEEN

# A patch of ground

I continued to explore East Anglia, drifting between shabby towns and quaint villages and thinking about the difference between the real rural past and what Ronald Blythe had called "people carefully doing things in the old ways". There was clearly much of the latter in both Suffolk and Norfolk: in heritage centres, museums, craft shops and "working farms". (I'm told that 30,000 people in the UK now earn their livings from "crafts".) But then, as the proprietor of one of the many lay-by cafés that line the region's narrow roads put it: "None of that's really real, is it?"

Then, as I came to the sandy country north and west of Thetford, I found myself thinking about shooting. It was hard not to. Every few miles, I would see a sign reminding me that I was near one of the vast shooting estates that developed there in the 19th century: Sandringham, for example, where Edward VII had the clocks set half an hour early so he could get more shooting in; Elveden, whose most famous owner, the Maharajah Duleep Singh, once shot 789 partridges in a day; Stanford, where the 6th Lord Walsingham once killed 65 coots, 39 pheasants, 23 mallard, 7 teal, 6 gadwall, 4 pochard, 1 goldeneye, 3 swans, 3 snipe, 1 woodcock, 1 pigeon, 2 herons, 2 moorhens, 16 rabbits, 9 hares, 1 otter, 1 pike (don't ask) and a rat — all in a single day, while wearing a snakeskin waistcoat and a hat made from an entire hedgehog.

It seemed odd that such an essentially unnatural leisure pursuit (in the sense that the quarry has to be artificially nurtured in order to be slaughtered) should have come to play such an important role in the rural economy. Yet in East Anglia, at least, it had, and, as such, presumably had some relevance to the "lost world" I was seeking. But then so, in that case, did the darker Norfolk known by Frederick Rolfe, self-styled "King of the Norfolk Poachers", who conducted his lifelong struggle against poverty and gamekeepers in much the same area. Rolfe's semi-ghosted autobiography, *I Walked By Night*, describes growing up at a time when "the worken classes were little better than slaves" and "the Children was sent out at an early age into the fields to work, scaren crows and such like Jobs", while a man "would stand in the field with a stick or whip to keep them at it". He had, he wrote, "seen many a Poor woman go to the fields in bitter winter weather, cleaning turnips and beet for the cattle, for the sum of ten pence a day. They would come home up to there knees in mud and whet, and then they would have the house hold work to do . . . Small wonder that so many were crippled with rhumatics, and brought children into the World with rhumatics bred into them." Small wonder, either, that a British Medical Association report of 1867 — around the time that Rolfe was writing about — spoke of "there not being a labourer's house [in Norfolk] without its penny stick or pill of opium and not a child that did not have it in some form". (Godfrey's Cordial, a mixture of opium, treacle and sassafras, was popular for quietening babies.)

It was interesting, looking at all the hedges, walls and fenced forests, to consider how much of the rural landscape was developed with the specific purpose of preventing the peasantry from spoiling the upper classes' fun; and interesting, too, to remember that it wasn't always thus. Before it was enclosed and dedicated to the slaughter of wildlife, the Breckland, as much of this area is known, was a desert. In the 17th century, travellers were reluctant to cross even by horse for fear of sandstorms, which in 1668 were so bad that the village of Santon Downham was entirely buried. The soil was so unproductive that fields were only cultivated one year in 10. In the 18th century, the local economy was mainly sustained by 15,000 acres of organised rabbit warrens. I don't suppose anyone lived very comfortably then. None the less, I was sorry that the 21st-century landscape felt, by comparison, so tame.

I threaded my way through mile after mile of neatly planted Corsican pines in Thetford Forest and could sense only an overwhelming normality: no desert, no rabbit warrens, no prickly-headed toffs; just real estate ripe for domestication, dissected by standard Suffolk roads and cables and decorated from time to time with big billboards — for golf courses, campsites, high-ropes adventure courses, a Center Parcs holiday centre at

Elveden, and so on. Stanford had become a military-training area. Pountney, where Rolfe was born, appeared to consist largely of caravan parks.

Such developments were clearly desirable from the point of view of the prosperity of ordinary Norfolk-dwellers. As a traveller, however, I felt that something was missing.

Eventually, drifting southwards towards Cambridge, I came to Bartlow, where I met a gamekeeper.

Bartlow is a small, low-lying, leafy settlement, arranged around a crossroads in a damp valley where the rivers Bourne and Granta — and the counties of Cambridgeshire, Essex and Suffolk — almost converge. About 100 people live there. I found David Peters on its edge, in the cottage he rents from his employer, the Bartlow Estate.

He was a small, broad, big-forearmed man, with ginger hair, lively brown eyes, a big smile and a crushingly firm handshake.

"Shall we go for a ride?" he said, indicating a muddy pick-up truck. Yes please, I said, and climbed in.

"You see the state it's in now . . ." He grinned. "But it never goes out on a shooting day dirty. It would be like wearing a white shirt that's covered in mud — you just wouldn't do it."

The inside smelt of dog, then of smoke. He hand-rolled and lit cigarettes frequently, with scarcely a flicker of distraction as he sped us roughly over bumpy tracks and field-edges. The only flaw in his technique was a failure to take enough drags to keep them alight, thanks to a running commentary too passionate to allow pause for inhalation.

"The shoot's shaped like a butterfly, with the village at the centre, so you have no roads, just these tracks and field boundaries. I have to do a lot on the quad bike, because you can't get the truck there in winter. You're covered in mud all winter. It's just over 2,000 acres — about 120 acres of woodland and the rest of it is arable. Between August and March, I travel about 12,000 miles on a quad bike just around that 2,000 acres, and I do about the same in the truck."

Outside, beneath a clear East Anglian sky, the cause of this passion stretched out around us: square mile after square mile of green, wind-ruffled farmland — his pride and joy — all intricately managed to facilitate the slaughter of partridges and pheasants. Leaving the village, we thundered through what looked like a farmyard, past two enormous tractors, and up on to higher, emptier ground. Suddenly, there were no buildings, no roads in sight, just an overpowering sense of space; even — if you discounted the roar of his engine — a sense of silence. Did he look after all this himself? "There's a lot more work to it than people realise. You can go out at 4 or 5a.m. and get home for breakfast at 9a.m., knowing that you really haven't got time to have breakfast, and then dinner time — you'll think this is pretty sad — but dinner time would be 1.45p.m., you'd get home and you watch the Anglia weather, watch a bit of *Neighbours*, and then it's time to go because you'd have had 20 minutes. What you can't eat and drink in 20 minutes, you don't really need anyway. Then when the birds come, I'll be out there from daylight really, which is 4.30a.m., and you'll still be out there chasing things about nocturnally till 1.30, 2, 3am. People always say 'I don't know how you do it', but it's only for a certain time, and I can do all the sleeping I need to do when I'm dead, can't I? I did a nine-to-five job once." He paused for a rare drag. "I found I couldn't sleep at all. I simply wasn't tired. I had to hand in my notice."

That was when he drifted into gamekeeping: first in Surrey, then in Hertfordshire. Before that, he had worked in an abattoir. Now, 18 years later, aged 41, he was in his seventh year at the Bartlow Estate and pretty much at the top of his profession — the previous year, he had won a Gamekeeper of the Year award from *Farmers Weekly* and the Country Land and Business Association. This, he explained, was because of the shoot's exemplary conservation record.

He waved out of the window at a broad, grassy field margin, spreading uphill alongside a ragged hedge. "This would have always been swiped down years ago and kept all nice and tidy — nothing's going to nest in it if it's all nice and tidy. When I came here six years ago every headland was ploughed to. There was no grass strips or anything. You can imagine all this ploughed right to the hedge, and it was just like a prairie.

"Everything I do really is for pheasants and partridges: I admit that. But everything else is going to benefit even more, because they're all up in the hedges and it gives every songbird a habitat. You can imagine: a little songbird flies along the top of there — those little

174

white flowers in there are lamb's-foot — and they'll just take insects off the top of them and take it to the nest."

A hare bounded out from the hedgerow; he slowed to let it go. "When I started here, there was four hares around the whole estate; there was two on this side of the road and two on that side. Now there's hundreds, because of the fox control and the predator control. And there's still lots of foxes. Look, there's another hare sat in the middle there."

We were over the crest of the hill before I could spot it, and so, in his train of thought, was he. "I like to have quiet spaces — look, you can just see a different colour of green underneath that hedge where the artichokes have come in, just below the beans. We never shoot that. It's just a quiet area for the birds to go so they're not always terrorised."

It's hard to convey the meaning of his conversation without the surrounding landscape to make sense of it. Every "this" or "that" or "there" referred to some curve in the fields, some hedge or copse or patch of grass or crop; all of which flashed rapidly in and out of view as the Land-Rover bounced along. It occurred to me that, to many people, what I could see out of the window would be simply a view: fields, perhaps, or hills. To him it was a living landscape with which he had a close and dynamic relationship.

"When you go out in the morning, it's absolutely brilliant. You see flocks of birds coming off your game covers, just songbirds which wouldn't be there if it wasn't for the game covers, but you don't see them anywhere else. We have sparrowhawks, we have buzzards, we have a kite that comes through now and then. We have short-eared owls turn up and you see them, because they roost on the ground. We've got tawny owls, little owls, we have the odd barn owl comes and visits. Because in these grass margins, where there used to be nothing, now you've got mice."

He sighed. "There's so many things you see all the time, and the sad thing is, because you see it all the time, you think nothing of it. It's not until you actually take someone out there that you realise that you've made it a haven."

He relit his cigarette, then pointed up to a tall, swaying wood on the hillside. "Look, up here, the game cover's situated on the side of the wood, so as they've got a nice sunny area to go out, and there's food value there, and you bring that downhill and the birds will come across here, trying to get over the top of these trees. So you're going to be 35, 40 yards high, and then the partridges, if the wind's like it is today, they'll come down and curl round and you'll have guns out here to the other side of that ridge."

We were moving so fast — from subject to subject and from vantage point to vantage point — that he was beginning to lose me. To him, we were moving through an intricately planned, transparently logical ecological masterpiece; to me, it was more like a sea of blurred green slopes. Indeed, what with the broad crests of hillside in all directions, and the wind sweeping through the wheat like a Mexican wave, and a kestrel tossed above it like a seagull, and a faint sense of nausea induced by the smoke and the choppiness of our ride, it was hard to dispel the conceit that we were actually at sea. There was, however, no danger of getting lost: to my navigator, every blade of crop was a landmark.

"The longer stuff in the middle, you can see the darker greens, that is maize, then 3m down the outside and at the front is a dwarf sorghum that will only grow to about 3ft, but the maize will just go up to 3ft or 7ft, and the other side there is artichokes . . .

"There you are, there's a jay — you don't see them round here very often. I don't do anything to those because we don't have many . . .

"This is heavy ground, so it'll take longer to come. And you see that row there, that's shorter? That's where the tractor wheel went along and made the ground that much tighter for it to push through.

"Look," he added, pointing to some brown flecks half a mile away. "There are three hares sitting down there gnawing on the sorghum — one on the edge, one just on the edge and one down a bit lower." As we drew closer, I saw that he was right.

Down in the valley, we stopped by an unkempt grassy strip with a stream beyond it. "These are always kept short, and for the last two years there's been millions of cowslips. We found an oxslip here. One of the Cambridge colleges phoned up and said, 'Do you have any oxslips?' — because years ago there were oxslips at Bartlow — and we said no. Then we looked up oxslip in a book, and we found one just there, so we phoned them up and they came and made a record of it. I'd already been along banging in hazel sticks by all the cowslips so they didn't mow them down. The boss says, 'Why are there stakes everywhere? It's a bloody eyesore.' So I told him, and I said if you mow them down, them cowslips, they won't be there next year. 'Oh,' he said, 'that's fine.' It didn't matter it was an eyesore then."

We drove on, in, I think, a figure of eight, although my sense of direction was falling to pieces. So were several of my prejudices. Aren't people who spend their lives working alone on the land supposed to be brooding introverts? Aren't gamekeepers meant to be mainly concerned with plotting against predators and poachers?

The tide of words continued. "Yes, I shoot things as well. I've killed 1,198 rabbits this year. Last year I killed about 1,300, and the year before I shot 1,700 in about six weeks. So we're getting on top of it. But three years ago it was just like carnage — you can be doing 40mph on the quad bike, you can shoot two, get loaded and snap the gun up and still be doing 20mph and you haven't got to change gear.

"I'm not going to tell you how many foxes I shoot a year because people can get the wrong idea. But it's nothing sometimes to see 15 or 20 foxes in a night here. Look, you see this line of trees? It's 153 paces to the end, and at the end there's usually a pool of blood. Every fox in the area walks past there to drink, and when they do they play catch with my bullets.

"I'm not proud of the number of foxes I kill, but there's a very high population round here, and if they get in among the birds then the restaurant's open.

178

There is a hunt next door, but the best form of fox control is a speeding bullet.

"In the end, there's no getting away from the fact that what this is about is people killing things for pleasure. There's no point in pretending otherwise. But what would happen to the countryside if this wasn't happening? What would this place be like, without all the things I've done here?

"It's like hunting — I don't think hunting would have suffered quite as badly as it did if they didn't try and blow wind up people's arses and say it was just about fox control. It isn't. But if you stand up and be counted for what you're doing, if you tell people the truth, then people will judge you fairly.

"Everything's benefiting on this estate from what I do for pheasants and partridges. But if you don't educate people, then those who are against you are going to stay against you.

"A lot of people who live in the village, they've come there from towns, and they need educating. Sometimes I've taken friends out lamping with me when I'm out at nights, and they can't believe what they've seen. I took one chap out and in one night he saw fallow deer, muntjak, roe deer, a couple of badgers, which are pretty rare round here, and we saw hundreds of hares, a few rabbits, eight or nine foxes, and you've got skylarks getting up in front of you on the tracks . . . You could turn the countryside into a safari park just showing people things because they'll never get the chance to see it otherwise.

179

"Other people will phone up and ask ridiculous questions, like 'How can I get rid of swallows?' I say: 'Why would you want to get rid of them? Why don't you move back into the town?' They say: 'They wake us up in the morning.' I say, 'Well, tough, they've flown all the way from Africa to come and nest in your house.' It's ridiculous. When we renovated the barns outside my house, they lost the eaves that the swallows used to nest in, so we spent about £500 on bird boxes just to keep them coming.

"But most people, to be fair, are happy to be educated. I'd got one chap who used to walk around with binoculars, who wouldn't really stop and speak to me, wouldn't give the time of day at all. He'd got RSPB stickers on his binoculars. Anyway, one day I stopped and I said, 'Did you see the buzzards?' 'Oh,' he said, 'we won't see them for very long — you'll shoot them.' I said, 'You've got the wrong impression about what we do. Are you busy?' He said, 'No.' I said, 'Jump in.' I took him into the big wood and I had a nest of buzzards in there and I've got poults in a pen. I've got a thousand pheasant poults in an area and these buzzards were flipping about. He said: 'I can't believe it, why don't you —' I said: 'It's not doing me any harm. The pheasants have got used to them — they take a little while to get used to them, but it's horses for courses.' "

What about poaching — the gamekeeper's traditional preoccupation? "It's not a big thing. People do still poach a bit. But not for money any more. They do it to see who can get the most heads in one night and whoever's got the most heads doesn't buy a drink. They leave the bodies where they fall and just pull the heads off them. That's how it's changed — the value of everything has gone down."

His previous job involved regular run-ins with illegal hare-coursers; some of whom, from the travelling community, took a dim view of gamekeepers who tried to curtail their fun. "I remember one time, we got a phone call saying there was a load of hare-coursers down the bottom. So we go down to these fields and they've got Range-Rovers, Discoveries, all parked on the edge, and there's 40 or 50 hares going round these three fields, and there's men with wodges of notes as thick as your arm, and the biggest men are at the gateway where the cars are going in and out, and one of the blokes we knew comes up to us and says, 'Right, you've got a choice. You can either stand and watch, or you can lay in the ditch and bleed. It's entirely up to you: take your choice — it means nothing to us.' What do you do? We stood and watched. They was telling you how it was.

"There was another keeper I knew, Brian, and there was this really scary man, a bare-knuckle champion, who used to phone him and say, 'Don't be out looking for me tonight. I'm going to get some pheasants and I don't want to see you.' And he didn't. You don't mess with them. I've known keepers who've got home and found their dogs skinned and pinned on their doors and all sorts of things. There was one keeper just packed his things and went to Scotland after that."

Such shady confrontations once formed a major part of the gamekeeper's job description. Today they are just a footnote. So too with vermin. For nearly 450 years — from the Vermin Act of 1532 until the Wildlife and Countryside Act 1981 — the whole tenor of rural society was geared towards the extermination of any wild animal or bird that wasn't game, and gamekeepers — armed with a shocking variety of traps and poisons — were the stormtroopers of the anti-vermin campaign. Take away those two *raisons d'être*, and the modern gamekeeper is a very different creature from his rustic forebears. Is he, in fact, a comparable creature at all?

"Gamekeeping has changed in all sorts of ways. Not just because we're now looking at conservation, but also because of motorisation, and because the estates don't employ so many people. An estate like this, 40 or 50 years ago there might have been six or seven keepers looking after what I'm doing by myself. So you work differently. I've read bits in old estate books and things, records that say things like: 'The keeper saw the stoat go in the hole at 7.50a.m., he shot it that evening at 9.25p.m.' — so he's sat there for 13 hours waiting for that stoat to come out the hole. Can you imagine that? There are old gamekeepers who can say to me, 'I've forgotten more than you know.' And they're probably right. But it isn't all the same stuff.

"But, that said, a lot of it is, and you've got to be prepared to learn. The trouble is, a lot of the old boys are going to be bowing out over the next 20 years, and a lot of knowledge will go with them. But it's a hands-on sort of job, and you pick up bits and pieces as you go along. You learn by your mistakes. It's like, when you're out at night, you put your lamp on, and there's a muntjak 250 yards away. How do you know it's a muntjak? By the eyes. Then there's a fallow deer. How do you know it's a fallow deer? It's got the same colour eyes as the muntjak, but the eyes are this far apart . . . How do you know that? I don't know. You just do. You know all the different eyes. It's your job."

So what does it take to be a good gamekeeper today — apart from good eyesight? "You've got to have a passion for it. If you don't, you might as well be stacking shelves at Asda."

You would probably earn more if you were. There are just over 3,000 full-time gamekeepers in the UK — down from 10,000 a century ago — and perhaps as many again working part-time. And although shooting is booming as a sport — around 480,000 people participated in 2006, and spent about £2 billion among them — the average full-time salary for a gamekeeper is about £11,000 a year. Is it worth it?

"Yes. Because it's like having a 2,000-acre back garden. There are so many things that only a gamekeeper sees. Like, there's one piece in the middle of a field here, it's in open country, there's no trees around it or anything, and I came down the track one morning and I could see a fox out on the ploughing, and it was walking away and there was a grey mass behind it. I couldn't work out what it was and as I went round, you suddenly cotton on that there was about 300 partridges walking after this fox. Because where it's early in the programme, the birds are all together and they stay in gangs, and he must have had his dinner, so he's no threat to them. So he's just walking across the field and they're just walking after him, because they're as inquisitive as a cat."

Back at his cottage, we stood for a while on his small lawn, letting the juddering of the long drive slip from our limbs. "I had this bloody mole here for a long time, and I couldn't get him. You can see what he's done. Anyway, I had to go to a funeral the other day, so I had a shower an hour or so before, and then when I got out I looked out the window and I saw the earth moving. So I've gone down the path, and I had a towel wrapped round my waist, and I stood there and it moved again, and I got closer and closer, and I'm literally that far away from the ground when it just moved, so I pulled the gun back a bit and shot, and of course I got it. I was so chuffed . . .

"There's just always something to interest you," he concluded. "My job's not going to work: I go to play on a quad bike and a truck all day and pull the trigger at a few things, and that's a lot of people's dream. OK, it's daylight to dark, and you don't do it for the money, and the fun bit stops when you're out half the night getting soaking wet. But that's what it takes. It's not a job: it's a way of life. For the last six years," he added proudly, "I've had two weeks' holiday. And I don't have time to get ill."

What about a personal life? "I had a family for 22 years and we separated a few months ago, I'm afraid.

No reasons — there was no one else involved. But things weren't going according to plan. That's a big sadness because we've got three children and we'd been together for 22 years but that was just the way it was. We got on well, but the communication had stopped. But they still live in the village."

Could his work have had anything to do with it? "No. Because they had a 2,000-acre back garden as well. But it's a big sadness. I like to think I gave them as much as I could, but the one thing I've failed at in life really was the important part."

He said nothing for a while, but the silence soon began to seem peaceful, like the old, broad-leaved quietness of the big band of trees beyond his garden.

"You see that ash tree?" he said eventually. "Well, you know how swans, when they're mating, do that thing with their necks, and they put their heads together but never quite touch? Well, we have a few green woodpeckers, because there are a lot of ants in the lawn, and although they're very private birds, they're used to you being here, so you can look out the window and just watch them. And I came in one morning and I could hear this ha-ha-ha sound they make, and this woodpecker come round the side of there, and it was making this sort of ha-ha-ha, just as quiet as that, and another one come round the other side and they stood there giving it all this neck stuff. I never, ever seen that before, and I shouldn't think there's 20 people in the country who've seen it, because it's such a private thing. I didn't even know they done it.

**185**

"That's what makes it all worth while — all the stuff you see. That means much more than money. I don't need expensive holidays — everything I need is here. When you've lived in the country properly, it drags you back. The truth is, I'm like a duck out of water away from here, simple as that. You know when you've been on holiday somewhere and you're coming home, and it's nice when you get back? I get that when I've been to Cambridge."

He paused again, and gazed again at the trees and the sky. Then he said: "I've got a mate who works on the farm next door — he started working there when he was 16. He's 52 now and he's been ploughing them same fields all those years, and he'll do it until he's 65. But he never gets bored of it, and he's always got something to say. Every year when he turns them fields over, I go and see him and say, another year done then, mate? He says, 'Yeah, it's another year done but a new one just starting, and, do you know what, I've been ploughing this for 30 years or whatever and it's never ploughed as good as what it did now.'

"That's what work means, to me. There's a difference between going to work in an office and going to work on a piece of ground that you can treat as your own, even though you'll never own it. At the end of the day we'll all die — it's just what stamp you can make on your little patch."

# CHAPTER
# FIFTEEN

# Poppyland

I arrived at Weston Longville, 5 miles north-west of Norwich, on a cold weekday morning. I had read the famous diaries of James Woodforde, who spent 27 tragi-comically uneventful years as rector here between 1776 and 1803, and I vaguely expected to find the place full of the local characters he wrote about: Cobb the rat-catcher; Andrews the smuggler; John Springle with a skep of bees tied to his head; widow Pratt; "saucy, swearing" John Brand, the profligate servant boy; Betty Dade the head maid; Reeves the tooth-drawer, who was "too old I think to draw teeth, can't see very well"; the "2 large Piggs" who broke into one of the parson's beer-barrels on 15 April 1778 and were too drunk to stand for a day and a half ("I never saw Piggs so drunk in my life").

It wasn't.

Instead, I found a Dinosaur Park and a plant nursery and a golf club (membership £670 a year plus £500 entrance fee) and a smart pub full of tourists (where the Stag Owners Club meets on the first Tuesday of every month) and a relentless torrent of Bernard Matthews lorries raging ear-splittingly along the lane at the southern edge of the village from the nearby turkey factory, and the same pedestrian-free lanes and neat, forbidding hedges that I had noticed through much of Norfolk.

I also found villagers, including some born-and-bred ones whose family stories stretched back almost as far as Parson Woodforde. Peter Howlett, for example, was an 85-year-old smallholder whose father was a farm steward on the estate owned by the Custance family — mentioned frequently in the diaries as local grandees. There were Howletts in the village in Woodforde's day, too, so Peter was probably descended from people who met the parson. But for all his links with the past, he seemed no more out of place in the modern world than I did.

He lived in a bungalow on the edge of a village, where until recently he supported himself through a mixture of market gardening and turkey-rearing. (Woodforde, by contrast, lived in a large rectory — now a private house — with extensive grounds and a well-stocked cellar and larder.) The bungalow was built by Peter's father, on a 3½-acre patch of land he bought in 1926, when the last Custance died and the estate was sold off, mainly — as was happening a lot in England at that time — to its tenant farmers. The smallholding had thrived for three-quarters of a century, but now Peter let out the land for grazing and survived mainly on his pension. Much of his time was devoted to looking after his wife, Diana: "She had back trouble for a long while and now it's caught up with her and she can't walk."

He had an old man's big nose and ears but a rather small, birdlike head, sitting on big, bony, athletic shoulders. When I asked him how the village had changed, he thought hard about it. "Well, everything different, ennit, if you go back to things. Everyone's moved around and mixed up — that's what happened, ennit?" He tossed his head, as if pleased with the point. "One of the biggest changes was all the farms being sold off, because now those farmers have sold 'em too, and what used to be farmhouses are all just private homes. Top Farm, where I was born, is part of the riding school; the dairy farm is part of the Dinosaur Park, and of course up at Church Farm, that's been sold off and the land is all private houses."

The Weston Longville he grew up in had neither electricity nor a proper water supply. At the farm where his father worked, "they hadn't got much water, but there was a pit up the dairy farm, and the younger son used to take a horse up the dairy farm with a three-wheel waterpump and fill it up from the pit, then bring it back down". When his father bought the smallholding, "he did put a well down", but "he never had a bathroom, and he had an outdoor toilet till 1982".

Like most people then, Peter began farm work immediately after — or strictly speaking slightly before — leaving school. The work varied. "I can turn my hand to most things. We used to farm a field up past Weston Hall and grow sugar beet, barley and hay and all that. But the farm work used to be done by hand, didn't it, with the horses and the ploughs and

**189**

everything — but now with the sugar beet they want 30 tonne an acre. So this big machinery is altering everything."

Such trends — which were evident when Ronald Blythe was writing *Akenfield* — were less important to smallholders, but they had still had to adapt with the times. "We did a lot of market gardening, and during the war we were milking three Jersey cows, so we always had milk and butter and everything. But the main thing we did was kept poultry." These were chickens at first, Rhode Island Reds, but in 1959 they had to slaughter them all "when we got the pest". Then they started breeding Norfolk Black turkeys, which Diana's parents had already been breeding. "This was around the time Bernard Matthews was starting — I think my wife's parents supplied him with his very first turkeys. Anyway, that was quite good, but we've more or less stopped that now, and the last year or two we been growing only a few vegetables in the garden."

He paused for thought, then continued: "It was a harder life we had in some ways, but it was the life we was used to. People worked hard, but they were happy in what they were doing. Life was slower but people knew it was slower and they were more contented, whereas today everybody's in such a hurry."

Social life consisted of the Young Farmers' Club — where he met his wife — and, later, occasional events in the village hall, which he was instrumental in creating after the war. "We had a youth club and did whist drives and barn dances and things. But now the younger people want to be doing other things. They'd

190

say we didn't have much entertainment, but you'd make your own. You'd walk up the pub for a drink and you'd play cards or you'd think up some games. But you always had plenty of other stuff to do. Dad was always catching rabbits everywhere, because rabbits, during the war, and pigeons, they were the main meat for us, weren't they? And of course rabbits used to eat a lot of crops. So Dad always had his traps out, and wintertime they were going round ferreting and digging these rabbits out. But the other thing we used to do when we was young was, at night-time, we used to run a net out round the wood and then they'd go round when the wind was right and drive 'em in, and then we used to pick 'em out the net and just break their necks."

It struck me that there were probably people in the village today to whom that would sound grotesque. Peter wasn't sure. "I don't know what a lot of them think. A lot of them I don't know. Years ago everybody knew one another, and they intermarried, didn't they? And now of course if there's a house for sale, that's mostly bought by someone from anywhere. And some of them, you see, they're just there and you don't see or hear nothing: all they want to do is run their own life. A lot of them you don't know who they are, you don't even know names."

This was — as you will have noticed — becoming a familiar theme. "I used to play in the cricket team," he added, "when we had one. And the football team. There was young people in the village then, you see, and if we wanted to do anything we had to do it here.

**191**

In younger days we used to walk down to Weston school when that was there, and of course that's now an artist lives there doing painting. A lot of my school pals who I went to school with, a lot have passed away now, or else they moved away. There's still one or two, but that's about it."

One of his near contemporaries was an 82-year-old widow and farmer's daughter called Marjorie Futter, who lived on the opposite side of the village: about 400m away as the crow flies but a good mile and a half on the busy, pavement-less road. This all-but-impossible divide meant that they rarely saw each other. "I don't know half the people in the village," Marjorie told me; which was odd, because scarcely a decade earlier she had spent the best part of a year researching the village's history, publishing the results in a booklet in 1997. "I did it because people's memories were fading and they'd be lost if we didn't write it down. And I must have met most people in the village when I was doing it. But that was 10 years ago and it's changed a lot since then. People are different now. Seven or eight people have died, and a lot of others have moved. There's a whole new lot of people now."

She proudly showed me her collection of old photos: a horse-assisted harvest, a threshing machine, a wooden-beam gallows plough, a horse-turned pug mill for making bricks. She seemed a sociable kind of person, but she clearly felt cut off in her little thatched cottage on the edge of the village. "People don't mix an awful lot. The shop's just closed, the post office has closed — we miss that terribly. The school closed years ago — I think that probably killed the village more than anything, because people meet through their children. But it's progress I suppose."

Her father was a smallholder: "Just agricultural farming with a horse, wheat and that, and then sugar beet." Like many villagers, he lost his home and land in World War II, when a substantial chunk of land was taken over to become a military airbase; the airfield was later acquired by Bernard Matthews, who uses it as one of the main production centres for his controversial turkey empire. "My father never got his land back."

She had fond memories of her childhood in the village, but most of her old friends had moved or passed on. "It's a long time ago, nearly 80 years. And the village has changed so much. We didn't worry about traffic in those days — we'd walk or cycle everywhere. But I don't think we did as much playing together as you might think, because the days were short and there was no electric light, and there were probably chores that you had to do.

"Nowadays, of course, people drive their children everywhere. But I don't think there actually are very many young people in the village. I suppose some of the newcomers have got youngsters, but I don't know them. I don't really know much about most people. I suppose most of them commute into Norwich.

"There's an awful lot more money in the village than there used to be — it's a completely different way of life. It was hard when I was growing up: we didn't have electricity or water for ages. Now some people have almost become millionaires just because of property prices. But people seem so isolated, I often think. It's a shame."

One thing that hadn't changed, though, was her sense of a connection with the more distant past. "Oh, it's lovely to walk to and fro in the rectory garden and think, just imagine him [Parson Woodforde] coming in with his horse and trap. And I can remember speaking to older people in the past who would say, I used to be the cook at the big house, I was the chief cook and under me I had so-and-so and so-and-so. But you can hardly visualise that now. It seems incredible, really, that life was ever like that."

The current rector, Selwyn Tillett, lived next door to the church in an altogether more modest modern building than Parson Woodforde's delightful rectory. He only came there in 2005 but was already being spoken of as a rejuvenating influence in the village. "It's a very scattered community," he told me. "They say there's a population of 300, but if that's true it's difficult to know where they all are. There's no centre to the village. The school went in the 1970s, the shop went early in our time, and the post office has gone too, although they tried to keep it going. There's no other public facility, apart from the church, the village hall and the pub."

Like most rural priests in the 21st century, Selwyn had more than one church to think about: "I'm responsible for nine communities, five parishes, seven working churches. I do a service at 8a.m., 10a.m. and 6p.m. every Sunday — but which church each service is

194

in varies from week to week. At Weston, we have a 10a.m. Eucharist on the first Sunday of the month, which brings in between a dozen and two dozen, including two children of primary-school age. We have an 8a.m. prayerbook service on the second Sunday, which typically brings in six or seven — and, at 52, I'm by far the youngest. And then we have a very traditional Book of Common Prayer evensong on the fourth Sunday, which brings in about eight to 10, with the same provisos about age."

Keeping the church alive and keeping the village alive are, in his eyes, part of the same mission. "Here, much more than in south London [his previous beat], you have to get used to being rector for the whole community — in exactly the same way that Woodforde was. But the sense of community is much less than in his day. The number of people with any real sense of the village's past — people whose grandfathers or great-grandfathers worked on the fields — is very small: maybe four or five."

Tillett was not a Parson Woodforde fan when he arrived. He felt — as I did — that the journals show rather too much concern for the parson's own physical comforts and rather too little for the poverty beyond the well-tended rectory garden. ("We had for dinner a Calf's Head, boiled Fowl and Tongue, a Saddle of Mutton rosted on the Side Table, and a fine Swan rosted with Currant Jelly Sauce for the first Course. The Second Course a couple of Wild Fowl called Dun Fowls, Larks, Blamange, Tarts etc. etc. and a good Desert of Fruit after amongst which was a Damson

Cheese . . ." reads a typical entry.) "I thought it might be a terrible obstacle," said Selwyn. Gradually, however, he came round, as he came to see that his well-fed predecessor had also had good points — perhaps even including his lack of saintliness — that helped him act as a focal point for village life. Weston Longville could do with such a point today.

"I think a lot of the current villagers are not people who feel that village society is really something that they're part of or want to be part of. The society they see themselves as belonging to is as likely as not to be the town where they work, or where their children go to school. This is really just as much of a commuter dormitory as anywhere in south London or Croydon.

"The number of children in the village is absolutely tiny. Any teenagers would rather spend their time in Taverham or Reepham, where they go to school and where their friends are. So it's largely a population of people of retirement age and above, which is typical of a lot of Norfolk.

"House prices have got a lot to do with it. Well, there's no work here, for a start. And even if you could get a job, you couldn't afford a home. We could really do with some affordable housing, but whenever there is any new building it's always modern private houses."

In such circumstances, even a parson as emphatically out of date in his attitudes as Woodforde can make a valuable contribution, by reminding people that the village has a past. And, of course, by putting bums on seats. "The Parson Woodforde Society treats us very well," Selwyn concluded, "and every few years they have big events. We had 170 at evensong the other day: 150 of them and 20 of us."

At Sidestrand, I stood on the beach and thought to myself some of the bitterest words a married man can think: my wife was right. This wasn't a quest. It was a midlife crisis. I was travelling not because I was achieving anything thereby, but because of some ill-defined inner urge.

The admission proved curiously soothing. I was a tourist. I could relax. I pottered about below Sidestrand's cliffs, which for many years had human bones sticking out of them after part of the coastline fell into the sea in 1916, taking a church and part of a graveyard with it. I bought an ice-cream. I chatted with a woman — a hospital worker from Manchester — who told me that she came back to these parts twice a year to visit her mother in a nearby old people's home. ("There's no point in coming more often because she has no idea if I've been or not.") I wandered, too, through the streets of Overstrand, which before World War I had seven millionaires living in it, as well as such distinguished regular visitors as Winston Churchill and Albert Einstein. Their presence was largely attributable to the Victorian drama critic Clement Scott, who almost single-handedly created the north Norfolk tourist industry after falling in love with the local miller's house and daughter, christening the area "Poppyland" and writing a series of articles about it. Today, I understand, Overstrand is one of several villages on that stretch of coast that the government is resigned to losing to rising sea-levels within the next 30 years. (Evacuation is more cost-effective than investing in sea defences.) I couldn't find Mill House, but I did find a field that seemed to answer reasonably well to the description in Scott's original 1883 article: "It is difficult to convey an idea of the silence of the fields through which I passed, or the beauty of the prospect that surrounded me — a blue sky without a cloud across it; a sea sparkling under a haze of heat; wild flowers in profusion around me, poppies predominating everywhere."

I felt better after that.

At Houghton St Giles I left my shoes in the car and walked barefoot down a muddy path towards Walsingham. This is what pilgrims did for centuries, in the old, forgotten England before the Reformation. It was a bright, cold morning, and there was something unkempt about the village — with sagging cottages with mossy roofs, soft as the turfed verges — that made me curious about what it felt like to be English in Norfolk before Henry VIII and his cronies forced through their programme of modernisation.

A silk sheet of dew gleamed on the grass, and here and there bright primroses shone. Can Chaucer have been thinking of a very different morning when he began *The Canterbury Tales*? Who knows? But his opening lines more or less came back to me ("Whan that Aprill with his shoures soote / The droghte of March hath perced to the roote, / And bathed every veyne in swich licour, / Of which vertu engendred is the flour"), and I could almost understand why, as he put it, "thanne longen folk to goon on pilgrimages".

So I walked for a few hundred yards and tried, in my head, to go back a few hundred years. It was a futile experiment: not just because the path — the Peddars' Way — had been diverted from its original route to allow for road traffic, nor because Radio 1 was drifting from a distant window; nor because a real medieval pilgrim would have left his shoes in Houghton's Slipper Chapel rather than in a car parked near by; but also because — well, because there was no mystery. The track, which seemed to follow the route of a disused railway, was well signed and straight, with well-kept verges and benches at regular intervals for the infirm. I couldn't even ask myself, as exhausted pilgrims must once have done at this point, what numinous wonders I might encounter from this point on. I had already driven through Walsingham, with its Christian traffic jams and gift shops, on the way.

Back at the Slipper Chapel there was a big, sensible car park with several coaches in it, together with a well-laid-out visitor centre, with neatly mown lawns, well-signed toilets and sensible, non-slip brick pathways.

In the gift shop, one fat lady was opening her heart to another: "There's not much you can say really, is there? It's hard. You've just got to be brave. For him, really. He started trying to tell me in the service station, but he just went, so I said come on, tell me outside, but then I went too. But I just kept telling myself, go on, be brave, be brave for him."

In the car park, a white-bearded man with an unnaturally red face was berating a tired-looking woman who seemed to have brushed against his Volvo while parking.

In the chapel itself, a young French couple were whispering, over piped music.

No one had left any shoes.

A long time later, about 30 miles further east, after many forgettable stops in villages whose local industries appeared to consist mainly of art galleries and tea-rooms, I parked in Potter Heigham outside one of Norfolk's oldest churches, where, on a patch of damp grass adjoining the gap-toothed graveyard, I met one of Norfolk's oldest eel-catchers.

I say old. He was 70 but looked younger, with a plump, upright figure, a bright smile, thick arms and a healthy tan on his round, bald head. He was called Chris Nudd, wore an anorak and tracksuit trousers and seemed to glow with good humour and health. The only sign of wear and tear was a copper bracelet on his wrist, worn to alleviate the torments of arthritis.

The damp entered his joints about a mile east of the village, where until about 20 years ago he was in the habit of spending countless frozen nights manning what is thought to have been Norfolk's last working eel-sett.

"A sett's basically just a net across the broad," he explained, as we approached his old haunt along a rough, soggy track. "Except that it's a bit more complicated than that. I took it over from old Tom Cable. Broadland Tom they used to call him. He could have told a tale or two. I don't know how long he'd had it for, but I think it's been here at least a hundred year. There were two of us when we had it, and you needed two — we were catching that many. We had it for about 15 years, I suppose, and after that it just wasn't worth it — not enough eels. It's not been used since, as far as I know, until the Broads Authority started doing demonstrations. But it's changed a bit since we had it."

"It" turned out to consist mainly of a wooden hut, about the size of a small garden shed, painted green, with a wooden jetty beside it, a small rowing boat moored alongside and, somewhere beneath the smooth, silvery water of the broad, an old-fashioned system of nets, ropes and chains. This unseen bit is the bit that matters. Imagine a tennis net stretched across a river, protruding slightly from the water and stretched down to the bottom with weights, with three big, round holes in it, from which protrude three further nets shaped like giant traffic cones, with "no return" cross-nets within them, like valves, so that fish can swim away from the tennis net and towards the point of the cone but not back again. That, in essence, is how a sett works. When the tide is moving in the right direction — back out towards the sea — every eel that moves with it will pass into the net system and should, with a bit of luck, end up in the points of the cones. All that remains is for the eel-catcher to bring them ashore.

"They've raised it all up, I think," Chris continued, surveying his former territory like an old dog. "We used to have the water coming in the hut sometimes. And

**201**

you couldn't have walked down here without getting your feet wet."

He seemed more interested in the hut than the net. It was largely inside the hut that he had practised his craft. "There's not all that much to it apart from laying out the nets, and then pulling them in when they're full, or when a boat come past. But you had to keep yourself awake, which can be hard if you been doing it for a few nights on the trot. We did have an old gas cooker that someone had thrown out — we used to fry herring. And sometimes we'd have some rum or something to keep us warm."

He and his partner would generally man the nets from August to November, throughout the final quarter of each moon, from dusk to dawn, after which he would drag himself into work at Woods boatyard in Potter Heigham, or, latterly, as a self-employed builder.

"That's very hard, doing that, but it depends how long you have to stick it. But, oh, we used to catch a lot, especially at first. We used to go out and empty the eels every two hours or so — we used to keep them in the water in two big wooden trunks. We used to have two guys from Cooke brothers' eel and pie shop in London come here with big boxes — they'd go off to their shop with 200 lbs of eels. We didn't get rich — we got 4 shilling a pound. But I really enjoyed my time what we had here, 'specially when the weather was good. The noises you'd hear outside . . . it used to be lovely just to sit out here. Of course, it wasn't always good: I remember the great storm of October 1987 — I thought the whole shed was going to be swept away,

202

with me in it. But it was a lovely place generally. You can only stick it for so long, though."

The sun had been sinking as he spoke. The pale reeds on the far side of the broad were almost indistinguishable. Soft layers of pink and blue sky were fading into one another before seeming to melt into the mist-touched, pearl-grey river. "I would say that's slowing down now, by the look of it," said Chris, which amazed me, because to my eye the water was utterly still. But sensing the nuances of the tide is a crucial part of the eel-catcher's art. You leave the nets down on the river-bed until the tide is about to ebb, then raise them and hope that the tide will fill them with eels as it goes out.

How had he learnt his craft? "I was a builder by trade, but I'd done a lot of eel-catching. I grew up around eels. My grandfather was an eel-catcher, my father was an eel-catcher. I saw them lining eels, babbing eels, spearing eels." I couldn't quite grasp what "lining" was. Babbing involves threading wool through bunches of worms. Spearing is probably illegal now, Chris thought, although there was a rusty old eel spear — a bit like a giant toasting fork — propped up outside the hut.

Above it was a strange sign that said:

```
S     N
T E   E
O E   T
P L
```

I was about to ask Chris what it meant when we were distracted by the arrival of a pair of ducks. One landed on our side of the net, one on the other, and the one nearest us then spent a long time quacking and trying to work out how to rejoin his mate. Chris was on the point of lowering the net when the one on the far side flew back. The ripples of its landing slid gently away, the reunited couple drifted silently after them, and the dusk was still again. Some time later, I realised that the sign was meant to be read from top to bottom.

"We're lucky tonight," said Chris. "The water's been very high, so the cruisers haven't been getting through Potter Heigham bridge. Sometimes you had to keep letting the net down, because you've got quite a few fishermen used to fish at night." Potter Heigham's bridge is famous — partly for its age (623 years) and partly for its sheer unsuitability for modern traffic, above and below. On at least one occasion, a pedestrian has leapt down into the water to avoid being crushed by a coach. On another, the local vicar was dropped down as ballast into a boat that was stuck, in the hope that his weight would force it further down into the water and thus free it. And tonight, it seemed, there was no way under it.

None the less, the broad was not deserted. The Broads Authority was staging one of a series of historical demonstrations of the sett system for the benefit of the general public, some of whom could now be heard tramping their way up the path from the village. A young Broads Authority ranger from Norwich, Eilish Rothney, was setting up the nets in preparation, and before long we were joined by about 15 locals and holidaymakers, escorted by a couple of volunteer assistant rangers.

They stayed for an hour or more, during which time no eels were caught but people got to handle some from a bucketful that Eilish had brought from elsewhere, as well as to eat pieces of fresh eel that she had fried on a stove just outside the shed. Some were too squeamish to try either of these delights. But everyone seemed awestruck by the experience — so unfamiliar to so many — of being out in the semi-wilderness on a dark night. They milled around, looked at and fiddled with the shed and its bunks and with the ropes and chains and eel spears, and asked any number of questions, some more penetrating than others.

"We think it's the only eel-sett in the world," said Eilish at one point.

"What is?" asked a posh woman.

"This one," said the deerstalkered man with her.

"What about it?"

"They think it's the only one in the world."

"The only what?"

"Eel-sett."

A bit later, however, when Eilish's demonstration was in full flood, something odd happened. She had been talking about the mysterious life cycle of the eel — how they've been around for millions of years but no one has ever seen them breed or be born; how they can grow to be as thick as a man's arm; how they change shape when they're ready to breed and then swim

3,000 miles against the Gulf Stream until they reach the Sargasso Sea; how they change into glass eels when they return to our waters.

Then she said: "But the sad thing is, we've been recording catches, and the numbers reaching our waters, in the past 40 or 50 years, have dropped by 99 per cent." There was an audible collective gasp of what I can only describe as physical pain. It looks silly in print, but there was something about the way she said it that conveyed to all of us the full enormity of that cold fact: that a species that had sustained countless thousands of English country folk over countless generations had, simply, been all but wiped out.

For a shocking moment, the world stopped feeling tame. We were just helpless human beings, bewildered and frightened in the darkness like our ancestors, wondering what on earth we had done to provoke such a catastrophe, and where it was all going to end.

"It's very hard to know exactly what the problem is," continued Eilish. "It could be global warming affecting the Gulf Stream. It may be pollution, ending up in the Sargasso Sea. We know they've caught eels that have PCBs. There's also loss of habitat."

But the moment had passed. Before long we were joking and laughing again, wondering at the eels in the bucket — writhing like snakes in slime, but with the curiously innocent, wide-eyed faces of baby seals — and picking Chris and Eilish's brains for eel-lore. "When it's very cold the eels just bury themselves in the mud and wait till it gets warm in springtime," said Chris. "They don't all go across to the Sargasso Sea.

Some of the ones we used to catch must have been there for years."

"It's weird, isn't it," said someone, "when you think of all those different nature programmes and things you see on the television, how they know every intimate detail — they've got cameras in the nest, cameras underground — yet with eels there's still so little that we actually know about them. We don't even really know that they spawn in the Sargasso Sea. They think they do, but they've never actually seen it."

"When I first started fishing," said one of the assistant rangers, "eels were a flaming nuisance. You'd be trying to catch something else and you'd keep getting flaming eels."

"Good to eat, though," said someone else.

This led to a discussion of fish flavours.

"Bream? They always taste of mud," said Chris.

"Yet they do take them up to London," said one of the locals. "Did you see that piece in the paper?"

"They'll eat anything in London."

"It's a foreign country, Chris."

"I know."

"You been up there lately?"

"No, but I seen it on the telly."

I spent the night on a farm on the edge of the village, and was intrigued in the night by a red glow coming from somewhere below my bedroom window. It turned out that the farm doubled up as a pet crematorium. "I do between 9 and 13 ton," the owner told me. A year? "A month."

He had, it seemed, drifted into it over the years, but business was now thriving. It wasn't just a question of incinerating corpses but of providing a whole range of funeral-director-style services for bereaved pet-owners. The thought "TV sitcom" appeared in my mind, as I'm sure it had to many visitors before — especially when he told of the time when a distraught but wealthy customer had persuaded him to bury a much-loved pony in his (the customer's) front garden. "He said he didn't want it cremated — his wife was too upset. So I hired a digger and we went round. Couldn't get through the gate. Ended up having to drag it round on a rope. Oh, my godfathers! The mess!

"We cleared it all up and dug a hole, and just as we were finishing the chap turned up. 'Hello, guv'nor,' I said. 'We've just popped him in the hole and now we're just covering it up.' He said, 'I'll go and tell me wife then, to come out.' So off he went, and I turned round, and just as the digger was putting the last bit of soil on the top — his back legs popped out the top. I could've had a heart attack. I said, 'I told you you should have dug deeper.' Somehow, we managed to get them back in — but I think we virtually had to break 'em off in the end."

He laughed, but not cynically. He seemed proud of his work. He was, he said, due to be doing a lot of "taking back" the next day. By this he meant returning the ashes, in caskets, to their owners. "We do about 20 different sorts of caskets. In fact, people are taking advantage of that, because they're solid mahogany, inlaid with brass — so they're buying an extra one to put their mum and dad in that they've got in a plastic jar from the crematorium."

Mortality had never seemed less threatening as I drove away on a clear, almost traffic-less Sunday morning. A few hours later, in a noisy lay-by near Northampton, I clutched my mobile phone to my ear and heard my father speak to me for the last time.

# CHAPTER
# SIXTEEN

# Ghosts

The chopped earth on my father's grave was still rough and unsettled, but the grass around it was bright as a smooth golf-green. A few pink buds remained on the hawthorn branches above him; from the surrounding leaves, a light breeze brushed occasional drops of rainwater on to my face. Even the withered flowers from the coffin showed traces of life.

We had buried him three weeks earlier. Now I was back in his village to continue the miserable ritual of clearing his cottage. The rain, which had been falling for days (despite the worst front-page drought headlines in memory), had temporarily stopped; and so, after many hours of sorting through drawers and bundling familiar clothes into bin liners, had I. A two-minute walk to his graveside seemed a logical way to take a break.

Actually, the grave wasn't all his: my late mother (who was never late in her life) had been waiting for him in the same hole for six years. The thought of them being together again, slowly being absorbed into the Hertfordshire soil, was a comforting one. They had been a close, gentle couple, and it felt right —

disconcertingly so — to think of them as a couple again. Yet the very rightness reminded me how much I had lost.

I bowed my head, then looked up, breathing in the peace of the early evening. On the far side of the cemetery hedge, larks still sang crazily over a field of short green wheat; beyond, where the hilltop sloped down into the river valley, ancient-sounding sighs rose from the high, ruffled treetops of Bluebell Wood. The sun sank towards them, seeming to wash the sky as it did so, and the hawthorn leaves gleamed golden-green in its light. Somewhere, children were squealing at play in the now cloudless evening; somewhere else, a lamb bleated. For a brief, hypnotic moment, everything — sounds, sights, even my inhalations of rain-wettened blossom and grass — was exactly as I would have experienced it, in this same village, 40-odd years before, in the evenings of my own early memories.

A thought struck me: was that what I had been searching for all this time? My childhood? Perhaps; perhaps, too, it had been fear of bereavement that had propelled me. Yet in the nakedness of my grief I saw clearly that there was more to it than that. I had been seeking other childhoods too — any that had been lived in the old countryside that I had grown up believing in.

That sounds foolish. My country childhood was a comfortable, middle-class idyll; most traditional rural childhoods were full of hardship. Yet I was convinced that, in some sense, my feelings of bereavement were tangled up with a wider loss that affected a whole rural generation. I couldn't quite say how. But I knew that a world was passing.

The idea of more house-clearing suddenly seemed even less palatable than usual, and I walked back by the longest-possible route.

Before I knew it, I was in the rape-fields behind Green Tye, on an overgrown path half-hidden from the village by a fringe of ragged trees and hedges, thick and frayed as an old sofa. The rape was a recent innovation, but apart from that not a leaf seemed to have changed since I used to sneak teenage cigarettes on this exact spot and dream beautiful daydreams about a world still huge with possibility.

In one direction, Green Tye lay sprawled across the field-edge exactly as it had always done, the low cottages settled comfortably among the vegetation like a pride of well-fed lions. It was, as ever, impossible to say with any certainty where the landscape stopped and the village began.

The other way, flat fields stretched to a high blue horizon, beyond whose hopeful haze my younger self had always imagined adventures waiting. (In fact, that was roughly where they had been building Stansted Airport at the time, to be followed soon after by the M11, the M25 and 50,000 executive homes.) I could make out the scrap of woodland officially known as Thorley Wood, although we used to call it the Harry Roberts wood, after the East London murderer who was caught there in 1966: he'd been sleeping rough while on the run after killing a policeman, and was caught after one of my six-year-old schoolfellows drew her parents' attention to the smoke from his campfire. (Apparently he was drawn there by his own childhood memories, having spent time in the area as a wartime evacuee. He has been in jail ever since.)

Further over, I could see the fields where I had earned my first wage-packets, picking wild oats or heaving bales on to trailers, before cycling home exhausted towards the welcoming coolness of home. I could even discern — I thought — the roof of what used to be Old Harold's cottage, over by Ashwell's farm. I smiled. Harold was an extravagantly wrinkled and foul-mouthed labourer who specialised in finding loathsome tasks — such as trying to kill rats with a stick — for teenage casuals. I wondered what had happened to him. My father might know: he was the kind of person who did. Except — I remembered miserably — that he wasn't any more.

Then I thought: maybe those weren't my very first wage packets? Maybe my first job was helping John the Postman, on icy Christmas dawns? My fingers burned with the remembered cold of those frostbitten cycle-rides; my chest ached with the thought that this was another question that my father would probably have been able to resolve.

I looked back towards the village, thinking how pregnant with meaning its physical fabric suddenly seemed to me. The scenes of childhood often appear pale and small to the adult eye, but today it was all saturated with colour and memory, as if each roof still concealed the familiar villagers I remembered from the days when this was the centre of my world.

**213**

They didn't: those villagers were all long dead. But as I walked back towards Perry Green, through a muddy tunnel of overhanging trees, I felt an overpowering sense of their presence: Old Harold, John the Postman, John the Poacher, the Braces, the Shipps, Mrs Alexander and her goats, Chris Glyn and his woodwork, Mr Felsted and his giant ferret. Imagine what layers of meaning this landscape must have held for them — and, indeed, for any number of previous generations of villagers, most of whom must have wandered at some point along this very same village fringe.

High, familiar boughs leant overhead. Fresh leaves stuck in moist clusters to a roof of light branches. The old wood stirred and creaked as I passed. Birds cheeped brightly. A warm breeze flowed gently in with the light at the end of the tunnel. Could anyone have passed this way without noticing these things?

The very act of growing up here, and of living and working in this landscape, would predispose you to thinking in a certain way. Perhaps it wasn't even possible to say where the village stopped and the villager began ... I imagined a whole series of Hertfordshire-born boys, from earlier generations, treading this path before me: cloth-capped and woollen-shirted in the 1950s, waistcoated and hobnail-booted in the 1920s, linen-smocked and leather-gaitered in Victorian times, fustian-jacketed in Napoleon's day, and so on in a long, mesmerising parade all the way back to a ragged Saxon churl. They were young men, just as I was once a young man, so presumably they must have had at least some thoughts and feelings that might have been recognisable by me? They would have smelt much the same smells that I was breathing in now and grown old feeling much the same spring breezes brush through much the same kind of green trees, and heard and recognised that peculiar rippling dialect of birdsong that I am convinced is unique to Hertfordshire. They would, I daresay, have gazed across fields much like those I was just leaving, sloping down and then up towards Thorley Wood, and the contours would have felt, as they did to me, reassuringly familiar, like the shape of one's own home. Each in his turn would have picked his way through undergrowth much like this, and noticed the damp and cool of the leafy shadows. All — probably — would have experienced dog-weary harvest evenings dissolving in warm beer while cold shadows blackened on the green, just as I had once done. They would have had the same sense of a continually rejuvenated landscape, whose texture would have caked their skins as it used to cake mine. They would have buried their parents in the same earth. They might even have reflected that, in experiencing these things, they were sharing in experiences that previous generations of villagers had had before them . . .

I gave up imagining. It was fanciful to pretend that my life had more than the most tenuous resemblance to those of Green Tye's former inhabitants. They were true villagers and I was not. Yet perhaps that very admission defined the wider loss that I had been trying to pin down. I was cut off from their experience not by class but by time.

The villagers of the past were all, in social terms, members of the same species. All lived and died in an agricultural society, dependent for their survival and their sense of self on their village and the landscape around it. Yes, some had ploughed with horses, some with tractors; some had known electricity and telephones while others had been mud-caked peasants shivering and scratching in stinking huts; a few had been relatively well-off. But they all shared an organic relationship with the village, whereby it sustained them and they sustained it. And in certain crucial respects they shared a world-view. They saw, mostly, the same wildflowers, heard the same birds, winced at the same frosts and slipped in the same mud. They shared a distinct accent ("toime" for "time", "iker" for "acre", "barn" for "born") and a distinct body of largely local knowledge: about the properties of plants, the inclinations of animals, the idiosyncrasies of the soil, the rhythms of the seasons, the lore and myths of the locality, and the memories of the village families. Most crucially of all, they felt their lives bordered by much the same horizons.

By this I mean that the bulk of each life's drama was set on the same small stage: a few square miles of fields and woods, with this particular thatched village growing (complete with villagers) out of its centre and, on its edges, a circle of neighbouring settlements: Perry Green, Much Hadham, Allen's Green, Thorley. Obviously, many would have known and done much

216

beyond that circle; conversely, events beyond it would have affected the lives of those within. But normality — for most people, most of the time — was local. If a young man went off to seek his fortune, or to fight in some far-flung war, that adventure took place off-stage. If he returned, he would once again participate in the very particular shared experience of normal Green Tye life.

So it was, too, with temporal horizons. The life of the 1950s farmhand was defined by the same boundaries as that of the feudal churl. Ahead, as for us, lay death; behind, likewise, birth. And beyond both remained Green Tye and its families and fields, scarcely altered except by that particular villager's own absence.

And that, I reflected, is where a great gulf appears between their world and ours. Modern lives are lived on a stage without boundaries. Road, rail, air travel, telephone, television, internet, mass education and multinational marketing have stretched and homogenised our world-views to the point where most of us consider the whole planet to be the backdrop against which the drama of our lives is played. Our horizons stretch deep into the past and future, too: popular science has shown us the empty aeons that preceded humanity's sojourn on the planet and the more troubling likelihood that further empty aeons will soon follow it. Do any of us seriously imagine that our grandchildren's lives will bear more than a passing resemblance to ours?

My previous generations of Green Tye-dwellers, real and imaginary, shared the comfort of a small context. Barring the collapse of Western civilisation, we shall never know such a context again. That may or may not be a bad thing. What it does mean is that, unlike almost any previous set of deaths, the passing of the last of those generations represents the passing of a world. Behind me lies birth; ahead, death; beyond — who knows? But not, at any rate, Green Tye.

# CHAPTER
# SEVENTEEN

# Lost worlds

One day, still tying up loose ends in Hertfordshire, I went to Ashwell — accidentally — and, stopping to look at the church, was surprised and moved by the worn graffiti on its walls. This had been carved in the 14th century by survivors of the Black Death — apparently desperate to leave some sort of record of themselves before they too perished. You could still feel their desperation. "*Superset plebs pessima testis*", moaned one. ("The dregs of the people survive to tell the tale.") "*In fine ije ventus validus*", said another. ("At the end of the second [plague] was a great wind" — possibly referring to a terrible storm in 1361.) Who were they talking to? Me, presumably, among others. And in a strange way their words struck home. Yes, I thought: that is what this is about. Confronted by oblivion, those monks had grasped something: if you don't write it down, it can vanish utterly — not just you, but your whole world.

My father had gone and had, as the old Akenfield farrier put it, "taken a lot of the truth out of the world" with him. But it wasn't just him: millions of others had gone too, or were about to go: people who knew the old

England, the old countryside. Fewer and fewer of the truths they knew remained for subsequent generations to learn; a sea of other truths was flooding in to take their place. And that — as much as the bitterness of each individual death — was what I still wanted to confront. For what does mankind have to fling back in the face of death, apart from our ability to hold on to things on each other's behalf: to pass down to those who follow the fact that this happened, or that this was how things used to be?

A new sense of urgency seized me. Somehow, while I still could, I wanted to discover more of my country — the land, the people, the past — and to write down some of what I found there: so that a few more voices, at least, might be preserved from oblivion; so that, when my turn came to die, some trace might remain for my children of this vague idea of rural England that still floated in my head.

On the northern edge of Northamptonshire, I spent a morning in Newton, where John Padwick, a cheerful teacher in his mid-forties from the adjoining village of Geddington, was trying to organise a celebration to mark the 400th anniversary of the Newton Rebellion. I'd never heard of such a rebellion, despite Newton being barely 40 miles from my home. According to Mr Padwick it was a pivotal event in English history.

"It was," he explained, "the culmination of the Midlands Revolt" — which wasn't much use to me because I'd never heard of that either. But Mr Padwick — who specialises in teaching children with behavioural and learning difficulties — was a patient instructor, and by the end of the morning I had more or less grasped it.

The Midlands Revolt of 1607 was the first great popular backlash against the enclosure of common land — a process that had begun three years earlier, in Radipole, Dorset, and would continue for three centuries. This process was at its most intense between 1750 and 1850, but continued until 1914, by which time some 21 per cent of all the land in England — 6.8 million acres in 5,400 parishes — had, in effect, been privatised, under 5,265 separate Enclosure Acts. Piece by piece, all over England, land that had been common became privately owned; fields that had been open were hedged and fenced; former common-holders were compensated with paltry allotments and — in theory — regular wages. The physical landscape changed, and so did the social landscape: the powerful grew richer; the poor, without necessarily becoming poorer, grew less powerful — or moved, in their millions, to the cities. The increased agricultural efficiency that tended to result from enclosure meant that the process could often be presented as, in material terms, a benefit for everyone. In many cases it palpably wasn't. And, in any case, the bitter resentment against enclosure that was widely felt by the labouring classes wasn't just about poverty: it was about disenfranchisement. Many of the "inefficiencies" of the old, communal system — for example, the need to reach agreement about endless little farming decisions — had also acted as a social glue, with even poor peasants being able to feel that, in some sense, the land around them was theirs. In the new, modern countryside, they couldn't. The land, and everything that lived and grew on it, belonged to the landowning classes; and the main choice facing the landless was between doing the landowner's bidding and destitution. But the landless, despite perceiving what was being done to them, never quite worked out what to do about it.

The Midlands Revolt came to a bloody end on 8 June 1607 on the fields of Newton, when 40 or 50 scarcely armed peasants were slaughtered in cold blood by soldiers loyal to the local landowners. Several hundred others, including women and children, fled. The rebel leader, who went by the name of Captain Pouch, was captured and executed; he had inspired his followers with the claim that the great leather pouch he always carried at his side contained "sufficient matter to defend [you] against all commers". But when he was arrested "his Powch was seearched and therein was onely a peece of greene cheese". About 150 rebels subsequently put their names or marks to an apology that secured them an amnesty; the rest presumably just melted away, as rebels do. As for the dead, no one knows what happened to their bodies. They were probably dumped in an unmarked grave; after which the massacre was largely written out of history. As a character in J. L. Carr's novel, *The Battle of Pollocks Crossing*, puts it: "No use to look for a stone or for mention in books because the chaps that shovelled them in wrote the books and put a stop to stones."

"We don't even know their names," said John, with an indignation that made me realise that, as far as he was concerned, he was talking about his fellow villagers. "The only names we have are those on the apology list. That's why we're doing it really. It doesn't seem right that 40 or 50 people should have been killed, right here in the village, and there isn't even a memorial to them. We should at least try to find out something about them."

Quite how he was going to put the record straight remained, at that stage, unclear. He had recruited a committee, secured various grants (a sure sign of a village activist with his roots in the modern world), and recruited a professional researcher — a young historian called Lisa Newth — to spend a few months trying to fill in the historical gaps. He still wasn't sure where it was all going to lead — "It sounds like we're working towards some sort of stone monument, and maybe some re-enactment. But the main thing is simply to help people to find out about their past. We're not interested in heritage-industry history — you know, where you have visitor centres and things. We want to keep it as community history: something that everyone can get involved in. Because there are a lot of things that go on in villages that some people don't really feel are open to them."

John, a friendly, talkative man with close-cropped thinning hair and a toothy grin, was, it seemed, a pillar of the community, with an array of parish-council responsibilities. As he showed me round the village, he talked not just about history but also about the social problems of today: the lack of affordable housing, the shortage of local employment, the tensions between local grown-ups and local youths. ("But who wants a village without youngsters?") Many of these, he thought, were problems "about who the village is for. And one of the things we're quite keen on is to use this rebellion to actually give something to all the people, even people who maybe have problems in the current system." In other words, to suggest that there is no such thing as a villager whom the village isn't for.

Accompanied by Lisa Newth, we wandered out of Newton, past the little church that inspired J. L. Carr's *A Month in the Country* and across the fields towards Geddington. Carr, who taught in nearby Kettering for much of his life, used to take local schoolchildren on walks in these same fields, explaining to them that members of their families had probably been among the peasants massacred there. (This was despite a warning from school inspectors in 1985 to avoid such words as "massacre" and "peasant" in this context.) The meadows were peaceful and empty of anything much apart from giant clumps of stinging nettles and the remains of a Tudor dovecote — which John was keen to have preserved. It had belonged, it seemed, to Thomas Tresham, the local grandee whose enclosure of common land up by Geddington woods had been the local rebels' main grievance.

Lisa filled us in on some of the details. The peasants' insurrection consisted of little more than tearing down hedgerows and filling in ditches, but its spread, had it continued unchecked, could have been catastrophic for the landowning classes. The rebels also wrote an appeal to James I, in which they compared their plight to the dark days of Edward II's reign, "when people were forced to eat cats' and dogs' flesh and women to eat their own children". The king, unmoved, ordered his deputy lieutenants to crush the rebellion once and for all, flavouring his order with the observation that "since that lenity hath bred in them rather encouragement than obedience, and that they have presumed to gather themselves in greater multitudes . . . we found it now very necessary to use sharper remedies".

The showdown took place in the fields where we now stood, beside the stream known as Ise Brook. We don't know much about what happened: only that it happened on the eve of Shakespeare's wedding; and that the first scene of *Coriolanus* may well have been inspired by it; and that that was the end of the Midlands Revolt.

Perhaps there was no need to know more. Perhaps it didn't matter. Perhaps, after 400 years, it was time to move on. But the crushing of the Newton Rebellion was — even in an age when life was cheap — a Tiananmen Square kind of moment, which the victors might not have brushed under the carpet so successfully had the victims not been so firmly at the bottom of the social heap.

In a sense, we all agreed, it was a bit ridiculous that we should be standing in a field, three otherwise sensible adults, worrying about something that had happened 400 years ago. We also knew that, in another sense, it mattered. "People care about the past," said

225

Lisa. "That's why you see so many local-history projects these days, and interest in genealogy, and things like that. Maybe in an age of mobility people feel a need for a sense of rootedness."

For John Padwick, it was simpler: "We just want to get what happened written back into history."

Such thoughts led me, a few weeks later, to Dorset and Somerset, to other famous scenes from the centuries-old struggles between those who worked on the land and those who owned it. I went to Radipole, on the edge of Weymouth, where I looked in vain for traces of that first Enclosure Act of 1604. I went to Tolpuddle, too, and stood on its scrap of village green — Dorset's smallest — beneath a huge, 320-year-old sycamore that once gave shade to six famous labourers — George and James Loveless, Thomas and John Standfield, James Hammett and James Brine. They stood there shortly before their arrest, in 1834, for illegally combining to form the Tolpuddle Friendly Society of Agricultural Labourers, in the hope that, as George Loveless put it, they might "preserve ourselves, our wives and our children from utter degradation and starvation". The "martyrs" are well commemorated there, by a plaque, an annual festival, a museum and shop — where I bought a book (One From the Plough, by Brendon Owen) about George Mitchell, one of the founding fathers of the first trade union for farm workers. This in turn led me to Montacute, in the south Somerset hills, where Mitchell lived out the bitter early chapters of his life during the agricultural depression of the 1830s.

226

I called what I had read to mind as I walked through the village's empty, sunlit, spotless streets. Mitchell began work at the age of five. He would start — on Windmill Farm — at first light and continue until dark, scaring rooks, whatever the weather; and, at home, would sleep in the clothes he had worked in, even if they had been soaked by rain. His diet consisted largely of bread and hot water, supplemented occasionally with scraps scavenged from the fields — snails, acorns, perhaps the occasional turnip. The farmer beat him so often and savagely — apparently as part of a general policy to inculcate obedience — that, at the age of eight, he moved to the nearby Abbey Farm, where the beatings were fewer but the other hardships were much the same. By the time he was 19, he was working up to 18 hours a day as an ordinary farm labourer, which earned him 4 shillings a week plus as much low-grade cider as it took to deaden the pain and the hunger. This was a common "perk" for Somerset farm workers, but seems to have been roughly equivalent to supplementing wages with heroin. Their health was typically so bad that they were known derisively as "skeletons at plough". One day, Mitchell was kicked and sworn at after being found lying on a hay-stook, too exhausted to move, at the end of an 18-hour day of harrowing and hay-lifting. After that, he quit the farm, successfully sought a new life as a stonemason and subsequently became a much written-about figurehead of the labour movement.

The farms that Mitchell worked on were still there when I visited — or, at least, the grand stone farmhouses were — but the only farm worker I could locate was far away in a giant field, thundering up and down the flat soil in a high, inhuman tractor like a giant insect, oblivious to the world outside his cab. The village was absurdly smart: full of upmarket pubs and bed-and-breakfasts catering for visitors to the National Trust-owned Montacute House. Ham Hill quarry — where Mitchell began his second career — was a country park. A bronze plaque on the village drinking fountain mentioned his name, but otherwise Mitchell's world seemed to have vanished utterly — along with all the other farm workers' lives, which, because they made no mark on history, were never preserved in print.

A little way to the south, however, I met a man who was well acquainted with Mitchell's life, and who had worked both on the local fields and in Ham Hill quarry. James Crowden was a cheerful, vague-looking man in his mid-fifties, with sagging trousers, big glasses and tousled, thinning hair. His old blacksmith's cottage in the village of Winsham felt much as you would expect such a cottage to feel, with low ceilings, thick, uneven walls, a solid wooden table in the cool front room and a faint aroma of apples and muddy spaniel. Just a few details hinted that this might be no ordinary English cottage-dweller: the statue of the Buddha on the mantelpiece, for example, or the faded prayer-flags hanging from the washing-line outside.

He had, he told me, done all kinds of outdoor manual work over the past 40 years: as a shepherd, a sheep-shearer, a cider-maker, a peat-cutter, a quarryman, a forester and a general farm labourer. He had also travelled widely; been a soldier; and studied ethnology and, to a lesser extent, anthropology and archaeology. And he had reinvented himself, with some success, as a poet and oral historian, who strove to preserve the stories of those who worked on the land around him.

We talked for a while about Mitchell, and about Ham Hill, and about another shared interest, Richard Jefferies, the great Victorian chronicler of rural life and poverty in 19th-century Wiltshire. Increasingly, however, I became interested in Crowden himself. He had, he told me, become a labourer by choice, after years of "looking for something" in exotic locations such as Kurdistan, Iran, Afghanistan and Tibet. He wanted to "get back to my roots" and felt that he needed to work on the land — as he had done as a teenager in Devon — in order to do so. After a spell as a peat-digger in the Outer Hebrides, he settled down on the Somerset-Dorset borders in the 1970s — and had supported himself pretty much ever since by the sweat of his brow. "It wasn't hard to find work then, if you were prepared to work hard, but the jobs came and went with the seasons. So I met a lot of people." This was an eye-opening experience. "The people I was working alongside had learnt their farming — or their rural skills — prior to World War II, prior to the tractor age, and had a very, very different outlook. Most of them were self-employed, free spirits, sheep-shearers, hurdle-makers, very skilled, and their knowledge — their manual skill — was a key part of their life. I was aware that some of the things they wanted to say about their lifestyle were important." So he started to write them down. "It started with a particular hurdle-maker. I'd decided I was going to interview him, because hurdle-making is one of the most ancient of all agricultural skills. And then he died suddenly, and I thought, Shit, I can't interview him. So I then wrote a poem about him instead, documenting how he worked."

Other poems followed, and before long he had a literary career running parallel to his manual one. Most of his writing documented the lives of those who worked on the land, either imaginatively in verse or, increasingly, in straightforward oral-history interviews. "It's a bit like emergency archaeology," he said, earnestly. "When I was a teenager I spent some time helping on a dig. This pub was going to tarmac over a field to make a car park, so we only had two seasons to find whatever was underneath. It's the same with this. There's only a short amount of time left for getting the stories, before they keel over.

"What interested me about archaeology," he added, "was that you were looking for clues to provide answers to basic questions about how people lived — which were questions you could simply have asked them if they had been around to ask. But they weren't." This made it all the more important to ask such questions of people who were still around. "I was very interested by something my tutor said when I was studying ethnology in the early 1970s. He said that in 50 years' time people would accuse today's anthropologists of not having done enough basic fieldwork, because tribes were disappearing so fast, and in 50 years' time it would be

**230**

too late." The tutor had been talking about tribes around the world, but the implication was plain: tribes were disappearing in England too.

No one could accuse James Crowden of being a Little Englander. His discussions of rural life draw on first-hand experience of such life from all over the world. He speaks half a dozen languages and has lived and worked in many different cultures. His poems and essays include some intriguing explorations of, for example, the relationship between Zen Buddhism and agricultural labour. (Skills such as sheep-shearing and hurdle-making, he argues, "cannot be taught directly" but are perhaps "on the very threshold of a wisdom that is beyond words".) Nor does he yearn sentimentally for an unreal past. "The old village life would have been terribly claustrophobic," he admitted. "And farm work is sodding hard work, especially in winter — and it used to be a lot harder. I know a lot of people who are crippled in their sixties and seventies. They pushed themselves far more than they should have done because they were afraid of getting the sack." No one in their right mind, he felt, would want to return to "the real peasant experience".

None the less, he was convinced that something had gone badly wrong in the relationship between the English countryside and its inhabitants. "We've lost the link between the land and the rural population. I'll never forget when I was working on a farm near Shaftesbury, and the farmer had sold the old cottages, so there was this farm worker there who was living on a grotty council estate in the town, and every morning on the way to work he would pass the solicitor who lived in the farm cottage, who was going to work in the town. It was only 2 or 3 miles, but it was beautifully ironic: they were both commuting, but in opposite directions."

He believed that it was vital "to understand the local past to preserve a healthy relationship between people and the landscape. Otherwise, it's just the countryside at one remove: something you look at without understanding what it's for. That's why oral history is important.

"It's also a question of respect. Sheep-shearers used to be gods. Now they are like drain-rodders — no status at all. And farmers — one reason why so many of them became so isolated during foot-and-mouth was that they were right on the edge of their communities. Once they *were* the communities.

"Everybody who lives in the countryside should work on the land for at least three months, on a farm worker's wage, and learn the real meaning of work and the real meaning of food. Only then will we have a society that values its farmers and farm workers and not just its middle-men and accountants."

He wasn't, he stressed, blaming incomers. "In terms of keeping skills or traditions alive — or things like village shops alive — the injection of incomers is good, bringing in energy and nous when the aspirations of locals are often towards the towns. And farmers themselves have a lot to answer for. A lot of people want to re-connect, but often they don't even know their local farmer because he's just someone who drives around fast in a four-wheel-drive." The problem was that "mechanisation has divorced men and women from the land" and that a conscious effort was needed to restore the connection. "Farmers have for too long had the attitude 'Get off my land!', when actually what they should be saying is 'Get on my land!'"

Things were, he thought, getting better, what with farmers' markets and the organic movement and the local-produce movement and the whole tendency of middle-class rural consumers, at least, to want to "know the stories of their food". But a lot more conscious effort was needed. To this end, he was now spending increasing amounts of time visiting local schools, initiating discussions between pupils and old countrymen, and encouraging children to think about what went on in the landscape around them when previous generations were young.

His mission was, he explained, as much about land as about people. "We need to value the land, as well as those who farm it. We just blast roads through, and lay concrete and tarmac and encroach on the flood plains, and destroy orchards and build an excess of supermarkets . . . and then expect the landscape to be forgiving." What we should be doing, he argued, was rediscovering "the role of the landscape as mentor — a chart of how man has used and evolved it. Every rural school should have a map of the parish and walk it regularly, so that children know the parish bounds and know every field and farmer and what he is producing." He had had some success in interesting local schools in this idea, although it was hard to imagine it catching on more widely in the current results-obsessed educational climate.

He himself had more or less given up manual work in recent years, devoting his time to writing and, specifically, to collecting local stories. I read many of them: stories of shepherds and cider-makers and thatchers and hurdle-makers and farmers and charcoal-burners. Few fitted neatly with my preconceptions of lost tribespeople: the subjects were rarely untouched by the normalities of modern life. Most made at least some use of modern technologies; had travelled; had links in other places; had carved out career paths in a distinctly modern world of career options. None the less, these lives were, more than most, entwined with the land on which they lived and the creatures and crops that grew on it; already, according to Crowden, "a lot of these people are no longer with us". In the absence of families and jobs that remained rooted in the same place for many generations, writing their stories down was the only way of preserving what they knew from oblivion.

Of course, I thought, as I left. *Stories*. That was what had *really* been worrying me about the transformation of rural life. Not modernism. Not the possibility that we and our children would have to adapt our ways of living to meet the demands of a changing world. Not the appearance of new faces in the countryside. Not technology or globalisation or progress, or the spread of urban sophistication, but the fear that rural places are losing the stories attached to them. It didn't matter what kind of stories: how Alfred defeated the Danes; how the monks of Mottisfont outwitted the Pope; why the Harry Roberts wood is called the Harry Roberts wood; how the parson's pigs got drunk on beer; or who's who in the graveyard. They didn't even need to be stories about the past — they might equally well be about who is related to whom, or what different fields are used for, or why that tree is broken off halfway up, or who lives in the little cottage on the hill, or where particular wild creatures have their resting places.

Big or small, important or trivial, they're all stories that give places meaning. Villages without such stories are like people with amnesia: it's hard to have a deep relationship with them. And because hardly anyone stays in the same place any more, and local living has been replaced by national and global living, growing numbers of villages are losing their memories.

Passing back near Tolpuddle, I met an old man who looked back on the local martyrs not just as history but as family too. His name was Alan Brown and he was, he thought, related on his mother's side to James Loveless. He, too, worked on the land: he'd been doing so for more than half a century, and used techniques unchanged since Loveless's day. He was a hurdle-maker and was, he reckoned, the seventh generation of his family to practise the trade.

"We've been living round here since at least the 1500s," he explained, on a muddy, wooded hill on the edge of Puddleton Down. "There are hurdle-makers on both sides of the family." He knew this because, despite spending nearly all his waking hours out here in the woods, he had studied local history. There had, he added, been 11 hurdle-makers living in Wool — his home village — in the 1880s.

This impressed me. I suspect that many modern countryside-dwellers have never seen a traditional hurdle, let alone a hurdle-maker — which tells you a lot about the landscape-transforming effect of wire fencing. But you would probably recognise his hurdles for what they were if you saw one: 6ft × 6ft sections of fence, woven tightly as a basket and amazingly strong. Alan made two every day, and sold them for £54 each. "It don't stretch the pocket over much," he grinned, greying hair flapping in the north wind.

But it had, until recently, been a viable business, supporting not only Alan but also his son, Steve — the eighth generation of the family to make hurdles. Then came an unforeseen peril: cheap hurdles imported from Eastern Europe. "They use a band-saw instead of splitting them, and once you cut through the grain it allows the water in, which is no good, and they fix them with nails as well. So they fall apart after three months — ours last seven to ten years. But it's much quicker, and so they're much cheaper."

They had lost client after client to this competition. When the last one said he was going over to "the European stuff", they realised that something had to change. "Steve said, 'Well, that's it, I'd better go.' He was reluctant to leave — he'd been doing it for 11 years — but needs must when the devil drives." He was now commuting to London to earn a living, leaving at 5a.m.

every day. "The trouble is, you want around £1,000 a week to get a mortgage just to buy affordable housing round here, and you can't get that sort of money on hurdle-making. It's sad, but what can you do?"

Alan worked as we talked, patiently building up his hurdle exactly as his forebears had done: splitting each 6ft length of hazel with absentminded confidence, weaving it in through his uprights, forcing it downwards with his knee, then twisting and weaving in the overlaps at the ends with his bare hands as nonchalantly as if they had been made of spaghetti. He wore hobnailed leather boots, torn overalls, ex-army gaiters, battered knee-pads ("knaps, we call them — these ones are 27 years old") and an old green sweater beneath the overalls whose sleeves had been worn to rags by the constant friction. He used three different billhooks ("they're all older than I am") for cutting, splitting and trimming, and a great lump of ancient ash for bashing things into place. But his most striking tools were his hands: huge gnarled objects like tree-roots, covered in the same dusting of green and brown as the weathered trees around him. The ring-finger on his right hand was particularly misshapen. "I broke it once," he confessed, "cutting wood. I repaired it myself with a bit of tape." He didn't get round to showing it to a doctor until 40 years later.

He was 70 now but seemed unwearied by his years. "I reckon I'll do this for another 15 years," he laughed. "I enjoy it. Of course, you got to keep going every day, regardless of how you feel. But I don't think I can remember a day that I really haven't enjoyed. It's a bit cold this week, but it's not a bad spot to work.

"You see how bare this is here?" He gestured at the desolate-looking patch from which he had cut his current crop of hazel lengths. "You come back next summer and there'll be a mass of bluebells and foxgloves and primroses. They've been dormant for two or three years, as the hazel's grown up, but now they'll come back. And then you'll get the butterflies as well — the butterflies follow me around." So, in the past, did the flies. "But now I have a Marmite sandwich every day and they don't bother me. They don't like the vitamin B.

"Apart from that," he added, "there's no difference at all between what I'm doing and what my great-great-grandfather did. You need nothing: you needn't bring anything into the wood other than your tools." What made him sad was the prospect of not being able to pass the tradition down to future generations. Yet he wasn't sentimental about the past. "In the 19th century, Dorset was the worst place in the country for poverty — they say it was as bad as for the people in Ireland. Even in the 20th century it was hard. My father was from a family of ten, and they had a pint and a half a day of milk between them. He used to try and creep out and get a bit of milk at night in the fields, milk the cows. And his mother, she died of septicaemia in 1917: they couldn't afford hospital, so the local doctor operated on her on the kitchen table at home . . .

238

"So of course it's good in the respect that we haven't got the hunger and the poverty any more. It's just sad that so much else is disappearing with it. I live where I was born: I built a house in the garden of the house I was born in. But not many people can say that. In most of these small villages round here, you may have lived here for generations but you can't afford a house now. So the town's moving into the countryside, that's how I see it. I think what's sad is, even people who came from the country, they've been infected with the town mind now. I think perhaps they're a bit ashamed of their background or something. But we tolerate each other — live and let live, really.

"But it's a shame that everyone's so materialistic. I think our parents, they saw the poverty of the early 20th century, and the war, and they tried to make it better for us, didn't they? But now? I think that people have forgotten something."

At Coate, in Wiltshire, I stood on an earthy lay-by at the edge of the village, watching the dust swirl in the slipstream of yet another 4×4. It seemed an uninspiring little place: just a few comfortable bungalows and crowded car ports behind windswept leylandii, set among plain fields of wheat, with assorted wires criss-crossing the sky and a business selling inkjet and toner cartridges. It seemed hard to believe that Richard Jefferies drew inspiration from the countryside round here.

Jefferies is largely forgotten today, but his accounts of the downtrodden lives of 19th-century farm labourers (in, for example, *The Toilers of the Field*) remain vivid and sobering, while his thoughts on the relationship between man and landscape still sometimes stir my heart: perhaps because my father loved him; or perhaps because he understood some fundamental truths of existence. "The endless grass, the endless leaves, the immense strength of the oak expanding, the unalloyed joy of finch and blackbird; from them all I receive a little. Each gives me something of the pure joy they gather for themselves . . . The hours when the mind is absorbed by beauty are the only hours when we really live. These are the only hours that are not wasted — these hours that absorb the soul and fill it with beauty. This is real life, and all else is illusion, or mere endurance."

I asked a middle-aged couple with a dog to point me in the direction of Jefferies's farm. "Don't know him, I'm afraid," said the man. "Is he new?"

It turned out that I was in the wrong Coate. The Coate that Jefferies lived in is about 15 miles to the north-east and does, indeed, remember him: there is an occasional museum in his farmhouse, and a country park based on the lake that first inspired him with a sense of the timeless romance of the English countryside. It didn't seem so timeless when I visited. Both house and park were long ago engulfed by Swindon, and the atmosphere was unashamedly suburban. There was a café, a car park, toilets, a play area, pitch-and-putt, mini-golf, a picnic area, barbecue hire, a model railway, a cycle path, various hard-surfaced "walks", earnest

240

warnings that other paths might become muddy ("take suitable precautions"), and Easirider buggies for those who weren't up to walking at all. It was hard to get much sense of what Jefferies (writing about his childhood) called the "magic in everything, blades of grass and stars, the sun and the stones upon the ground", and my first instinct was to feel disappointed.

The longer I stayed, however, the more I fell under the place's spell. Everyone I looked at seemed to be taking pleasure in being there. One young mother was excitedly telling another about a bird's nest her little daughter had found. A hoodied teenager was riding his BMX bike in careful circles, tenderly balancing a toddler on his handlebars. Some Muslim women laughed delightedly at the wide-eyed wonder with which one of their children kept drawing their attention to a swan.

"Penguin!" shouted a middle-aged father as a fat magpie hopped across his young family's path.

"I only cheated twice," said one teenage girl to another as they emerged, arm in arm, from the crazy-golf enclosure.

An elderly black couple stood hand in hand, looking out over the lake.

"Please don't push me in," laughed a white girl of about five, balancing teasingly on the water's edge. "I was going to throw you in head first," said her huge tattooed father.

The wind ruffled the wide lake, and the shadow of a cloud suddenly vanished; birds glided across the water like toy boats; two fishermen sat patiently under some trees.

A tired-looking young father noticed my glance at his two bedraggled boys — smeared with mud and ice-cream and flushed with happy exhaustion — and rolled his eyes as if in a kind of apology.

"I'm walking better now," said one shuffling old man to another. "It's my sticks."

"You coming here tomorrow?" said a fat white boy sitting with his feet in the water to the Asian boy standing beside him.

I felt suddenly ashamed to have sneered at the place. Really, I thought, of all the achievements of our civilisation, what could be more noble than this? All around me, people of all classes, races, ages and religions were enjoying themselves in the most innocent, harmless way imaginable. Who was I to patronise them for not having an authentically wild rural experience? What did it matter that the past of the place had been packed away into a museum, or that a piece of ancient countryside had been tamed, in effect, into a giant suburban park? At least people were rejoicing in it.

# CHAPTER
# EIGHTEEN

# Walking by night

The clear evening sky was changing colour over the hills of the Althorp Estate in Northamptonshire. The day's rain clouds, emptied, had sunk to the horizon, while the lower sky behind them had acquired that strange aluminium brightness that shines when the last light is fading fast. The summer air felt deliciously cool.

"Some of these trees are 700 years old," said Steve Caple, freelance pest controller, gesturing at a series of enormously thick sweet chestnuts near by. They were widely spaced around us in the traditional manner of English parkland, but the grass itself was closely mown, in the traditional manner of an English golf course. "All this used to be part of a stately home — not Althorp, but another one. But then they lost their money and it was pulled down." I think this must have been Harlestone Hall, sold by the Andrews family to the Spencers in 1830 and demolished in 1939. "You can still see the old stable block, look, over there, but the house itself has gone. That's where the clubhouse is now." I couldn't imagine its chalet-style design delighting many country-house enthusiasts. Then again, connoisseurs of rural charm might find much to displease them in these parts: from the coach parties that still flock to the shrine of Diana to the thousands of new homes that are due to be built on most of the fields on the far side of the woods. Time leaves heavy footprints as it passes through southern Northamptonshire.

"Of course," Steve added, taking an armful of net from the back of his car, "most of the trees have got rabbits under them." That was why we were there: Steve had a contract to keep the rabbit population down. "I've had it for 10 years. I come out here most nights. I probably kill about 2,000 rabbits a year here. But you can see why they pay for it. The rabbits head straight for the greens, because they're watered, and they do incredible damage with their claws.

"The trouble with rabbits," he added, "is that you can never actually eradicate them. They breed so fast, and new ones just move in from somewhere else. But you can keep their numbers down."

We wandered over to one of the larger trees and Steve began to lay out the net around it. "OK. This is what we call a long net. This is what the poachers would use at night — not like this exactly, but they'd run it along a hedge and then drive the rabbits towards it off the field. Not that you get many poachers these days." He arranged his net in a large circle, about 20ft in radius, with the tree at its centre and a dozen poles, about 10ft apart, holding the net upright like a baggy, knee-high tennis net.

Then he produced a small, apathetic-looking jill ferret, which had been dozing in a wooden box in the back of the car, and popped it down one of the holes near the base of the tree.

We waited in silence. A faint grinding of distant traffic floated over the thick treetops from far away, interrupted by the occasional — much louder — bird squeak. "If it was really quiet, we might hear thumping," Steve whispered.

Then a rabbit exploded from a hole and, within a second, was hopelessly entangled in the net. Steve hurried over, extracted it, broke its neck with a quick, dispassionate wrench, and deposited its twitching body on the ground. A big, bald, tanned man, with a greying moustache and the kind of medium-sized beer-gut you'd expect on someone who spent much of his youth playing rugby and chatting over pints in country pubs, he moved with surprising speed and economy, and killed the bemused rabbit with an efficiency that made squeamish thoughts seem irrelevant. "It's pretty instantaneous," he said. "They'll be terrified in the net for a second or two, but they don't actually feel anything."

The process was repeated a few minutes later. Then the ferret emerged, with what looked like a self-satisfied expression on its snub-nosed face, and Steve said: "That may be all that's down there for now."

We had already caught several rabbits through "purse-netting" — when a single net is pegged over each hole — and Steve thought that a doe might have shepherded her young down a blockhole (a dead end) and blocked the tunnel with her body to protect them. This would have reduced the ferret to scratching,

245

vainly, at the doe's bottom — bits of which appeared to be caught in her tiny claws.

It was time to move on to the next method: shooting. This was done from the car, with a .22 rifle pointing out of the driver's window as we drove slowly around the course. Initially, however, it involved simply sitting very quietly, waiting for the rabbits to emerge into the twilight from the long grass. "You mustn't look at them," he said. "They're watching us, and if they see you looking at them, they'll run away."

We sat. Nothing happened. The twilight blurred.

"You've got to be patient for this job," murmured Steve. "You can't rush it. You're not working against nature — you're working with it. But this is the side of the job that I love. I've been doing wasps' nests all day, which brings the money in, but this is the side that's pleasurable. Look at that" — and we gazed for a moment at the old lake, with swallows still swooping over it and a pair of swans gliding with their cygnets. "I'm out here, getting paid for it, and a lot of people are stuck in an office all day working.

"My dad worked in a factory, in Northampton, and after seeing him coming home every night after spending all day indoors, I vowed that I would never work inside if I could possibly help it. It's odd really: I must have been the black sheep. One of my brothers ended up becoming an academic. But it was a very happy childhood — a typical country upbringing."

He grew up in what was then the small village of New Duston, a mile or so from the golf course, just beyond the wooded hilltop we were now facing. He still lived there but, he said, "it's not the same village I grew up in. Where I live, it all used to be fields. There were meadows, hedgerows, a lake — we'd spend our whole time playing in the woods, making dens, climbing trees, scrumping, or bird-nesting, or pond-dipping. Now we're virtually part of Northampton — that's what I hate about it. And of course they're building all these houses up the road — they're building homes all the way down to the roundabout, all the way down to Weedon Road, in the flood plain, everywhere." This was, I already knew, one of the parts of the country most dramatically affected by the official drive to build hundreds of thousands of new homes to ease the housing "shortage". Those who object to poorer families being priced out of the villages they grew up in should hesitate to object to this. None the less, the sheer volume of new building proposed is staggering. The last I heard, the government's official advice was that nearly 60,000 homes would need to be built in villages and greenfield sites every year from 2007 to 2011. Only around half of these (oddly) would be "affordable".

"Back then it was a proper country village. We grew up with lurchers, ferrets, rabbits; we didn't have computers or gameboys — there was barely any TV — but we all had catapults, and I can still remember getting my first ferret. My love of wildlife developed at the same time as my interest in catching things.

"I don't enjoy killing things — of course I don't. If I ever thought I was starting to enjoy that side of it, I'd get help. Killing is just something that has to be done:

you do it as quickly and efficiently as possible. But I love being part of the countryside. I love being in touch with nature, getting inside the heads of wild animals. And that's what it's all about, really.

"For example, when we were lads walking in the fields, you always carried a stick, and often you'd see the rabbits scurry into certain clumps of long grass, so every time we walked past we'd routinely thump down on to those clumps of grass. Nine times out of 10 there'd be nothing in there, but the other time you'd get a rabbit for your dinner. But you couldn't look at it, because it's watching you, and if they saw you looking, or pausing to raise your stick, they'd go. So you just had to go wallop without looking . . ."

As a much younger lad, he once attempted to catch rabbits by digging several deep pits and covering them with twigs and leaves. His first victim was an elderly gentleman walking his dog. He never tried that again, but he did, thereafter, begin to think more carefully about how different creatures might be caught.

"It's amazing how much there is to know about what goes on in animals' heads. I've caught rabbits with my bare hands, when a ferret's been down there, but I've heard of people who've plucked a hare up out of its form, which I've never managed. The trick is to put a walking stick in the ground with a hat on it, and hope that the hare will keep watching that. And then you very carefully get behind it in a big, decreasing curve, and it will be so focused on what it thinks is the main danger that it won't notice you, and at the last minute you fling yourself down and grab it.

"That's what catching things means: you've got to understand how your quarry thinks. Anyone can put bait down for a mouse. But I never want to see the last mole, or the last rabbit, or the last fox. What I enjoy is that I'm pitting my wits against a wild animal and it's pitting its wits against me. Sometimes they escape, they slip the net, and I think, well, good luck to you, chap."

Since the hunting ban, he said, the gamekeepers at Althorp had been shooting every fox they saw. He, by contrast, was happy to leave in peace — and even to encourage — the vixen who had been raising five cubs in the woods adjoining the golf course. "She's helping me with my work, and I'm happy to watch her. I even dumped some rabbits I'd shot for her the other day."

He paused. A breeze was no longer ruffling the barley in the sloping fields beyond the golf course. Nearer us, there were various brown-grey smudges on the edge of the long grass that might or might not have been rabbits.

"Yes, it was a lovely country childhood," he said. "I remember waking up to the sound of lions roaring."

What?

"Fossett's Circus — do you remember Fossett's Circus? — they used to have their winter quarters on the edge of the village. The circus children used to come to our school for the winter. It was a village school then — if they weren't from Duston, they were from Harpole or Kislingbury — everyone was from a village . . .

"I still see a few of the lads I was at school with," he added, thoughtfully. "But most of them have gone away."

Now in his early fifties, Steve had done various jobs since leaving school: builder, glazier, even a nurse in a mental hospital. "So I did work indoors for a little, but I enjoyed that bit. I love talking to old people and hearing their stories. Even if they are crazy." Gradually, however, he reverted to his first love, working outdoors with — or, if you prefer, against — wild animals. It began part time but for the past decade or so he had been self-employed, full time, as a pest controller.

"This was always what I was interested in, and I was always doing a bit of it on the side. So when I set up on my own I had quite a lot of experience. You learn stuff as you go along, but it's also about tapping into stuff that people have always known.

"You'd be amazed how many pest controllers don't have a clue about rural pest control. The modern pest controller — the Rentokils of this world — if they were doing this, they'd just get some aluminium phosphate pellets, put 'em down, fill the holes in, kill everything down there with the gas and move on. I don't like that side of it — there's no skill in that. I just think there's something sort of cowardly — unsporting, if you like — about not giving them a chance. I'd rather use traps — it's a skill.

"One of the things I like about netting rabbits like we've just done," he continued, "is that this is how it's always been done — for centuries." He knitted most of his nets himself. "I didn't do this long one, but I've done long ones in the past, and I do all my own purse nets. It's nice on a long winter's evening in front of the fire, just knitting away. But that'll die away soon, too, I expect. An old fellow taught me, and I've taught one or two. But that's the kind of knowledge that doesn't get passed down any more."

This — the passing down of knowledge — was a subject he felt strongly about. "I was lucky. I had a wonderful teacher: an old man called Bert Andrews, who lived in Little Brington. I used to love listening to him. He only died a couple of years ago — he was 93. I was very fortunate to know the old chap. He must have been the last person in these parts who'd done the harvest with a scythe, and ploughed with a horse."

Little Brington was just down the road, a pretty village right outside the gates of Althorp Park, with a famously beautiful church and a thatched, honey-stoned pub called Ye Olde Saracen's Head. "I spent many a happy night in that pub with Bert, just listening to him talk. Of course, that was back in the days when they still had pubs for the agricultural working man. You could walk in in those days in your working clothes and your muddy boots, with your dogs. I remember Bert's dogs — shepherd dogs, he used to call them — they used to worship him. He'd come in and they'd go straight under the long bench where he sat, and they'd not move all evening, until he said the words 'Good night, landlord' — and out they'd come. He once told one to 'stay' in a field and then forgot all about it for several hours. By the time he remembered, it had started snowing, and the dog was still sitting there under the snow.

"I could listen to Bert for hours. He'd seen so much — there was a whole world that he'd known, that most people don't know about. He reckoned a good ploughman could plough an acre a day, and that meant walking 9 miles a day. Apparently the thing he worried most about when he was ploughing was that he would plough through a wasps' nest. He did that once, and of course all the wasps burst out, and then they don't just sting him but they sting the horses and the horses panic and bolt . . .

"He worked from first light until it was dark, seven days a week, and never once had a holiday. And when he wasn't ploughing he'd be a shepherd. It was a lonely life, and of course by the end of his life his knees had gone. But no one dared complain back then because there were that many people would jump into your job.

"But the sad thing was that then when he was about 60 he gave it up and switched to building. He'd had a falling out with his boss, you see. I never saw him lose his temper — no one did — but just this once, he'd had a hard day, and the farmer said, haven't you done so-and-so, and Bert turned round and said, 'Don't I ever bloody do enough for you?' And the farmer said, 'If that's your attitude, you can go.'

"So he did. And then many months later a message got back from the farmer that, if Bert wants his job back, he can have it. But Bert wouldn't take it: he said, 'What's been said has been said.' But it used to prey on his mind. Years and years later, I remember him saying to me: 'What a bloody fool I've been — I should have gone back.'"

He had, luckily, bought his tied cottage by then — for £500. Towards the end of his life, Steve suggested that Bert might try selling his vegetable patch, for which — he had reason to believe — he could expect to get about £36,000. "So Bert said: 'What the bloody hell do I want £36,000 for, at my time of life? I'd rather have a bloody garden.'

"Oh, I miss him a lot. But it was a different world then, of course. A farm-worker's life wasn't really his own: everything belonged to the boss. If Bert saw a rabbit, he'd just grab it and wring its neck and have rabbit pie that night. But if his boss saw him he'd have to give him the rabbit — because that was how those squires were then: everything was theirs."

Steve wasn't averse to a bit of poaching himself, once. "I was a terrible poacher on the estate when I was younger. Some weeks I got more pheasants than Earl Spencer had. One thing we used to do was, for a few days, where we knew the pheasants were roosting, we used to go up the hedgerows and scatter corn and soaked peas, and after about a week the first thing the pheasants would do when it got light was flock down from the trees straight out into this ride and feed on the corn and that. So what we'd do then, we'd go out before it was light in the morning, and we'd hang little fishing-line nooses in the little grass runs through the hedges. Because a pheasant will always run rather than fly, you see, if it can: they look to run through cover. So you can play on their natural instincts.

"So we'd just go off and wait somewhere where we could watch them, and they'd come through, and some would be caught as they came out. And we'd walk down through the wood with a sack and a knife, and then we'd run at them and they'd all run like mad, and those that hadn't been caught coming out would be caught going back the other way. We didn't even kill them at that stage — there'd be no time, because the keepers would be watching out for us. We'd just cut the line with the knife and put them in the sack and disappear into the woods, and then we'd kill them and sell them. It was never like big poaching gangs — they raid the release pens and sell them all and get a lot of money. We used to get like a sackful. It was only the bravado of youth really. We got caught a few times — I've got one conviction for poaching. But that's what kids did in those days.

"You don't get so much poaching now. I don't think there's much money in it. When we did it, there was nothing else to do. So you were out to this time of night every night, building dens, getting up to mischief. Now they've all got their computers and their television. The exercise would kill half of them and, anyway, they wouldn't know what to do.

"But at least when I'm old I'll be able to look back and think, I had a childhood. I did a million and one things. What will today's kids be able to look back on? Sitting on a computer.

"What makes me sad," he added, "is when I take my daughter out in the countryside — she's 15 — and she says, 'Dad, this is boring.' She just wants to be back on her computer, chatting to her friends on MSN. She's not looking at it through the same eyes as me. She's not seeing the beauty of the hedgerows and the fields and the flowers and the trees.

"But maybe she'll appreciate it when she's older."

We sat quietly for a bit longer, until I, at least, no longer had a clue if any rabbits were about at all. An owl drifted past in the gloom. "A little owl," said Steve brightly, with the confidence of someone who often sees such things.

At one point, he leaned over the grass with me and patiently explained how to make a snare. "A rabbit will always follow exactly the same run: every step. Look, you can see how the grass has been worn down — one there, one there, one there — it always puts its foot in exactly the same spot, every time. As soon as it's frightened, it runs off on the route that it knows leads to home. So you put the snare straight across one of those, and the bottom of the noose wants to be about 5in off the ground, and then as it puts its foot there its head goes through the loop, and then when it jumps to the next one the noose is pulled tight."

I was struck by the sense he seemed to have of the romance of his role. Most people, I suggested, wouldn't think of pest controlling as a very glamorous job. Did he feel himself to be an outsider? "Oh, you get the odd person — women, mostly — starting rows — 'Oh, you're so cruel . . .' But anyone who thinks about it can see that what I do is necessary. But, yes, of course, you've got to be a little bit sensible. So I tend not to let people see what I do.

"But I'm not embarrassed about it: I'm proud of it. What I do is what country people have always done, using the knowledge they've always had. And I'm keen to tell people about it, because if nobody passes on that knowledge, then sooner or later it's going to disappear." He was, he said, "a passionate supporter of keeping country traditions alive for future generations to understand and enjoy". His favourite reading included Frederick Rolfe's *I Walked By Night* and the *Journal* of James Hawker, a less well-known poacher of the same period (he lived from 1836 to 1921) who operated in Leicestershire and Northamptonshire. "I've been reading about him in the public library. He lived for a while in Duston. He talks about poaching and snaring rabbits around Nobottle and Brimpton and Harpole — the exact places where I go out today catching rabbits. You can learn so much from books like that.

"What worries me," said Steve, as we finally headed for home, "is that all this country knowledge is dying out. It's important to save country traditions. What's going to happen when we all run out of oil, and people have to learn to live off the land again?"

# CHAPTER
# NINETEEN

# Milked

On a windy, tree-crested hill on the eastern edge of Wensleydale, in North Yorkshire, an old farm looks down over a green river valley, with Leyburn — a tidy market town full of tea-rooms and hairdressers — perched comfortably on the slopes below. I stopped in its cold stone yard, where I met a dairy farmer whose family had, some said, farmed there for 600 years.

"Actually," said Jonathan Sunter, "that's not entirely true. We've been in this dale since the 1600s, and I think even further back on my father's side, but a lot of our roots are in Hawes" — about 15 miles to the west — "and we've only had this farm since my grandad came down here in the early 1960s." But they had, he admitted, been in the area "as far back as we can trace". As far as he knew, they had all earned their living from the land.

He feared, however, that he would be the last of his line to do so. "I'd be happy to see my children go off and learn to do something else. I'd urge them not to leap into this. The last few years have been absolutely soul-destroying." Which was worrying, because by the standards of his industry Jonathan should probably be considered a success story.

"Just in the last month or so," he explained, as we took shelter from the wind in the tiny, muck-splattered cabin that served as his office, "I've started to feel that there might be light at the end of the tunnel. But for the past few years it's been pretty black."

He was in his early thirties but looked older, with a slight puffiness to his face and bags under his eyes. I wasn't surprised to learn that he had once been a keen rugby player — the England shirt beneath his body warmer was a giveaway — but I wouldn't have guessed that he had played on the wing. He had, he said, been working on the farm all his life, apart from a brief spell at college in York in the early 1990s. "I came back in 1996, just as the first BSE outbreak was starting, and since then it's just been downhill ever since."

There had been various low points, from foot-and-mouth in 2001 to an epidemic of abortions that affected 25 per cent of his herd in 2007. But the real problem had been simple economics. "Milk prices have dropped and dropped and dropped, while the cost of producing milk has gone up." By 2006–7, the average price of a litre of milk was 17.9p, whereas the average cost of producing a litre of milk was 21.32p. No dairy farmer could hope to achieve a profit: the best they could aim for was to limit their losses.

"It's been really tough. Just a few months ago, we were sitting down, going through the figures, and, basically, if we didn't see a price rise right away, that was it for us — we were going to have to wind up the enterprise. There isn't a lot you can cut back on, because there's an awful lot of fixed costs you don't have control over, like electricity and diesel and feed — feed prices have absolutely rocketed this year."

Like most dairy farmers, he sells all his milk to one of the three big farmer's cooperatives, which in turn sell most of it either on the international market or to the big supermarkets. This provides a degree of stability, but almost limitless scope to be screwed down on price — something that the supermarkets have exploited ruthlessly. "With milk, you take what price you can get. You can't just decide not to sell it."

What kept the farm going — and what qualified it to be considered a success story — was the fact that Jonathan and his wife, Helen, had had the initiative to start a new line of business, producing a range of upmarket jams under the label White Rose Preserves. "We started three years ago, and it's done well. It's been incredibly hard work, but we're now selling to about 50 different shops around the country." The irony is that these are luxury products, sold in upmarket delicatessens and farm shops to the new rural rich; whereas the farmer's traditional business of producing necessities — the food that England needs in order to keep going — has proved an economic disaster.

"Once, on this farm, you could support two or three families. Now it barely provides me and my dad with a living. The work's still there, but not the money. My brother, Michael, used to work here too, but he gave it up a few years ago to become a fireman. If he hadn't, one or other of us would have to have gone out and found outside work by now.

"Sometimes I look at my friends who don't farm, or those who used to farm but have decided to call it a day, and I think: Why am I doing this? You kind of think that if you work hard, you get rewarded. But it's just not been like that for a while.

"I've been cutting back and cutting back and cutting back for as long as I can remember," he continued glumly, as he showed me round the distinctly dilapidated farm. "We've been under-investing drastically for years. There's so many things you know you've let go, like roofs leaking and gutters needing mending. And then when something goes wrong, like the restrictions resulting from the foot-and-mouth and blue-tongue incidents in the south, you've nothing to fall back on. Three pence off a litre of milk doesn't sound much, but when we lost [all those cattle] to the abortion outbreak, the cost of that ... I stopped counting when I got to £45,000, and that didn't include the vet's bills. It's just mind-boggling thinking of it — it gave me a sick feeling in my stomach. It was quite devastating, to be honest. After a while, you just can't carry on like that."

Like most dairy farms, Hilltop Farm has achieved staggering improvements in efficiency in recent decades. Without increasing either its size (about 220 acres) or its herd (about 130 Holstein Friesians), it has almost doubled its output. "Forty or 50 years ago, you might have produced 5,000 litres of milk per cow per year. Now they're producing 9,000 to 10,000 per cow."

This isn't just a question of technology and streamlined management: the cows themselves have become more productive. "You see this," said Jonathan, leading me into an old and apparently abandoned milking parlour. "These are the cubicles that we used to use. My dad put this in 40 years ago. We would have Friesians in those days. But the modern cow" — having been crossed with the notoriously big-boned, big-uddered Holstein — "is so much bigger than the cows this was built for that they've just outgrown the cubicles. So we had to build this new one to accommodate them." And he led me into a neighbouring building whose cubicles were visibly several feet longer and wider. "The old building wants flattening really," he muttered. "That's another thing . . ."

We moved on to a big barn, with young heifers on one side and calves on the other. Each already had a yellow tag on its ear, to enable every aspect of its wellbeing and yield to be monitored by computer from birth to abattoir. It seemed odd, I said, that such dramatic leaps forward in efficiency should have coincided with such financial disaster.

"Yes," said Jonathan. "But that's what's happened."

The reasons included rising feed and fuel costs and cheap foreign competition in the international market for milk derivatives (e.g., cheese and powdered milk). But the main cause, as I understood him, had been years of ruthless negotiation by supermarkets, in pursuit of their price wars. Not only had the cost of producing milk risen faster than its retail price, but also the farmers' share of the retail price had fallen. There has been a lot of obfuscation about this — with conflicting claims and counter-claims by farmers' representatives, supermarkets and the Competition Commission. But as I write, the Office of Fair Trading has just fined supermarkets and other retailers a total of £100 million for price-fixing. And there is one other simple figure that brooks no argument: between 1995 and 2007, the number of dairy farms in England and Wales fell from 28,093 to 12,695 (with a further 2,000 farmers indicating in a 2007 Milk Development Council survey that they planned to quit in the next two years). That's three dairy farmers packing it in every day — with "it" representing, in nearly every case, generations of family history and investment and accumulated expertise. It seems unlikely that they were all just making it up.

Why had there been no outcry about this? "There has been, but most people aren't interested. The government doesn't give a monkey's about agriculture. The public just wants cheap milk. You can shout as loud as you like, but it won't make any difference. Nobody's listening to you.

"A few years ago we were picketing with Farmers For Action outside Tesco's and Morrison's distribution centres — in Teesside and Doncaster — but it didn't make any difference. Or if it did, we didn't see any of it. The trouble was, a lot of farmers obviously thought, this won't make any difference, so I won't bother. So eventually you give up."

That didn't mean he had forgiven the supermarkets. "That's one thing with the preserve business: I won't deal with supermarkets. Someone phoned from Asda asking if we were interested, and we've been invited to attend 'meet the buyer' days with Tesco. But Helen answered the phone and said: 'My husband's a dairy farmer. I don't think that'd be a good idea.' They knew what she meant. They control us in the dairy industry. I don't want them controlling our other business." His voice was as bitter as the wind.

What had made all this worse was that even the North Yorkshire public seemed largely indifferent. "It's changed a lot round here. In a lot of the villages, the locals, or what were the locals, are becoming a minority. They've kind of lost their voice. House prices are extraordinary — that bungalow over there, they're asking £300,000 for. I don't know anyone who could afford that. But it's not people round here who buy them: it's well-heeled professionals, or people who are retiring. And some of the newcomers struggle to accept our way of life, i.e., they complain about the smell of the slurry, even though we've been doing it for generations."

The abortion outbreak among his cattle was caused by a parasite called *Neospora caninum*, which is transmitted to cows after getting into the land from dog excrement — in other words, as a direct result of people walking their dogs on grazing land. "There's a popular walk through our land that comes up from the town. We ended up having to fence part of it off." Were the public sympathetic? "Not really, no."

He shrugged. "You do get quite isolated. The community isn't as close as it was. I don't think anyone

263

I was at school with goes to the auction mart any more. Most of the friends I used to see there when I first left school have dropped out of farming now. It's not the same as it was."

Behind the farmhouse, two young bull calves, scarcely bigger than Great Danes, were amusing themselves as he spoke by pretending to be sheepdogs, chasing a dozen or so sheep up and down a small field. Normally, they would have been exported. (One unfortunate side-effect of breeding for high milk yield is that it produces animals that are useless for beef, having a very poor bone-to-muscle ratio; so bull calves are good for nothing except to be exported for veal.) "But there's a ban on exports at the moment because of these bluetongue and foot-and-mouth incidents, so now there's nothing I can do with them. I'm shooting them at the moment. I don't like having to do it, but what else can I do?" And I thought again how tired his face looked.

"I start work at 6a.m.," he explained. "Not as early as some. But I'm often working until 9p.m., especially with the preserves. So it's not an easy life. But it's not a bad one either. I much prefer working outside, especially when you get to springtime and the grass turns green and you turn the cattle out. It's nice to be out in the fields. And it's nice to be your own boss, and to be able to drop in and see your family every now and then. I'm not looking to get rich doing this. I just want a decent quality of life."

Despite Jonathan's slightly dejected tone of voice, the future of Hilltop Farm actually looked rather bright.

After all those years, the market forces that had brought it to its knees had begun to push in the opposite direction. A huge increase in demand for dairy products in China in 2007, combined with a drop in production elsewhere in the world caused by increased demand for biofuels, had produced a dramatic rise in milk prices — around 35 per cent already, and no sign of stopping. With so few dairy farms remaining in England, those that did survive could look forward to a future of, in theory, fat profits.

Jonathan had his doubts. "Some of these things, like the biofuel things, are going to force up production costs as well. And although you hear about these increases, we haven't seen much of it yet. They're really quick to take it off you, but they're slow in giving it back." None the less, he added, "I don't intend ever to sell milk at a loss again."

I wasn't sure whether to feel sorry for him or not. The troubles of the past decade had clearly bruised him — as one might expect — and yet his future seemed more assured than most people's. The real problem — I reflected as I left him — wasn't his but Britain's. We now import more than 40 per cent of our food — compared with 26 per cent in 1995 — at a time when, all over the world, food is getting scarcer.

The running down of the dairy industry is just an extreme example of a process that has affected most parts of the farming industry — it was reported in 2007 that one farm in four was running at a loss. We haven't listened to the individual farmers as they have been squeezed out of business. But when we find ourselves needing a degree of self-sufficiency again, we may be alarmed to find that we no longer have the farmers, or the land, or the livestock that we need in order to achieve it.

That evening, many miles to the east, I was crossing the Yorkshire wolds by twilight when I noticed a sign to "Wharram Percy: deserted medieval village". I turned down a rough-edged lane and, a mile or so later, abandoned my car in a deserted car park.

It was pretty much dark by then, but a big moon was rising, and it seemed a shame not to have a look. A steep, narrow, overgrown footpath led down the side of a wooded valley for half a mile or so, eventually crossing a river and a disused railway. Some black-and-white cows glowered at me at the bottom of the hill with what I felt was unnecessary surliness. Shortly afterwards, the path emerged on the other side of a brush of woodland, with a hill of lumpy turf sloping up to my right. Here was one of the most studied villages in England.

Identified in 1948 by Professor M.W. Beresford and subsequently pored over by innumerable archaeologists and historians over a period of some 40 years, Wharram Percy is the most famous of an estimated 3,000 deserted medieval villages around England. (Many are in my own county: Professor Beresford, with others, wrote a whole book — not a bestseller — entitled *The Deserted Villages of Northamptonshire*.) If you wanted a physical symbol of the passing of a rural civilisation, it would be hard to think of a better one than this.

Once, Wharram Percy had two manor houses, as well as a street with houses on both sides, and a village green. About 150 people lived there, and worshipped at the large parish church. Today it is just a series of lumps in the ground on an empty, windswept hillside, with only a half-ruined church, a Victorian farm-building and a few English Heritage signs to suggest — to the untrained eye — that human lives were ever lived there. I sat on one of the lumps and inhaled the rich, damp scents of evening. It was, I realised, cold. It was also rather pleasant. On one side, an immense, low disc of moon glared from the navy-blue sky; on the other, the cooling air seemed to dampen the tips of the nettle-clusters with a delicate, pearl-grey foam. A creature was rustling insistently in the woods; some rabbits chomped on the turf, and the occasional low flapping indicated a bird's late homecoming to roost. But as for humanity — the human race might as well never have existed.

I pottered around, exploring; it was hard to make much sense of the lumps in the half-light. I suspect I would have found it hard in broad daylight, too. To me, a lump is a lump. For academics, however, the site is prized because of what it has taught us about how villages evolved. As I understand it, it appeared in its final "nucleated" form on the site of an older dispersed settlement. Its peasants (who had a tendency to be left-handed and ate lots of sea-fish) lived in well-built houses with stone footings. It thrived for centuries, surviving both the Harrowing of the North (William the Conqueror's post-Hastings semi-genocide) and the Black Death; but finally succumbed to the one power

**267**

that, it seems, no human community can resist: market forces.

For me the moral seemed simpler: the days of man are as grass. The village on whose ruined foundations I was standing endured for about 600 years — and was itself built on the site of much older settlements. Throughout those centuries, it would have seemed as permanent as anywhere in England — as safe as houses. Warnings about gathering economic storm-clouds must have seemed as remote and abstract to them as they do to us today. Why, for a century or two the village was owned by the then all-powerful dukes of Northumberland. Who could ever have imagined that this — this world — would not go onward the same until the end of time?

But it didn't. In the 15th and early 16th century, the economy of sheep-farming swept through the place like some savage army. A community built on the assumption that life should be sustained by arable farming fell victim to the fact that it was becoming steadily more profitable for landowners to turn their land over to sheep. Thousands of villages became destitute in this way.

According to M.W. Beresford, writing in 1951, each such collapse "represents a landowner pursuing his advantage to the point of destroying a farming community, either inside or outside the letter of the law". Wharram Percy's last villagers were evicted in 1517 by the then landowner Baron Hilton (not to be confused with Barron Hilton, brother of Paris Hilton, of whom, sadly, the heartless landlord doesn't seem to

268

have been an ancestor). The church survived a few centuries longer but fell into disuse and disrepair in the 20th century. Its tower fell down in 1959, shortly after the lead was stolen from the roof.

I found another lump in the ground to sit on — once, perhaps, somebody's doorstep — and noticed that the turf had become damp. A clump of plants a short way away was now too indistinct to make out: I think it was ringwort. The silent moon glowed indifferently. I found myself thinking of a line of John Clare's: "where silence sitteth now on the wild heath as her own like a ruin of the past". There could not have been another human being within a mile of me. I could not even hear the road.

I stayed there for a while, trying to imagine what, if anything, a medieval villager would have felt about this spectral moonlight. I thought of death and ephemerality and the passing of old England. I thought of all my months of travelling and of all the old countrymen and women who had vanished from the land. And I felt . . . well, to be strictly honest, I didn't feel anything much, except that I was getting cold and that it was time to go back to the car and find a bed-and-breakfast in which I could get a hot bath and watch some television.

So I retraced my steps, feeling rather sad that I was too enfeebled by modern luxuries to be able to empathise properly with my rural ancestors.

At some point I must have taken a wrong turning, because I suddenly noticed that I was no longer on the footpath. I rounded a huge black tree that I took to be an oak and came to a more open area of bumpy pasture.

The turf was crisp underfoot now. Tiny particles of frozen moisture danced above it, like fine silver dust. I could sense some beasts breathing in the corner, but the shadow of a hedgerow obscured them. I realised that, though it felt almost as bright as day, the absence of colour limited what I could see. It was like being in a beautiful black-and-white photograph. Perhaps that was why it felt as though I were walking in the past.

Everything was sharply defined, yet subtly different, as if this were a different England, in a different universe, in which things had, in some profound but unspecified way, unfolded differently.

A rustle on my left — and a sudden, bittersweet tang of damp livestock — made me look to my other side. A wide-eyed cow was staring at me, spotlit by the moon. Her huge eyes gawped at me in amazement, as if she had seen a ghost. Perhaps, from her point of view, she had.

As I hurried off in search of civilisation I realised with sudden, uncomfortable clarity that, here in this strange, uninhabited world of moonlit half-tones, I really was just a shadow — a passing visitor whose time on earth was already half gone and would soon be over altogether.

Perhaps that is one of the defining insights of rural life. In towns and cities, everything is designed by and for humans, and you are too busy to notice your personal clock running down. When you live among the life cycles of other species — beasts, trees, hedges — it is easier to sense the bigger picture, and to perceive your own little cycle for what it is.

# CHAPTER
# TWENTY

# The horseman

Another time, I found myself driving through the same area by day, skimming across curved, green Yorkshire wolds. Wide, empty fields fell away in all directions beneath a pale sky; straight, low-verged lanes positively invited speeding. Then — not far from Market Drayton — I found myself slowed down by crowds of pedestrians.

These began in ones or twos: dog-walkers, I imagined, or perhaps ramblers. Then the clusters grew: couples, friends, parties, all warmly wrapped, with gloved hands clasping Thermoses or binoculars or else thrust deep into the pockets of olive-green coats. I looked around for a hunt. There was, however, no sign of either fox or hounds on the open slopes of short winter wheat.

Eventually, at a high crossroads, I found the lane lined with parked cars and binocular-users on both sides, in four different directions. I pulled over and asked what was going on.

"Kiplingcotes Derby," said a pink-faced, flat-capped man with rheumy eyes. The syllables didn't seem to make sense, even when both question and answer had been repeated.

"Britain's oldest horserace," shouted his companion, a tall, square-chinned woman with a bass voice and a military bearing.

What, here?

"Down that way," she continued, gesturing urgently. "There. Down there."

Not wishing to offend her, I drove down a thin lane that led to a small wood, where it became a bumpy, deeply puddled morass of muddy bridleway. Several clusters of spectators stood among the trees; my progress seemed to intrigue them.

The puddles deepened and broadened. In due course, I reached one so huge and glutinous that it seemed mad not to turn back while I still could. Three olive-clad men watched my nine-point turn with only the faintest suggestion of contempt on their not-quite-smirking faces.

Finally, one of them wandered over. "You lost?"

I explained that I was looking for the racecourse.

"You're on it. Better get off it, too, before you're stuck."

"Be along in a minute," shouted the taller of his two friends. I wasn't sure if he were talking to me or not — there didn't seem to be anyone else within earshot.

Was this a good place to watch?

"Not really. It's just where we always come."

"Think they've started," interjected the shouter.

"You can see the finish, if you're quick," continued the first man. And he proceeded to issue a complicated set of directions for driving to the northern end of the course in a normal, non-amphibious car. Again, it seemed ungrateful to disobey.

Ten minutes later I was standing in a crowd of more than 100 people on the wide, grassy verges of a wide, rutted bridleway, with a tall hedge behind us and an icy wind slicing through it.

Here I spoke to a short, red-faced octogenarian from Market Weighton who explained that the spectacle we were about to witness had scarcely changed in nearly half a millennium. The Kiplingcotes Derby was first run in 1519, from a stone starting-post on the edge of the village of Etton to this same wind-sliced spot between two fields on the edge of Londesborough. It still covers those same 4½ miles, in a straight line that mixes wide-verged road, flat track and rough, undulating path in measures that many would consider dangerous to human and equine health. It goes through four parishes, crosses two roads, and typically attracts about a dozen runners, ranging from serious racehorses to old hacks whose owners just want the thrill of taking part in Britain's oldest flat horserace.

"You can see the document in Malton, in the museum. Someone found it in a bank vault. It sets it all out." Specifically (I learnt later), it confirms the establishment of "a horse race to be observed and ridd yearly on the third Thursday in March; open to horses of all ages, to convey horsemen's weight, ten stones, exclusive of saddle, to enter ye post before eleven o'clock on the morning of ye race. The race to be run before two." The race must, however, be run every year, on the day and at the time specified: if it is once missed, the right to use the course will lapse.

This is what gives the event its romance. Whatever else happens, the show must go on. So in 1947, for example, when huge snowdrifts blocked the course, a horse and cart were driven through them to clear a way for a single, walking entrant.

"You have to hold on to these things," concluded my octogenarian, "or they're gone."

The size and enthusiasm of the crowd suggested that the Kiplingcotes Derby would not be going anywhere for a few years yet. But I was struck by the preponderance of grey heads. Yes, any event so rooted to the middle of a working day is bound to draw a disproportionate amount of its support from the retired and the unemployed. But where were the unemployed?

A few random conversations confirmed my impression that this was an old people's event. Among others, I spoke to an antiques dealer from Middleton-on-the-Wolds who had once been a jockey ("I always lived with horses — when I was a boy I used to ride to school, and a farmer let me tie my pony up in his field"); a vet's widow who had "been coming here as long as I remember"; a retired bookmaker ("But there's no betting here — no one even knows who's going to enter until they line up at the start, let alone who's going to win"); and an old lady who told me that her son had been born 50 years ago tomorrow, and that it had been snowing then, too. This last remark perplexed me until I looked up and noticed the snow, which had begun to flurry over the hedge.

I did see half a dozen younger faces, but closer inspection revealed them all to be journalists, covering the event for the local press, radio and television. One of the print journalists was complaining loudly to a fellow hack that his newsroom didn't appreciate his talents, which just goes to show that journalists are the same everywhere. Then, almost imperceptibly, the ground began to shake. A hundred pairs of eyes looked up, and those of us who had drifted to the centre of the track hurried back to its side. The shaking intensified, and abruptly the whole place thrilled with the thunder of hoof on turf; the air sweetened with scents of hot horse and freshly kicked divot; and a straggling file of nine impossibly muddy runners and riders galloped past to the finish.

The winner, by some distance, was a grey gelding called Etton Lad, ridden by 19-year-old Katie Croft; second was Cold Affair, ridden by Laura Crawford, who had won the race a few years earlier when she was 15. So there were some young people here, at least.

But the biggest cheers were reserved for the third-placed rider: a little old man called Ken who, it seemed, was riding the race for the last of many times.

After the weigh-in, a rather formal trustee presented the winner with her trophy, and then gave Ken a magnum of champagne in honour of his retirement — "for being a good sport". He was, he added, taking Ken's word for it that he really was retiring. "We can't do this every year."

There seemed to be a certain frostiness between the two men as they shook hands. None the less, there was renewed applause, and well-wishers rushed forward to shake Ken's hand.

"You know he's 75?" said my octogenarian. "Won it 10 times, and if he hasn't won it he's generally been second or third. Ken's more famous than the race, round here. You want to talk to Ken."

So I did: not there and then, because no 75-year-old in his right mind would want to stand around chatting in this wind while the sweat from a 4-mile gallop froze to his skin, but some time later, at his home in Cliffe Common, 15 miles to the south-west. He was, it turned out, only 74, but in other respects my information was correct.

A former stable lad, Ken Holmes had first ridden in the Kiplingcotes 24 years earlier, had first won it the year after that and had since become the event's undisputed king. His fame hadn't been matched with fortune, though. Though Cliffe Common seemed to be quite a desirable place, with developers rushing to meet demand for upmarket homes there ("The Maltings: a selection of 13 detached and semi-detached houses", said one hoarding; "The Hedgerows: four-bedroom houses from £249,950", said another), Ken's home — which he shared with his long-term partner, a glamorous Scottish lady called Moira — was a motorhome on the edge of the village, neatly tucked away inside a barn.

A pack of chained Jack Russells guarded it. "Don't worry about that one," he said, untucked shirt-tails flapping in the wind. "Her bark's worse than her bite. But that one" — he added in the nick of time — "will definitely go for you. And you want to watch that one too. She's blind, but if there's a scrap going, she'll pile in."

I made it into the motorhome, where we settled down in the main room to talk. Ken — a small, balding man with ruddy, leathery skin and light glasses resting uneasily on his flat nose — was still smarting at what he saw as a bad performance at the Kiplingcotes.

"If I'd ridden a race like that as a professional," he told me, "I'd have been sacked. I was sticking to the tail of the girl what came second, because she beat me once, and I was that busy watching what she was doing that we let that grey thing get away beyond recall. Generally when they go like that they come back to you, but this one didn't bloody stop."

He had once been a professional National Hunt jockey, half a century ago. He retired when he was 22 — "after I got sick of the St John's ambulancemen picking me up off the floor". Thereafter he worked in various racing stables, in capacities ranging from stable lad to assistant trainer; spent a period as an agricultural salesman; then, 20 years ago, became an equine dentist. He didn't have a formal qualification in this profession, but seemed widely admired for his mastery of it. He had customers as far afield as Newmarket, Lancashire and Wales, and was also in some demand as a lecturer.

There are, he explained, two parts to equine dentistry. "You have to know what you're doing. And you have to be able to handle horses. If you can't handle horses, you can't be an equine dentist."

"If ever anyone had a way with horses, Ken did," said Moira, who had joined us in the tiny room. "They only have to hear his voice and they're calm." She looked younger than Ken — and sounded more educated. Her eyes shone as she talked about him.

"Do you remember Lucius?" she added. The only Lucius I remembered was the 1978 Grand National winner. Apparently this was the one Moira had in mind. Ken broke him in in 1972. In 1995, Ken and Moira visited him in his retirement. "He hadn't seen Ken for 23 years. Ken just said, 'Hello, old man, let's have a look at you,' and I tell you, if you could have seen the way he pricked up his ears . . . it brought tears to my eyes."

"Made the hairs on my neck stand up on end," added Ken. "They never forget. Dogs are the same."

But even someone with the most profound affinity with animals takes his life in his hands when he starts messing around with a horse's teeth. "They're not all easy." The hardest, apparently, are Dales horses ("bargy") and Welsh ponies (liable to stand up on their hind legs and lash out). "I've had some narrow escapes — a couple have nearly killed me stone dead. The nearest squeak was near Whitby — he'd have kicked my eyeballs out if he'd had half a chance. His hoof went past my head and knocked a brick out of the wall. My throat went dry — it was that close."

Another time, "We arrived at this place just outside Beverley, we arrived there at 1.30p.m. and by 2.20p.m. Moira was in Royal Infirmary with a broken leg. It was a horse that I had wolf teeth to take out of. I took a

**279**

wolf tooth out at one side, and I was on the other side taking one out. Moira's got his head up, helping me to do my job. He put his bloody leg round Moira's leg, like that, and went down on his bloody knees like that. Snapped her leg as clean as a whistle."

"I just went down and went in and out of consciousness," explained Moira sweetly, "but of course Ken couldn't stop — he had to carry on taking the tooth out . . ."

"But," she added, "it's a super job. We meet some super people."

What about the Kiplingcotes? What was that about? Getting away from the tameness of work with a bit of horse-related danger?

"It's a great tradition," said Ken. "That's the main thing. A modern-day jockey would be reluctant to ride over there, because of the hard terrain. But if you've got a decent horse it can be exhilarating. He's got to be fit, mind, and so've you." He didn't add that both horse and rider needed to be fearless: the mixture of hard and soft going, and wide and narrow track, and relentless uphill gradient is enough to push all concerned to their physical limits. Over the years, he said, "I seen two horses collapse and die"; you could tell that he was the sort of person for whom that mattered.

"There's something special about it," said Moira, who had ridden in the race twice. "The fact that it's been going on all those years, and the fact that people aren't necessarily at the beginning and the end but they've all got their own special vantage point . . . It's eerie, somehow — when they're all waiting, and nothing's happening. And every time I'm there, I get a strange feeling that I've been up there before, long ago."

Ken has a record 10 victories to his credit (as well as five second places and two thirds). But he may be best known locally for his exploits in 2001, when he and Moira were the only riders. "The organisers decided to call it off, because of foot-and-mouth, even though it wasn't a controlled area," he explained.

"But if it stops at all," interjected Moira, "then that's it — it's gone for ever."

"Should you ever not gallop over the land, the race becomes defunct," said Ken. "That's why, since 1519, there's never been a break. You can't just say you'll do it another day instead."

So Ken and Moira turned up anyway and, to cut a long story short, overrode the organisers' objections and rode up the course. (At one point the police were mentioned, to which Ken replied: "It's got bugger all to do with police.") It's conceivable that this controversy might explain the frostiness I sensed when Ken was presented with his magnum.

On balance, however, the establishment approved of Ken. Since breaking the record he had been keeping the Queen in touch with his achievements, and replies had been sent on her behalf. She was, it seemed, sorry to hear that he was not planning to ride another Kiplingcotes.

He was sorry himself. But, he explained, "I'm 75 this year. If anything happened to me at my age, they'd say:

the silly old bugger, he should have packed up years ago."

It was an uncharacteristic admission of potential frailty. In general, he seemed as tough as an old riding boot. He attributed this to his upbringing. He grew up in a tiny house on the edge of Norton, about 25 miles to the north, one of 10 children. When he was little, his father "buggered off to Ireland", where he became a champion jockey — "but I never, ever did see him". Instead, Ken started work at 15 as a stable lad — and had been working hard ever since.

"The first trainer I worked for was a slave driver. I had two cows to milk, rode out four horses, cleaned the tack of the paid lads, swept the yards, crushed the oats, the dunghill to chuck back, the dogs to muck out, the logs to chop, cows to muck out. But I never minded hard work. What was hard was when he'd get me to waste, to ride a horse at, say, 7 st 4 lbs" — his Kiplingcotes weight was 10 st — "and then I'd get to the race meeting to ride it and find that he'd stuck someone else on it. That was hard to take."

He had no regrets: the mental and physical toughness he had developed had stood him in good stead. He had maintained his independence right through his working life, had raised eight children (and had more grandchildren than he could count), owed nothing to anybody and had achieved a certain kind of sporting immortality. What he did regret, he said, was that the world he grew up in was passing away.

He talked for a long time, rather sadly, about various rural types he used to know. "There were chaps who really knew nature then. I knew men that lived on the wold — real wild men. There was one bloke I knew — Tom Barron, he fought at the Somme — could whistle up hares to shoot 'em. He was wonderful — a bloody artist." There were others, too: Peter, for example, "an old countryman from York, used to breed shirehorses"; Old Frank, "an old country lad, lived in caravan"; as well as a "wise old stableman" who bequeathed the enigmatic advice that, "Son, there are three things in life that you will never see — a fat jockey, a bookie wearing bicycle clips and a dead donkey."

A more useful lesson that he learnt from his rural mentors was how to catch moles — an art he still practises. "When I first came here I did a silly thing. We were overrun with them — we were inundated with bloody moles. So I caught 18 of them and hung them on the fence at the end of the paddock. So then the farmers saw what I'd done, and I ended up catching moles for them, too. I still do it."

He sucked on his mug of coffee and sighed. "Country life was country life then," he reflected. "I remember the days when they were cutting corn with a horse pulling a reaper. And the roads always smelled lovely in summer. And the people you'd meet . . . When I was at school there was always the old roadsters — what you'd call tramps, I suppose — that used to go from village to village and sleep in farmers' barns, looking for casual work. Gypsies were gypsies then — not like these guys you see now in BMWs. And everyone had some tale to tell . . .

"But look at the world today. Hunting's gone, farm horses have gone. Farming's gone down the nick. Villages aren't villages any more: you can live three or four doors from someone and not know 'em, because they commute to work — do you get me? And there's no work locally. They're closing sugar-beet factory at York, that's been there for years, because it's cheaper to import sugar cane. What's going to happen to this country if there's a war? We import gas, we import food . . . You won't need guns to bring us to our knees."

He could — and did — carry on for hours in this vein. ("There's no discipline in schools, no respect for the police . . ."; "Young people don't know what work is — they don't know they've been born . . ."; "A lot of these yuppies are bloody troublemakers. I mean, they come in [to the village] and they want to take over. They can't bear to hear the sound of church bells ring, or they can't bear the smell of slurry . . .") They were what I was coming to think of as typical old countryman's views — and no less valid for that; but I hadn't met many old countrymen who were so keen to share them. "If the editor of the *Selby Times* goes three weeks without getting a letter from me," he admitted, "he'll telephone to see if I'm OK."

Then, just as I was leaving, he shared one other view: "In my opinion — and it'll be my opinion till I die — the biggest social evil of my time has been something that you've got, and I've got, and none of us can do without. And England will never be the same because of it. It's called the internal combustion engine."

284

For a moment I felt crushed by the weight of all the car-miles in my life: not just the wanderings described in this book, but also all those tens of thousands of miles — tens of thousands of hours — travelling to and from work, or the shops, or between families and friends and holidays in different parts of the country. Segments of wasted life flashed before my eyes. Was that what I evolved for? Was that what any of us evolved for? I imagined for a moment a world in which all my friends and relations lived and worked within walking distance, and my fellow villagers and I all worked together in the fields around our homes, and to travel — on the rare occasions when one did travel — really was to undertake a grand adventure. Will it really be such a bad thing, I asked myself, when the oil finally runs out?

Then I drove off.

# CHAPTER
# TWENTY-ONE

# Backward and forward

Cherry Burton, a few miles to the east of Cliffe Common, looked like a village of tomorrow rather than a village of yesterday. There was a basic winding ribbon of old buildings along its centre, with a friendly pub, a good school and a village pond with ducks on. But two enormous estates — one on either side of the main street — had been built since 1960, and there was nothing remotely sleepy about the way the traffic thundered between them. Initial inquiries suggested that, apart from perhaps four farming families, most people earned their living in nearby towns in service industries, local government, teaching and the NHS. There were also around 27 businesses based in the village, including a golf club, a motorcycle shop, a residential care home for the elderly, two driving instructors, several gardeners, a burglar-alarm company, a home-improvements company, a mobile butcher, a painter and decorator, a taxi service, and a creator of "dream kitchens" (whose clients, according to his website, included Premiership footballers). In short, it had much the same kind of mixed, post-agricultural economy as any other modern English village.

But it also had a past, and one person, at least, remembered it.

No one knew more about Cherry Burton's yesterdays than Peggy Webb. She came to live there in 1918, when she was five, having spent her earliest years in Bishop Burton, 1½ miles to the south; apart from a few years spent travelling during and straight after World War II, she had lived there ever since. She had seen it changed by the arrival of tractors, of motor-cars, of electricity, of mains water and drainage, and of new housing estates full of incomers from the towns. And she remembered the times before any of those things. Not only that, but she had observed sharply, and pondered, and remembered, and written things down; and, when I visited her, she shared enthusiastically.

She was a dignified woman, with a tidy home full of knick-knacks and little visible sign of deep rural roots. Perhaps she didn't need such signs. Her father had been a market gardener — the son of a head gardener and a maid at a nearby grand estate — and, since he was one of 13 and her mother was one of seven, the surrounding area had been packed with her aunts, uncles and cousins. By my estimate, the village would have been about half the size when she was growing up — that is, about 280 houses rather than the current 560. It included at least nine farms, each employing several labourers, as well as a blacksmith, cobbler, teacher, tailor, undertaker, joiner, postman, policeman and roadman, and more than a dozen people in service — as butlers, maids, chauffeurs, grooms, gardeners — in the village's two grand houses.

By modern standards, Peggy had a childhood full of physical hardship. But, she insisted: "It was a lovely life. It was beautiful. There were wells everywhere — I don't know where they've gone — and the water, oh, it was delicious, it was crystal clear, it really was. We could play in the street, all the children — it was a great playground — and that's where I learnt to dance, outside the pub while they played the piano with the windows open."

She leant back in her chair — gracefully, as if she were the Queen — and gazed slightly upwards before releasing a flood of childhood memories that seemed to be passing before her eyes.

"And then when the springs froze one February, all the meadows were covered and there was a terrific frost and it was all ice so you could safely skate on it and slide on it, and it was lovely. We didn't have skates — we just skated on our boots. The children would hold hands, and the one on the outside — which was me — would end up going really really fast . . .

"We were always welcome to go and play in the farmyards and we used to climb the stacks and we used to climb through the stacks — very dangerous . . . And then there was a wonderful chalk pit we had, we weren't supposed to go there, but it was like the white cliffs of Dover, and when we were let loose on a Saturday and had nothing better to do, we used to all go down to the chalk pit and see if we could find an old wash basin, and then we would climb up to the top and sit in this thing and slide down. It was the most dangerous thing . . .

"It wouldn't be allowed now. But then nothing would. I remember sometimes if my uncle Eric was milking he would squirt milk straight in our mouths, or we'd be eating swede fresh from the turnip-cutter." It didn't seem to do her any harm — but then "we always thought twice about complaining about aches and pains, because the cure was usually worse".

She looked frail, but much less so than you'd expect in a 91-year-old widow. She considered herself fortunate, she said; not least because both her children lived in the village. Her daughter, Rosemary, sat with us for a while, as did Ros Stanley, a prominent member of the local church. But it was Peggy who did the talking. It was almost as if she were in a hurry to share as many memories as possible before they disappeared.

The Cherry Burton of her early years verged on the feudal. She remembered meeting the local squire, who had "a red face and a rotund figure", in the street. He said, "You're a nice little thing," and gave her two-and-six. Her mother was furious with her for accepting it and made her put it in the poor box.

Later on, after leaving school, she briefly became a housemaid — "but to be honest, we didn't get on". After that, she worked for her mother, who ran the village shop. "It was supposed to be cash only — don't give credit, my father said, because you won't get the money. But of course we did, and we didn't get it. But we survived.

"Dad grew vegetables, so he would exchange Brussels sprouts for butter, for example — we did a lot of bartering. But he wouldn't work in the shop." If she and her mother were both engaged elsewhere, her mother would just leave a note saying "Down the garden" or "Upstairs" and trust customers to come and find her.

A married man used to come in and molest Peggy when she was left in charge. "I was the person with rosy cheeks, and he was very nasty. He would show you postcards — 'Oh, look at these,' he'd say. So I said to him one day, 'Do you like chocolate?' And he said, 'Oh, yes, I do, I do like chocolate.' Well, we'd just got a consignment, I don't know whether you know of Ex-Lax. I said, 'Would you like a bar of this then?' You're only supposed to take one of them. So he said yes, he would. So he took it — he ate it all. 'I was on the toilet for a week,' he said. He wasn't rude to me any more."

Many of her memories concerned her immediate family: being wheeled home in a barrow by her brother George, while he told her the names of "all the wildflowers that grew in the hedgerows, the names of the trees, and the birds"; snuggling up to her sister, Mary, for warmth, in their shared and freezing bed ("it was nothing to us to break the ice on the wash bowl before we could have our morning wash"); watching her mother "sitting in the coal house plucking chickens before Christmas, two for us and the rest to sell"; meeting her husband for the first time: "He was my cousin really, and he came to stay with his auntie, and we took one look at one another and that was it — strange isn't it? Bless him. There weren't anybody else but John. But it's funny how you know, don't you?"

But she also had a wider story to tell about the village as a whole. "It was such a wonderful community — the village people, I won't say they loved one another but they were fond of one another. And you knew exactly if he was ill or if she was ill and all about that, and I don't think there was one door in this village that wasn't open to me. Unfortunately they're all dying out now. The people who come here to live, they don't know anything about the village.

"But you see deep drainage came, and that was fatal, because it meant that they could build all over the place and take land from the farms. And farmers weren't daft — they sold up, which is rather grieving. We weren't happy about it but you've got to make the best of things, haven't you? But nowadays there are so many people in the village . . .

"But it's nice to remember, isn't it?"

Sometimes it wasn't clear which particular period a memory belonged to, but it scarcely mattered: the picture she painted was of a village — a lost village — somewhere in the past. She remembered sitting on a gate sniffing in the scent of a bean field in full blossom ("But they don't grow beans any more, do they?"); watching the ladies try to catch a greased pig at the Bishop Burton show; the tramp who used to sleep in her uncle's barn, who claimed that he had a title but "had spent all his money on wine, women and other things" and that the tin he carried contained a great secret; the little washerwoman in a cottage in the main road, who used to teach the village girls how to wash and iron when work was slack; the blacksmith's forge ("a magical place at the end of the pond"); the "delicious smell of steaming cloths" at the tailor's shop; where the village's two ice houses were ("There was one at the big house, and then at the farm at the top — but they've done away with them all"); how Arthur Grey made the dew ponds on the big open land on the Westwood ("You can still see those — there's one that still has water down the bottom"; how Art Starkey, who was "a bit, not dumb exactly, but not overbright", used to draw and paint "the most beautiful horses — I'd love to have one"); how Lady Boynton's chauffeur built himself a shed to live in at the end of his cottage's garden ("It was supposed to be because he had TB and didn't want to contaminate anybody, but we thought it was because he wanted to get away from his wife."); how her uncle Percy got hopelessly lost in the fog in his own field; and, best of all, how every five years or so "the springs would rise". The causes of this last phenomenon were obscure — possibly something to do with how much snow had fallen on the Pennines — but the effect was dramatic: "Springs came bubbling up in the road. You could catch it in your hands and drink it. It was delicious. Pump Cottage garden and the adjoining field would be awash, the old post office would have water pouring out of the front door, and the barrels of beer in the pub cellar would be floating around . . . But that never happens now."

She leant back in her chair again and smiled. "It's nice to be able to remember. I'm just so sorry for people who get this Alzheimer's and their memory's gone."

292

Then she said: "You shouldn't live this long, should you, really?"

Do such memories matter? I think they do. Obviously, each of us has personal memories that, like our dreams, are of interest to no one but ourselves and our therapists. But communities have memories too, and if individuals don't preserve them then the communities they belong to lose all sense of what has gone before. And when that happens, their whole character as communities can be called into question, because they no longer have a collective past.

Even so, one person's memories remain one person's memories. In another person's mind, a village may have an entirely different story. So it proved with Cherry Burton. After I left Peggy, I was shown round a bit by Ros Stanley, who sang the praises of the modern village.

Ros, an ex-teacher in her mid-fifties, was an incomer. "We came here from Sheffield, 30 years ago. So we almost belong now." She seemed to play a central role in community life, and it was easy to see why. As she showed me round the village, she stopped twice to pick up litter, which she carried home with her to dispose of.

The village has many things going for it, she explained. It has a "wonderful" school and a "very healthy outgoing church", in which she is active, and a drama group and a wine circle and "all sorts of other organisations" and a "very good, very positive atmosphere". It also has a decent number of retired people. "You'd be surprised how much difference that makes. Everyone agrees that villages thrive when people participate. But a lot of people who are working, and have young families, really don't want to participate, which is a pity, but you can see why. If they're away a lot, or working long hours, then perhaps it's understandable that they might just want to crawl back into a nice quiet hole and not be known by anybody or seen by anybody. But if your children have left home, and you've retired — maybe quite young, like we did — then you can suddenly find that you've got time to put something back in, and I think that's happening a lot. People around our age, or the ones that came here just before us, are retiring now, and so the village at the moment has got a lot going on.

"And that can be very rewarding for the people concerned, because I do think that to feel at home in the village, to be truly a part of the village, you need to contribute in some way."

Ros, who was jolly and auburn-haired and wore a crucifix and kicked off her shoes as soon as we reached her home, reckoned that around a fifth of the population was "actually frontlining, actually hands-on involved with running something", while nearly three-quarters would "at least go to something during the year", and the rest "you never see". By today's standards, she thought, that was "extremely healthy. And," she added hastily, "there are people who contribute in all age groups. Especially the young."

It was a group of half a dozen church-going village teenagers who kicked off the initiative that is, arguably,

Cherry Burton's greatest claim to niceness. "They'd been learning about the Fairtrade movement at school and decided to set up a weekly Fairtrade stall in church. It was a great success, and a few years later, during Fairtrade fortnight, they had a Fairtrade pancake evening and invited the whole village. That was a success too. And after that evening, somebody was walking down the road with me and said, 'You know, that was absolutely brilliant, what shall we do next?' And I said, well, I've heard of things called Fairtrade towns, perhaps we could become a Fairtrade village?"

So they did. It was hard work. They had to get the support of the parish council, and then set up a steering group (11-strong at its peak), and then persuade all the village's retail and catering outlets — in this case, the pub and the village shop — to stock Fairtrade products. But it worked. Both the shop and the Bay Horse now sell Fairtrade tea, coffee, chocolate and biscuits. "And the nice thing is that Fairtrade has been integrated into most groups within the village, so that if someone is organising an event, like the village panto, they'll always serve Fairtrade tea or coffee or chocolate bars."

They had had their Fairtrade certificate since 2003 but were still gaining momentum. They had, for example, recently raised several hundred pounds for the village school through a Fairtrade fashion show in Beverley Minster. Meanwhile, the village had added a further layer to its considerateness. Encouraged by Howard Petch — a "wise and erudite" villager who in addition to being (at the time) principal of the agricultural college in the neighbouring village of

Bishop Burton was vice-chairman of the charity Farm Crisis Network — they decided to become a Local Produce village as well. "We felt that, as a rural community, it was very important to support UK producers. And the closer to home, the lower the transport costs and the more you're supporting your local economy. So now we support local produce in the same way as we support Fairtrade.

"The shop has a variety of local products — it has local baking, it has local greengrocery — anybody that's got produce can bring it along. As for the pub, the owner is actually a butcher, and before he was a butcher, he was a farmer, and we have all local produce in the pub anyway — all local meat, fish from the fish market. So we're as local as local can be, and that's what a lot of people want anyway: they don't want something that's travelled halfway round the world. They want a Yorkshire beef-steak. So it's brilliant from every point of view.

"It's hard to get local milk at the moment, because we're losing dairy farms like there's no tomorrow, and none of the farms that I know of can afford a dairyman any more. But it's as much about revolutionising people's outlook as about changing the way they shop. Obviously we want to make a practical difference, but we also want to teach them to value the farmer again — because with oil prices going up, and self-sufficiency going down, it's crazy not to."

I asked where I might find some of the original teenagers who had started the Fairtrade initiative. Ros's answer was instructive: one was working on a charity project in Birkenhead, one was on her way to spend a year in northern India as part of her training to be a nurse, one was in Kenya on a Fairtrade project, one was about to go to Tanzania, one had been in Uganda. But none, it seemed, was currently in Cherry Burton.

Could she see any of them becoming permanent residents? "It's tricky. The trouble is, in a sense this village has been a victim of its own success. When we came here 30 years ago, it was cheaper in Cherry Burton than it was in Beverley. But prices have been pushed up as people have moved in, partly because the league tables have shown how wonderful the school is, and now Cherry Burton is more expensive, even though prices have been going up in Beverley too. So for children to continue to live here — we've got no shared-ownership schemes or anything like you have in London — it's very, very difficult. You've got families now with children that are grown up that are living at home because they can't afford to buy. So there's a kind of hidden poverty even in a basically rich place."

The same old story? In a sense, but Cherry Burton had chosen a more positive version of it than most. And perhaps it was foolish of me to focus too much attention on the past — on the dying village, if you like — when what mattered was the living village, and how it functioned in the 21st century. Or perhaps it was important to focus on both.

I drove away pensively. A few days later, I heard that, the night after talking to me, Peggy Webb had died in her sleep.

# CHAPTER
# TWENTY-TWO

# Middle England

Near Bedford, I stopped in Elstow and stood on the same green where, 400 years ago, the author of *The Pilgrim's Progress* used to wrestle on the sabbath, until a voice demanding. "Wilt thou leave thy sins and go to Heaven, or have thy sins and go to Hell?" persuaded him to be a preacher instead.

The green, and the high church beside it, couldn't have changed much since — apart from the various boards advertising the "Bunyan Way" and related attractions. And the various other boards that bossily admonished passing humanity to buck its ideas up: "No artificial flowers please", "Cycling prohibited", "All cars must leave by 5p.m.". And, of course, passing humanity itself — which on that particular afternoon consisted mainly of two sightseeing families of four, one of which was absorbed in eating ice-lollies while the other bickered furiously about some incident of childish misbehaviour in the church.

I tried not to hear them and, instead, looked up at the tall, breeze-brushed horse chestnuts on the green's edge and imagined how this place would have looked through John Bunyan's eyes. The sprays of cloud slipping past high, windswept cottage chimneys in the cold blue sky beyond can't have looked any different from the heavens he saw. And although the churchyard must be fuller today, it must have felt much the same, with its curiously uneven gravestones, like a mouth overcrowded with teeth, suggesting thoughts of graves giving up their dead on the day of judgement.

What could be more English than John Bunyan's England? Yet what else — apart from the sky and the churchyard — was there in common between his world and mine? In his day, almost without exception, life was nasty, brutish and short, textured by cold and poverty and circumscribed by fear of hellfire and the imminence of death. In mine, physical discomfort is rarely so close as to be easily imaginable, while spiritual insecurity is rarely so deep that it cannot be assuaged by judicious shopping or light entertainment. Death can usually be postponed or brushed under the carpet. As for boundaries, the only thing that circumscribes my world is the pale emptiness of agnosticism.

Then I entered the church and looked at the stained glass, which illustrates Bunyan's other great work: *The Holy War*. You don't hear so much about that one these days. Those to whom the phrase probably means most — Bedfordshire's growing population of Muslims — arguably have a world-view closer to Bunyan's than the mass of lapsed Anglicans (like me) who traditionally think of themselves as his spiritual heirs. I wonder if God notices the difference.

In Ampthill, a quiet market town in the otherwise noisy triangle of countryside between Bedford, Luton and Milton Keynes, I met a man who had grown up in Stewartby, a once famous village near by. Richard Holden was 75, and had spent all his working life in the brickworks around which Stewartby was built. (Well, most of it: a few cottages and farm buildings had been there for 1,000 years or so, under the name of Wootton Pillinge; the rest was created between 1926 and 1935 by the Stewart family, as a model settlement for workers in their new factory, which at one point produced 500 million bricks a year and provided most of the raw material for Britain's post-war building boom.) Richard — a tidily dressed, pudgy-faced giant of a man who was not in the best of health — had started as a dogsbody and eventually rose to be an office manager. He had moved to Ampthill on retiring but still recalled his early years in Stewartby as the happiest of his life.

"My parents came to Stewartby in 1935," he explained, eyes narrowing as he thought back. They lived at 200 Stewartby Way, one of the village's smaller houses, opposite the farm and the allotments. Like most villagers, his father worked at the brickworks. "He was a crane-driver. But he died at the age of 41. I was just three, and my younger sister was born less than three weeks later. So my mother was left with four children and 7 shillings' rent to pay, with just her widow's pension. Life was a real struggle. It was desperately difficult. I remember we often used to have

300

to go to bed at 7p.m. because we didn't have any money to put in the electricity meter.

"But then every now and then, especially around Christmas, there'd be a knock on the door and my mum would say, 'Could you see who's at the door?' So I'd open the door and say, 'There's nobody there, Mum.' But someone would have left something on the doorstep, because they wanted to help us. But because they didn't want any thanks, they just disappeared into the night.

"Usually it would be vegetables, or something like that. But I remember once there was a Christmas tree, or at other times someone would have wrapped a present, and I really had no idea where they came from. So it really was as though Father Christmas was real."

He moved his fingers on his mug of tea in an anxious sort of way and looked down. "I realise now that my mum had been a great friend to a lot of people — you know, a good listener and a comforter. So now, because we'd got nothing, other people willingly helped. It made a huge difference. I was a big lad and it was quite a job buying clothes to keep up with me. But I was lucky enough to gain a free place at Bedford Modern School, and I had some skill at cricket, and one day I found that someone had paid for a proper pair of cricket trousers and boots for me, at Foster Brothers."

I had only known him for 10 minutes, but there were, I realised, tears streaming down his cheeks.

"You could carry on all day telling stories like that. People cared about everybody then. There was no 'self, self, self'. Nobody was rich then, although some people were a bit better off because the wives worked in the canteen or as cleaners. But what got us through it was a devoted, loving mother and the support of the people of Stewartby."

He paused again to wipe away a tear, then continued: "Today, a lot of the friendliness has been diluted. I often go back there, but you ask my friends and they'll tell you the same thing: that kind of family atmosphere has disappeared. People keep to themselves.

"You used to walk through Stewartby and all the mums would be standing by the front gate talking, all keeping an eye out for who was doing what. So the children could all be playing in the street somewhere, and no one worried. If you go there now you might be lucky and see one person walking a dog, but that's about it."

What had changed? "Well, there's fewer people work at the brickworks, for a start. Hanson [which bought it in 1984] reduced the operation by 90 per cent, and the village was devastated. And then there's cars and television. When I was young our world hardly went further than Bedford. I remember when I first went to Bedford Modern I was amazed that they taught French. We had vaguely heard that there was a place called France, but we had no idea they spoke a different language.

"But now everyone's looking further afield for their lives. And, of course, since tenants got the right to buy their houses, something like a third of tenants have exercised their right to buy. And a lot of people have also realised that they're actually quite desirable properties to sell. So where there used to be this very fixed population, now there are always 'For Sale' boards up."

I began to think more about communities. Person after person had lamented the decline of villages in the social sense: the traditional equivalent of today's online social networks, in which large groups of people share the everyday banalities of their lives with scant regard for privacy or prudence, and derive a sense of belonging from doing so.

But how do you "find" a community? What does it look like? How do you measure its health? I have lived 16 years in my village and still have only the vaguest idea of the invisible and fast-changing forces that make it tick. It would be presumptuous in the extreme to pass judgement on the workings of other villages, on the basis of passing visits.

Yet I did, over the months, become convinced of two things. First: there are many villages in England whose inhabitants try hard to foster community spirit; some do so with considerable success. (You have only to study the archives of, for example, the Calor Village of the Year competition to find dozens of examples of this.) And, second: the impetus for such admirable efforts tends to be provided by incomers.

The second point isn't surprising. The villages of the old countryside had traditional focal points — school, church, farms, pub, shop, post office. In the new countryside, those points are vanishing. Small schools (i.e., for one village only) have been in decline for decades (and hundreds more are threatened with closure by new government spending priorities). So has the church. (It was reported in 2007 that up to 10,000 rural churches were now so little used, and would cost so much to maintain and repair, that they risked having to close.) Farm workers are now outnumbered by seven to one by National Trust members. As for village pubs, village shops and village post offices, in 2006 these were being lost at a rate of, respectively, 26 a month, 25 a month and 12 a month. (The post offices have since caught up: of the 8,000-odd rural post offices that survive at the time of writing, 2,500 are expected to have closed by the end of 2008.) So the traditional community figureheads — teacher, vicar, farmer, publican, shopkeeper, etc — have faded away, or, if they survive, are stretched to the point of invisibility.

Where communities have not died as a result, it is usually because a new type of leader has filled the gap: the website editor, for example, or the enterprising, business-plan-producing, grant-seeking high-achiever who is prepared to apply urban nous and know-how to rural problems.

I suspect that, a decade or two ago, such innovators were often shunned as outsiders who had no business "interfering". Now, even born-and-bred village traditionalists are increasingly recognising that anyone who attempts to breathe life into their community should probably be encouraged. Such life-breathers are found in many parts of today's countryside. In Stottesdon, for example, a remote, ancient village set deep in a maze of high-hedged, pot-holed Shropshire lanes, I met a woman who, having spent much of her life in the Home Counties, had set about reviving the village through its pub, the Fighting Cocks.

It looked like an ordinary pub at first, with low beams, faded cushions on wooden benches, a roaring fire and, shortly after what used to be opening time, no one much about. Then a man walked into the bar and ordered a pint of milk. No one batted an eyelid. He chatted to the landlady about the weather and a minute later a barmaid re-emerged with the milk. He paid and left. Then a young woman came in, bought some cigarettes and began to use the internet on a computer in the corner. She was comparing the prices of flights to southern France. In the next room, a group of customers was sitting down to begin a lavish dinner made entirely from local produce. And in the room next door to that a jolly lady called Lesley was just closing up a small shop that half an hour earlier had been full of other jolly ladies who had come in for organic chocolate, fresh meat, home-made chutney and, by the sound of things, a chat.

"What I've tried to do here," explained the incomer in question, Sandra Jeffries, "is make the pub the centre of the village." This might sound pretty straightforward, especially since the Fighting Cocks is pretty much at the centre of Stottesdon. But it isn't.

"I've been here eight years," said Sandra, a large, bespectacled woman with short hair and a no-nonsense attitude, who was working as a secretary in the Midlands before getting divorced and reinventing herself as a Stottesdon landlady. "And since I've been here we've lost five pubs within a two-mile radius, including the Fox & Hounds in this village."

Such closures reflect a nationwide trend. Fifty years ago, a significant number of country people would spend a significant proportion of their time in pubs: partly because they were comfortable compared with their homes, and partly because traditional manual agricultural work was not incompatible with long evenings of beer and cider-drinking. So pubs could make ends meet by providing drink and drinking space. Today, they can't. The drink-driving laws and the dwindling number of working-class villagers have meant that hardly anyone goes to a country pub to hang around and drink. So pubs can't make a profit unless they sell food — and not just any food, but food good enough to make them a "destination" gastropub able to compete with all the other gastropubs within driving distance of an increasingly choosy public. This isn't easy. As with farmland, a more reliable way of making money from a country pub is to sell it.

"But," said Sandra, "once a pub closes, it becomes a house, and the village loses a meeting place. There used to be a shop here, too, just opposite, but that closed years ago, and the shop in Durston closed in August. We have literally one or two buses a week: there was one today to Bridgnorth, and one yesterday to Leominster, and that's about it. We've no village hall. It would be very easy for people to get isolated."

Sandra's solution was to reinvent her pub as a pub-cum-shop-cum-post-office-cum-internet-café. She was in the process of expanding the internet element to include 12 broadband terminals. The shop, in a once derelict outbuilding at the side, sells meat, cheese, vegetables, juices, butters, smoked salmon, breads, fruits, jams, chutneys — in short, much the same local produce that Sandra uses for her pub meals.

"It's my policy to use local suppliers for everything, whether it's for cooking or for the shop. I buy local milk, local meat. The beer's local. We go just over the border to Worcestershire for our cheese, but it's still within a 30-mile radius. And the veg we sell in the shop tomorrow will only have been dug out of the ground today. It will still be covered in mud — you can't get fresher than that. So it helps local people as producers, as well as helping them as consumers.

"It's the opposite of what a supermarket does. Supermarkets kill communities — they don't pay farmers properly, and then the customers get food that's travelled thousands of miles. It's a mistake to think that supermarkets offer better value: they don't. But if you support small suppliers, it helps keep the community alive — and you get fresher food.

"You could pretty much do your entire weekly shop there," said Sandra, "as long as you didn't want too much ready-made stuff. But the other thing about it is just that it's nice for people to come to the shop and talk. They may only have a little chat, but it's important because you can get a bit insular if you don't bump into people.

"We still don't have as many regulars from the village in the pub as I'd ideally like, but we will.

"We've won a lot of awards," she added, "and had a lot of coverage. I think it's because it's local, it's unusual and the community is thriving and not dying."

It's hard to quantify the impact this has had. On the night I was there the customers consisted mainly of visitors from other villages who had come for a gourmet dining experience. And I did speak to one farmer — best left anonymous — who told me: "I don't go to the pub. I don't really think I fit in. I was born here, but these days I feel like a bit of an outsider. To be honest, I don't really feel it's my village any more."

But no one else had a bad word to say about it; and it would be absurd to argue that the new-look Fighting Cocks was anything but a huge asset to the village. If Stottesdon develops a stronger sense of community over the next decade or so, it will be largely thanks to Sandra Jeffries. Which provoked one obvious question . . .

"I'm not going anywhere," she said. "I nearly gave up in the first couple of years, but not now. It's hard work, and if I add up how much I earn it's not very much. You've got to like it or you wouldn't do it. But I'm here till I retire now."

There are several rural charities and grant-giving bodies that encourage initiatives of this kind. The Pub is the Hub — set up by the Prince's Trust in 2001 — has helped around 300 village pubs (including the Fighting Cocks) to add "community value" to themselves in one way or another. Similarly, the Village Retail Services Association has helped at least 150 villages to set up "community shops" as, in effect,

308

cooperatives. I also know of a pub, the Old Crown in Hesket Newmarket, Cumbria, which is community-owned.

Such schemes seem to work well, since they benefit not only the users of the service (who get a shop or pub they wouldn't otherwise have had) but also those who provide it (who have to spend lots of time cooperating together and are often surprised by how rewarding that can be) — and, when local produce is used, those who supply it. I think very highly of the community shop at Sulgrave, a village near us in Northamptonshire. But the trouble with these new mini-institutions is that — in contrast to the more permanent rural institutions of the past — they are, ultimately, as ephemeral as the populations that create them. There are other obstacles to community involvement, notably the increasing need for volunteers to obtain licences, qualifications, Criminal Records Board checks and the like before they can do their bit. (Parish councillors even have to disclose their financial interests.) But all these can be overcome, and often are, presumably because the human instinct to do things for the collective benefit is stronger than we think. Ephemerality is more problematic.

I spent an intriguing afternoon around this time in St Briavels, Gloucestershire, where a retired academic (and incomer) called George Peterken talked me through a scheme of common land use that he and about 70 of his neighbours had been running since 2001: partly as a way of reviving traditional "commoning" practices in the area and partly with a view to maintaining as many as possible of their different smallholdings as flower-rich meadow. It sounded inspiring. But, warned Peterken, "it only takes one or two people to drop out and the whole thing collapses. It's like a lot of things: there's a core group of perhaps four to six people keeping it going, and if any of them goes then things can fall apart. We had a bit of a crisis recently when our treasurer resigned. You'd only need a couple of us to move on, or die, or whatever, and you might find that you didn't have enough people to keep it running."

I noticed this again in Sheepy Magna, in Leicestershire, where I went to see a new post office that villagers had set up in their church. This had been described — by the regional director for English Heritage — as "an inspiring example of a local community and its vicar getting together to find creative solutions"; the *Sunday Times* had called it "admirable". Its beauty was that it killed two topical birds with one stone. On the one hand, the church was, like thousands of others, both poorly attended and in urgent need of repair. (The Church of England estimates that, nationwide, it needs to spend £925 million on repairing such churches over the next five years — which is £590 million more than it can afford.) On the other, its post office had, like thousands of others, given up the ghost in the face of overwhelming market forces. (In 2007, one rural post office in four wasn't making any money at all.) The then vicar, Annette Reed, put the two problems together to make a solution. A campaign was started;

money was raised, including £45,500 in grants from 12 different bodies (county council, district church council, Countryside Agency, etc); and the crumbling tower base at the back of the church was simultaneously restored and converted. The new sub-post office was opened in April 2004 — by the village's oldest resident, Lucy Wood — and people had been enthusing about it ever since. I decided to have a look.

But it turned out that there wasn't a post office in the church that day. The part-time postmistress was ill. "It's very difficult," explained the lady cleaning the church. "She's very poorly, and the Post Office have said she can have time off, and we've not got anyone to replace her, so we're in the process of trying to get hold of the Post Office to find out what we do. But you're welcome to have a look at it."

"It" turned out to be a neat oak-panelled room, about the size of a disabled toilet. (I can say this with confidence because there was a newly installed disabled toilet just next to it.) There was a Post Office sign, but otherwise no clue that this was anything more than a little back room.

In the main body of the church there was a trestled stall selling bits and pieces on behalf of the local hospice. And a kettle. "Our big worry," said the lady, "is that people will get out of the habit of coming here."

In a cottage just across the lane, I spoke to a church warden, Neil Jones, who was one of the prime movers of the scheme. A vaguely chaotic-looking self-employed printer — originally from Sheffield — who had lived in the cottage for 35 years and had previously been employed as a teacher, he seemed a bit depressed by the whole business. "I think it was three years ago the old place closed," he explained, "and the Post Office let it be known that they'd be willing to keep it in the village if someone was willing to take it on. So Annette Reed, who was our vicar then — she's now moved on — said, why don't we put it in church?

"We'd already had some plans passed by the diocese which divided the vestry into two, with a toilet on one side and a small room on the other, because we'd been wanting to make the church a more useful building. But the post office would give us a reason for people to go there during the week. So Annette and I looked at each other and said why not?

"Unfortunately, we'd just cleaned out the church fund repairing the church clock, but we managed to raise the money through grants, and, most importantly, we found someone to run it: a lady who was already running a post office in the next village. So it's been up and running for several years now."

Was it working well? "Two answers: yes and no. We had two good years, when on a good day maybe 30 people would come, and on a bad day 20. We got an ISDN line, because you've got to be online, so that people can draw out money, for example, and they can use Connect, which is the county council's outreach programme. We'd started to sell the *Atherstone Herald*. We always served tea and coffee whenever the post office was open — it was only two days a week — so there were always people around. We sold bread from a local bakery. Things were really beginning to move.

312

"But the bread was from an independent family bakery, and the son who was doing the baking became ill, and they stopped baking. So that cut off one of our strings, which was a bit of a blow. And now the lady who was doing the post office has been ill, so now that's teetering. She's been off for nine weeks, and we're not sure what we can do next. She didn't earn any extra money from it, you see, because she had to close her other post office in order to come here. But she's a local character, she's lived in the area all her life, and she wants to support the community. And she has. But now she can't do it. She can't hire anyone in, so if she doesn't do it, it doesn't get done. So the future's dependent on her health at the moment, and right now it's not looking so good.

"But, before that, it was working really well. I hope we get it back, because I really can't express how much less life you get in the village when it's closed. It's not that it's an unfriendly village: it's actually very friendly. But to be a community you need to meet, and for anyone who doesn't have children of primary-school age and isn't a big pub-goer, there's nowhere to meet. Before, when the shop was there, there was always somebody coming and going, and people would walk over there and get their newspaper and get their bottle of milk or whatever they wanted, and I would go two or three times in a week and say hello to five people each time I went. And the moment the shop shut, these movements, these little journeys around the village, ceased to happen, and it became noticeably quieter. I would place a shop much higher on a list of necessities for a village than it's generally put, because of this kind of random movement of people that it generates, which in turn leads to random interaction. That's really why we tried to step in with the church: we wanted to give people a reason to come out of their front doors at least occasionally.

"But, as I said, it all comes down to individuals. It's no good having a post office if you haven't got someone to run it."

In Edington, a medium-sized Wiltshire village that was voted Calor Village of the Year for England in 1999, I spent a morning looking round and talking to one of the prime architects of that triumph, an ex-sailor (and incomer) called David Perkins. There was clearly still a lot going for the place, including a famous annual music festival in the church. But David seemed no less depressed about things than Neil Jones had — as if a brief golden age in his village was already coming to an end.

It had started, paradoxically, when the school closed in 1996. "The village was thrashing around trying to find some way of keeping the premises available to the village. Eventually we formed a charity called Edington Villagers Limited — we had 44 villagers signed up to it. Then we rented the school premises from the county council and we set up a nursery school. My wife is a teacher, and the school happens to be right next door to us, so we ended up running it."

It thrived, as did the village. In due course, the Village of the Year title was mentioned. "That was great. Lots of people got involved, and we did wonderful things, trying to win it. We built a skateboard ramp, we renovated all the equipment in the park, we got things going around the village." He paused and looked wistful.

"Everything worked well up until about two years ago, but since then, because of government policies and things, schools have been sucking in all the four-year-olds and a lot of three-year-olds as well. So the nursery started losing money hand over fist. We pulled the plug while we still had money to pay all our bills.

"So now there's no nursery, and the primary-school children get bussed to the next village along, Bratton. It's only 3 miles away, but it does make a huge difference. In my perception, the school was fundamental to the village; in some ways it drew things together. The nursery managed to keep some of that going, but now that's gone it's rather knocked the stuffing out of the village again.

"It is still a good social mix, and the people do get on well together, and those that get involved all put what they can into village life. But over the past few years all the old gaffers who used to tell the old stories have been fading away, and you don't really have the family structure any more. You no longer have the parents with children with grandparents in the village who they can rely on to help look after the children when they go out to work, and that's the structure that is missing. We found that in running the nursery school — that there are so many young parents around who don't have immediate contact with their parents, that my wife was a sort of surrogate mother to the young parents because they were coming in for advice on childcare that, in previous times, they would have gone to their parents for. It's because people move around, I suppose. But that's why it was important to have a school.

"There's a saying — I think it's African — that it takes a whole village to bring up a child. That certainly used to be the case: everybody took an interest and if little Johnny stood out of line, then somebody would tell Dad and Dad would give him a clip round the ear when he got home. Nowadays, if a child steps out of line and a parent gets told, the parent will take the child's part. Kids know it, and what can you do? But that is the attitude of parents nowadays, and that, to my mind, is why a lot of it's falling apart. As with all these things, you're never very far from it all slipping away."

# CHAPTER
# TWENTY-THREE

# In the blood

In Barton, Lancashire, a group of what looked like anti-terrorist police in chemical and biological warfare protective suits were standing around on a triangle of land just below the point where the busy main street crossed a busy railway. They turned out to be dairy workers: about half a dozen of them, taking a mid-morning fag-and-coffee break. The cluster of sheds and farm buildings around them was the premises of J. J. Sandham, an old family business famous — in cheese circles — for its traditional Lancashire cheeses.

They seemed oblivious to the silliness of their uniform: white wellies, white overalls and white peaked caps over blue plastic bonnets. Or, at least, they were used to it.

"You've got to have your hair covered — everyone does," said one of them — a large man with a goatee beard. "There's so many strict guidelines they give you these days. We're always being inspected — everything from milk going in to cheese going out. Makes a big difference, when you've got a small workforce."

Constant, deafening interruptions from passing trains and lorries made coherent conversation difficult, but they seemed a happy bunch. Most lived outside the village but within a 10-mile radius of it. Two were staying temporarily in a large brick house on the edge of the site. They had recently arrived from Poland and didn't speak much English.

The longest-serving member of the group, Chris, had worked there for 10 years — although, as he said, "It doesn't seem that long ago since I first started." The most senior was Paul, the "cheese-maker", who had arrived recently from a rival dairy that had closed but had none the less taught many of those present. "Actually," he said, "most of the lads that makes cheese round here all learnt from the same people, you know, if you trace it back."

The rest were younger men — in their twenties — who seemed to see it as an OK kind of occupation until something better turned up. "I only came here for a gap between jobs," said one. "Trouble is, I'm still here."

Was it unpleasant work? "It's OK," said another of the young men. "Not 'specially skilled, but it's hard graft. Some of the cheeses are 20 kilos plus. A lot of the younger lads, who're used to computing and stuff, they can't stick it, sweating over vats all day. So some of them don't last long."

"It's a notoriously high staff turnover in this business," said Chris.

"Aye," said the young man. "One a day normally."

Everyone laughed.

"Trouble is, pay's not so good," said the first young man. "It's not terrible, but it's not premium wages, if you know what I mean. Not for the work you do. Just average."

"Still," said Chris, "as long as you've got money to pay bills, that keeps everybody happy. Plus you get all the cheese you can eat . . ." He paused. "If you pay for it."

"It's a good cheese though," added Paul. "One of the best."

He was on the point of saying more, but a huge train thundered past for the best part of a minute and, immediately afterwards, a small man in a white gown and what looked like a synthetic panama hat emerged from the shed behind us.

"Ah," said Chris. "Here's boss man. He knows a lot more about it than we do." And they went back to work.

Boss man was Chris Sandham, an energetic, pale-haired 45-year-old with calm grey eyes and an infectious passion for Lancashire cheese. He was of the third generation of his family to make the stuff on this little wedge of land. His great-grandfather built the house, in 1894, and his grandfather started making cheese in it in 1929. He himself had started work at the dairy a few days after leaving school and had taken over from his father in 1995; and although his own son, Thomas, was only one, Chris was already worrying about how to make the business a viable proposition for the next generation.

He invited me into his office — a little square structure cluttered with paperwork and framed award certificates — and, rocking back and forward on his chair, told me the story of J. J. Sandham traditional Lancashire cheese.

"We are a small firm. We're only producing 5,000 litres of milk a day, which may sound a lot to you but it's not, believe me. Some of these bigger lads will spill more milk on the floor in a day than we use. So we can never, ever compete on price because some of these places are making 100 tons of cheese a day. We're making 3 tons a week and we're bloody busy.

"It's always been a right family affair. Dad and Grandad would make the cheese and Mum would get the cheesecloth and sew the strings in round the top. They had no refrigeration when my grandad started — they'd just stack the cheese in the house, two deep on either side of the stairs, all the way up, with a little pathway in the middle. People would come to the house and they'd come with a jam jar and say, 'I've come for some cream,' and my mother or my grandmother just used to ladle cream and they'd pay half a crown. My grandmother used to sell a bit of cheese down at the canal to the passing barges, and Mum made butter outside in that lean-to, on a wooden table with a butter churn. She had the butter pats and she'd just make it and throw salt in and no hairnet and no apron and no washed-down walls with stainless equipment. It's just a different world, isn't it?

"Of course, even when we built the storeroom, we didn't have refrigeration for a long time — all you did was you opened the windows and got a bit of air flowing through. So you used to get flies would land and bluebottles would lay their eggs, and there was this old farmer across the road — he used to come and do a bit of work part time for us. He was a big man — his legs were so big they used to have to split his wellies down the back. Well, his job was to smear the cheese with butter, and he actually used to lick it off his hands as he was doing it . . .

"And I remember in the 1960s Dad used to go round with his little lorry and pick up milk from all the little farms, and then when he got back they'd just slide a window of the dairy open and they just used to pour the milk straight from the milk churns down a chute into the vat. Nowadays no milk company will collect milk unless it's refrigerated. But the odd thing is: we are so hygienic, we're so stringent with everything we do, but we have more outbreaks of food poisoning than we ever had."

His narrative was interrupted every few minutes by someone poking their head round the door with a query or bill or delivery. ("Just let me sort this lady out with some cheese . . ."; "I'll just pay this chap . . ."; "More green string? I'll do that in a minute . . ."; "Has anyone seen my keys? . . ."; "Why does everyone disappear when that guy comes? . . ."; "Fifty-six quid? That hurts, that does . . ."; "I still can't find my keys . . .") But each time we were left in peace he would pick up his narrative exactly where he had left off. It was almost as if he were reciting a tried-and-tested version of events — the family story, if you like.

"When my grandfather started," he continued, "he was better at producing cheese than selling it. He ended

321

up digging a hole in a field and burying a lot of it — he didn't want to sell it cheap and undervalue it. It's probably still down there. So it wasn't an easy business even then. And 13 or 14 years ago, when several clients went bust and my dad had had a heart attack, there were some very lean times for us then as well. So I'm very aware that you have to adapt: the minute you stand still, you go backwards. But at the same time this is the same business that my father and grandfather ran, and we make the same traditional Lancashire cheese. That's the point of it. We pasteurise our milk, we use a vegetarian rennet and instead of coating the cheese in butter or margarine, we coat them in wax. And we do, reluctantly, make a few special variations for the supermarkets. But apart from that, we use the same recipes, we use the same amount of salt — we do it exactly the same, we handle the curds by hand, it's not automated at all, and so we do everything as near as we can to what we were doing 77 years ago. I really am still quite passionate about it, which is a bit sad really."

He showed me proudly round various spotless sheds, some containing giant stainless-steel vats and others stacked with shelf after shelf of waxed round cheeses. We bumped into a couple of workers — both cleaning things — but the rest seemed to have vanished into the gaps between the buildings. "You'd never even try to build a dairy on a plot like this if you were starting out today," said Chris. "It wouldn't be allowed. But because we've been here all these years we're allowed to get away with it. We just have to make and mend.

"But there are so many regulations these days — that's the big change. Years ago we used to sell our whey to the pig farmer across the road. Now we have to pay to have it taken away. And we're always being inspected. Sometimes it does gall me a bit when I've been making the product and I know what's right for the product and I know what practices are best to maintain and attain a top-quality product, and it does sometimes get my goat when someone comes out of university and they've never done, I won't say a day's graft because that's not fair, but they've never worked in the industry. They've been around it and they start saying, well, this is how we should do it. Why does ticking the piece of paper and initialling who's cleaned what make me a better and more efficient firm? How does that make my product better?"

We found ourselves back in his office, where, during another interruption, I counted 21 different awards on the walls, studied the labels on the files near the door ("Analysis reports and certificates", "Accident reports", "Temperature sheets", "Customer complaints", "Scale verification records", etc) and wondered whether a man with a perfect work-life balance would have quite so many packets of Cup-a-Soup lying around. As soon as the visitor departed (saying "Thanks, Chris, you're a superstar"), he resumed his reflections on the changing face of cheese-making.

"We went to the pasteurising in the 1970s because it was being forced upon us. Also, we've never produced any of our own milk. When you're producing your own milk, you know how clean your milking operation is, how clean the teats on the cows are, but when you're buying it in from another source, you don't know. So we're not averse to progress — we just believe in the value of tradition. The thing about a family business is that you learn things that can't be taught. Just tiny things, like walking into the dairy and you think, it's a little bit cool in here, or you can walk in and you can smell whether the milk's got a high cream content. You can just sense it. And that's why I think it's important that we keep making cheese in the same traditional way — so that that knowledge isn't wasted . . ."

He paused suddenly, and, for a moment, all the energy seemed to have drained from him. Then he seemed to shake himself, and the flood of words resumed. "But the business has changed so much. The world has changed so much. Look at the farms — nearly all the smaller ones have gone under, or stopped being farms.

"But the other big change, of course, has been the supermarkets. Go up any high street and you'll see there are no food shops at all, and all the market halls have closed. So we've had to focus our attention on the supermarkets, and that's meant branching out from just making the traditional cheese that we've always made. So now we're making blocks, we're making 11 kilos, we're making 6 kilos, we're making 1 kilo, we're making cheeses with garlic, with sage, we're doing a smoked cheese . . . My grandfather would be spinning in his grave at some of the things we're doing now — even though we're still doing it to all the old recipes.

"But of course you don't want to put all your eggs in one basket either. We did have one supermarket that liked this garlic cheese we make now so much that they wanted it for their own brand on a national listing. Well, we just couldn't do it. Even if we got rid of all our other customers, we couldn't meet that demand. And, anyway, it would have been short-sighted, because what happens a few years down the line when they turn round and say, 'Chris, can you just tweak 5 per cent off the price?'

"So, we try to spread it all round. And we try not to stray too far from what we do best, which is making the traditional Lancashire. But it's a difficult climate — it is for all food-producers. We are paying less for our food now than we were 15 years ago, and how can that be? People are being forced into cutting corners and people are working for nothing, and I can't believe that that's the right way of going about it. But what can you do? What can you do about the world changing?

"All I know is that my dad was a good, honest, proud, decent chap, and so I think it's been instilled into me that you just work to the best of your abilities and try and make a good fist of everything you do."

We wandered out to the front and gazed over the roaring A6 to the village on the far side. "My great-grandfather built this house, my grandfather was born here, my father was born here and I was born here. I went to school in Barton. It's home — it's where your friends are, it's where your family are and I just feel as though this is where my roots are and this is where I should stay. I still play a bit of cricket on a

Wednesday evening through the summer — I'm absolutely crap, but I've got strong arms from making cheese, so I can throw a ball further than anyone else and they put me on the long boundary. But, having said that, it's not the village it was. When I was a lad it was still a nice family environment — even if your mum and dad were working, your grandparents were here to look after you. People didn't move away, you were born in the village and you worked in the village and you lived in the village — that sort of thing. Back then I knew who lived in every house in Barton. Now I haven't a clue. We have people live across the road and they've been in 24 years and I bet I've only spoken to them on four or five occasions. It's changed, hasn't it? We close our door and we have our own world within our four walls.

"I do sometimes wish," he added, "that I'd worked harder at university and got into a job where I could get weekends off, because it's a seven-day industry. You can't turn the cows off at weekend, and I think last year was my first Christmas Day off work since 1976. But then that's farming, isn't it?

"Still, it's looked after our family for all these years. And although people say the house must be worth a lot, how can you ever sell it? How can I sell it when it's four generations now — five, now we've got Thomas?"

He looked up at the house. "My dad would have been so proud the Sandham name has carried on," he said, dreamily. "And the business too," he added. "My dad died five years ago, but my mum had said, your dad is so proud of the way you've turned it round . . .

That's payment in itself: to hear your dad's proud of what you're doing."

The English countryside is full of such hard-working sons — not just cheese-makers but farmers, craftsmen, huntsmen, fishermen, you name it — all doing their best to be worthy of a late father's approval by keeping his craft going. From a certain sophisticated, metropolitan perspective, they might all be considered slightly pathetic: little boys who never quite dared to escape the parental shadow, and who kid themselves, as most of us do, that the happiness they remember from their childhood is attributable to the world having been a better place rather than the fact that they were children at the time. But such a view would — like most sophisticated, metropolitan sneers — miss the point. This is how much of England's culture evolved: through the passing down of knowledge, and values, from parent to child. Rural England's story is, in a sense, the story of endless variations on this process. And if latching on to the wisdom of previous generations suddenly feels a bit inappropriate in today's fast-changing world, well, perhaps it is. But in my experience people who do keep family concerns going tend to be among the most innovative countryside-dwellers I have met.

A few days after visiting Barton I spent a long time lost among the damp hills of Herefordshire, in a network of steep lanes where each thick hedge seemed to conceal a field overflowing with fruit trees. I could smell it, even from the car: not the fruit, most of which

327

had been gathered in by then, but a general ripeness in the air — a rich, rotting aroma of vegetal abundance.

Every now and then a roadside gap would reveal a thrilling panorama of lush, autumnal hills beyond, with a hint of mist playing over the lower fields and a brown smudge on the horizon that might have been Ledbury but might equally — for all I knew — have been Hereford or, conceivably, Ross-on-Wye. I'm not sure that any of those towns could be described as buzzing, but there seemed, that morning, to be something indescribably romantic about whichever hilltop town was caught in sunlight in the golden distance. I suppose it was that rare sense — mentioned before — of being back in an age when real distance existed, and metropolitan sophistications were found in exotic rural dreams rather than rural reality.

The gaps quickly closed. The tangled lanes kept me in their grip. In due course I reached Putley, which struck me as less like a village in the conventional sense than a scattered series of grubby signs and muddy gateways, most indicating the unseen presence of farms or orchards. There are, I believe, six different orchards in and around Putley. In one of them, through a relatively smart gate on the edge of the village, I found a man called Norman Stanier, whose family had run the orchard in question for generations. He was a short, wide, fit-looking man in his fifties, with close-cropped hair and the kind of clear, steady, narrow-eyed gaze that for some reason I always associate with PE teachers and outdoor-activities instructors. It turned out that he had once been both of these things, after leaving Putley in his late teens. Then, when his parents grew too old to manage the orchard themselves, he came back, realising, as rural sons often do, that he couldn't bear to see the family land taken over by strangers. That was 14 years ago, and he had no intention of leaving again.

"We didn't come back lightly," he told me as he showed me round the orchard's acreage one muggy morning. "I remember well discussing it on New Year's Eve 1990. But in the end we felt it was the right thing to do. I'd worked on the orchard as a child and a teenager. It had always been there. My parents had run it, my grandfather used to own it before, and our ancestors had been in the village for hundreds of years. If we hadn't taken it on, the farm would have died."

Norman had a family by then: a wife, Ann, whom he met while working as an Outward Bound instructor in Devon, and two sons. They built a house — "as green as we could: timber frame, with a brick skin stuffed with recycled newsprint" — and gradually took over the running of the orchard.

It wasn't easy: growing things never is. But his parents were there to advise (his mother still is), and, fruitwise, the orchard continued to thrive. The problem was making it work as a business. The art of growing apples hasn't changed much over the centuries, but the art of selling them has. "In my parents' time, you could sell fairly easily to the local wholesale markets, but that's changed fairly drastically because of the supermarkets. Nowadays the supermarkets buy in bulk from whoever can give them exactly what they want, when they want it, for the lowest-possible price."

You'll have heard similar laments a thousand times. Supermarkets may provide a ready outlet for farmers and growers, but their vastness makes for a wildly unequal relationship. The small producers don't have a leg to stand on in negotiations, and even winning a big contract as a supplier tends to be a route not to riches but to a future of fear and dependence. But from the Staniers' point of view, the problem was also an opportunity, which jogged them into creating what is now a highly successful scheme: "crop-sharing".

"It's simple, really," said Norman. "People — ordinary people — pay about £300 for an annual subscription. In return they get two 30 lb boxes of eating apples, two 30 lb boxes of cooking apples, a couple of dozen bottles of cider and apple juice, and an organic box of pears, jams, chutneys and jellies. It's not as cheap as buying apples from the supermarket, but you get something completely different for your money.

"In supermarkets, you can buy apples all the year round. They're just a commodity. But a significant number of people don't want to shop like that any more. They want to know where their food came from. Twenty years ago, there wouldn't have been that interest, but now it's important to people.

"So the crop-sharers get much more than the apples and things. They also get to spend four weekends a year at the orchard, one in each season, and each time we'll organise activities — wassailing, cider-tasting, a dance, a walk, a talk, a craft demonstration — and they'll get to know each other and the orchard.

"We started off with about 15 crop-sharers, and now we have around 50. Most of them come from towns, or at least from less rural parts of the country. So for them it's a way of reconnecting with nature. People love to reconnect with the seasons — to eat fruit that they've seen blossom. And nothing's more seasonal than an orchard."

It was, in a sense, a phenomenon that I'd encountered several times before, in farm parks and visitor centres around the country: agriculture as entertainment, I suppose you'd call it, or agriculture as education. But the crop-sharing at Dragon Orchard seemed to go a little deeper than that. "It's called Community Supported Agriculture [CSA]. It's been going for years — there are hundreds of projects around the world." Not many are in Britain, but this is changing. Campaigning organisations such as the Soil Association have been supporting CSA through their "Cultivating Communities" project, believing that (to quote the Dragon Orchard website) "reconnecting consumers with producers may be the single most important strategy for breaking away from industrial agriculture and moving towards more sustainable farming".

"What makes the difference is what the crop-sharers put in," said Norman as we paced through the long, damp grass. "We started the crop-sharing out of necessity, but it's taken on a life of its own. I suppose it came naturally to us, having managed outdoor centres and being used to leading people and explaining ideas and so forth. But it's amazing what the crop-sharers themselves have brought to it. We've become a really close community. Look —" and we turned into a section of orchard with a huge, thick, curved wall in the middle of one side. "We created this shelter with straw bales in the spring and now it's all plastered and lime-washed. It was a group project. We're going to put a wooden bench in it next.

"People don't just want to get fruit from us. They want to contribute. A lot of them sponsor trees — about 70 trees out of 200 are sponsored. Look, this little corner is called Sheila's Grove: the crop-sharers sponsored the trees in memory of someone's mother who died. Then there's the poetry trail, which a local poet set up. You'll see the wooden posts as we go round. And one of our sharers wants to make a traditional wooden apple press. They're full of ideas. In fact, next time they come I'm hoping we can brainstorm about what we should do next. I'm going to make an 'ideas wall' for people to put suggestions on."

In a big barn near by, Ann Stanier was busily packing fruit and jams into about a dozen boxes. "I've got to get these done this morning, because we're going down to London later and we can drop them off. Crop-sharers are meant to come and collect their crop, but there's no point their making a special journey if we're going past anyway." Both of their sons live in London and show, as yet, little sign of wanting to continue the family business. But that may change when the time comes, many years hence. Ann looked stressed, but in a cheerful, mustn't-lose-count-of-how-many-pears-I've-packed sort of way. "It is hard work," she admitted. "In fact, it never stops. But it's very satisfying."

I don't think the Staniers can have been getting very rich out of this. Norman still found it necessary to supplement their income with a side-business in which he used his climbing skills to provide "roped access" for maintenance work for inaccessibly high buildings around the country. But they seemed to feel that their project had enriched them spiritually.

"What we've found," said Norman, "is that people really like to be connected with a piece of the countryside. They don't just want to visit it: they want to be involved. In a lot of ways, for most people, the countryside really isn't very accessible at all. You can walk across it on footpaths, but you never actually get to know the land or the people who work on it."

He was right. I'd been travelling in Herefordshire for a while, not just in the Putley region but further north, where the fields glistened with sinister, slinky-like chains of polytunnel frames, and local traditionalists battled against faceless agricultural businesses to restrict their spread. I could see that such innovations might be necessary; perhaps even desirable, given that food needs to be grown and rural economies need to be sustained. But they neither looked nor felt natural: the fields around a village such as Marden, say, look as though they have been overrun by aliens from outer space.

Here in Dragon Orchard, however, with birds chattering through wet leaves and a pair of big Kune

Kune pigs munching peacefully in a muddy enclosure not far away, it felt altogether more natural — more like England. "It's really not very different from how it was when I was growing up," said Norman as we trudged around.

There were about 22 acres of orchard in all, divided into half a dozen sections. "This one's 35 years old," explained Norman, "and this one was planted in 1996. This one's for juice or for selling to the local farmers. This one belongs to the crop-sharers. And that one's just for cider. The cider boom's been good for the whole of Herefordshire.

"We're still quite traditional in our methods, because we're relatively small. So we grade and pack by hand, and of course the pruning's still all by hand. I suppose the other big difference is that when I was a boy we employed two people to work here, but now we do it all ourselves. But that's the story right across agriculture.

"The future? Good and bad. The good bit is that I think there's still a lot more potential in the crop-sharing side of things: a lot more diversification to be done — walks and talks and so on. On the bad side, climate change seems to be causing some serious problems with the weather. We hardly get any frost any more — just rain. We've lost a dreadfully large number of trees because it's all got waterlogged, and look at all this grass — it shouldn't be like this, but it never stops growing. And the lengthening of the growing season is very, very worrying. I'm afraid we'll have to do something else eventually."

I expected him to look worried as he said this, but he didn't. It was almost as though he knew that, even if the details changed, the combination of old land and new thinking would continue to sustain his family for a good while yet.

"I love it here. I love the work: I love to chat to people, and to explore new ideas with them. I'm happy we've been able to keep the farm and the way of life going. If we hadn't come back, that would have been the end of it."

He turned away and looked back at the orchard. "It's not just the people, it's the place . . . it's where we belong. The village is friendly, even though it's scattered. Not many people work on the land, but a lot work from home. It's not sexy, not like the Cotswolds. It's too far away from anywhere. I suppose you could say it's boring. But it's where I come from. It's home."

# CHAPTER
# TWENTY-FOUR

# The hunter

I stood on a wet brown Cumbrian fell and watched the Blencathra Foxhounds seethe through the bracken in pursuit of a man-laid scent. They looked as happy as a pack of fast-moving animals reasonably can.

It had rained for much of the morning, and sunlight gleamed on the damp wilderness known locally as "back o' Skiddaw". But it was the sight of the undulating pack of hounds that thrilled me: their pale backs surfacing and vanishing in the sea of wet vegetation as if they were porpoises, flowing down gulleys and bounding up steep boulder-fields, their body language vibrant with purpose, their positions relative to one another changing constantly, with the same obvious yet impossibly complicated logic that one senses in the movements of a football match.

A sandy-whiskered huntsman strode behind and among them in stout boots, directing the flow with occasional calls on his horn and, it seemed, the odd word and gesture. He wore a brown jacket — apparently red was considered too provocative — and an olive-green cap whose long brown peak gave a helpful sense — even from a distance — of the direction of his gaze.

I stood on the same spot for I don't know how long, watching the other side of the valley. (The great thing about following a hunt on the fells — rather than among the fenced and hedged enclosures of the flat south — is that you can watch the pack at work over really quite large distances.) Sometimes the hounds moved in straight, confident thrusts; sometimes they seemed to lose the scent and began to swirl chaotically; sometimes a ring on the huntsman's horn summoned them back to him. I could see what people mean when they talk about a "golden thread" connecting the huntsman to his hounds.

There were no horses. There were, however, 50 or more hunt-followers below us, strung in little groups along a mile or so of the north bank of the river Caldew: some on the boggy grass but most on the rough track that follows the river's curves. Many had dogs of their own. It was hard to be certain where the followers ended and the ordinary hikers began, although a good rule of thumb was that anyone wearing brightly coloured hi-tech fabrics was a hiker, whereas the hunt-followers were mainly in greens and browns, and showed a marked preference for flat caps, waxed jackets and corduroy trousers. Several wore tweed jackets and some wore ties as well. The master of the hunt, a big, firm-jawed man called Michael Thompson, wore a red waistcoat beneath his tweed jacket. "We dress appropriately for the conditions," he told me. "But we want to uphold our traditions as well."

The followers seemed to be pursuing a wide range of agendas and timetables, with some heading homewards while others were still arriving. Several had initially stayed at home because of the weather. Everyone I spoke to said that they were enjoying the day, and, indeed, there was a palpable air of pleasure in the valley. This was how communities feel when they come out to do something together: chatting among themselves, greeting and waving and catching up with close and distant friends; enjoying being out in the countryside. It was like a quiet village fair, stretched out in a long, thin line.

But the odd thing was that, although everyone seemed happy, whenever I asked about the effects of the ban on hunting mammals with dogs, the answers suggested that some appalling atrocity had been committed. "The final nail in the coffin" was mentioned more than once, the coffin apparently being occupied by rural life. "It's a bloody disgrace," spluttered a small (and previously good-humoured) man in a flat cap and glasses. "Absolutely shameful."

I found this a bit perplexing. Yes, I could see that it might be mildly galling that there was no fox to watch — no mysterious other who could be defeated only by the combined cunning of all involved. But it was still a hunt; they were still enjoying a day in the hills, communing with the landscape and with one another; there were still hounds to watch; and there was at least the possibility that they might see a fox. Did it really matter so much that there was to be no killing?

Perhaps I thought like that because I was an outsider; as another follower put it, "It all comes down to people who don't understand the country telling us how to run our lives. We just want to carry on living like we've always done."

To call this a familiar refrain would be an understatement. People had been saying such things to me wherever I went: everything was fine until the outsiders came . . . If you expressed such xenophobia in London, you would be pilloried as a racist. And, indeed, there were obvious racist overtones to a note issued in 2007 by a local group calling itself the Popular Liberation Army of Westmorland, which threatened to use arson and other criminal means to end "the occupation of Westmorland by incomers, holiday-home owners and encroaching leechlike scum of that ilk". Similar language was used around the same time in similar threats issued by the Cornish National Liberation Army, who proposed to burn the homes and cars of "English incomers". Obviously, not all natives of Cumbria or Cornwall sympathise with these views, not least because both counties would face destitution without tourism. None the less, it would be wilfully blind to pretend that such sentiments are not widespread and bitter in many parts of rural England; or, indeed, that "living like we've always done" does not, in most rural places, embrace habitual hostility towards outsiders. Academics call this "rural xenophobia"; it has been around for centuries, although it was traditionally directed at inhabitants of other villages and counties rather than migrants from towns. It isn't an attractive trait. Its persistence suggests there are still many people in England whose sense of identity is tightly tied to a sense of place, but perhaps also that that sense of identity is now so insecure that it easily feels threatened.

"The trouble is," said a tight-jawed, well-bred man from Bassenthwaite with a neatly pressed jacket and tie and an oddly resentful smile, "people come in from the outside, because they like what we have here. And then once they're living here they want to change everything."

Yes, I said politely, as I generally do on encountering such sentiments; yes, I know. Then, as an afterthought: "So which part of Cumbria do you come from?"

"What, originally? We came up from London ten years ago."

Barry Todhunter, the sandy-whiskered huntsman mentioned earlier, was rather more local than that. He lived a mile or so to the south, in Threlkeld — which is well known to lovers of the Lake District as lying at the foot of Blencathra, the great triple-headed fell also known as Saddleback. His bungalow must be a good half-mile from the pretty holiday cottages and retirement homes of the village centre, up a steep track beyond what used to be the council houses. But you could hardly say that he was peripheral to village life: he was even depicted — along with a previous huntsman and several hounds — on the sign of one of the village's two pubs, the Salutation Inn.

340

The bungalow went with his job, huntsman of the Blencathra Foxhounds, which he had held for more than 25 years. For five years before that, as the hunt's whipper-in, he rented even humbler accommodation in the same village. Yet he still thought of himself as, in some ways, an incomer. His birthplace was 10 miles away, on the north side of Blencathra, in Caldbeck, where the celebrated huntsman John Peel (with his coat so grey) used to live. "I have," he told me, "lost quite a lot of touch with my roots."

There was nothing old-fashioned about his manner: he was an affable, ordinary sort of bloke of fifty-something, sensibly dressed in an ageing fleece and solid, rubber-soled shoes, with short, greying hair, rimless glasses, and sideburns curved, curiously, in the shape of a Nike "swoosh" logo. But his childhood was steeped in rural tradition. His father was a farmer, and most of his fellow villagers were employed in agriculture in one form or another. He grew up in the 1960s: "an age of innocence. There wasn't a lot of money around: there were no farm subsidies or money from Europe. What a family lived on was what you produced. We owned a few pigs, and used to help out milking a few cows, and we had a few fell sheep — their fleeces helped pay the rent. So we all needed to help. It was the same with most of the lads round the area: before you went to school you did your jobs, and then when you came home from school you'd change out of uniform, feed the calves, the hens, mucking the barns out — all that. Homework came somewhere just before bed. At hay-timing we couldn't wait to get home from school to help with the hay bales. It was a different world." About the most exciting thing that could happen was to cadge a lift from someone's father to go to Wigton on Tuesday auction day. "And every other Saturday me mum would take me hunting — but the bargain was that on the Sunday I had to help at home: dosing sheep, marking lambs, moving cattle.

"There wasn't the comforts we have now. But you made more of what surrounded you. You played in the beck, you were climbing trees, you were rabbiting with your terrier. And you valued the company of your family and friends.

"But," he added sadly, "there's only a handful of the lads I was at school with that I still know. You see, I left home when I was 15 . . ."

His first job was as a whipper-in down in Lunesdale, near Sedbergh — about an hour's drive to the south these days, just beyond the bottom rather than the top edge of the Lake District. He had no qualifications and no experience of life beyond Caldbeck. It was, he said, "a bit of a culture shock — like going to work in France. The type of farming, the type of attitudes, were quite different to what I was used to." It was quite a relief when, after two years, "the whipper-in's job came vacant back here".

He had lived in Threlkeld ever since; married a Threlkeld girl (descended, as it happens, from John Peel, who eloped to Gretna Green and sired 13 children); raised two children in Threlkeld — both of whom would like to buy homes in the village, he said, but neither of whom could afford to do so. ("You saw they're building some new houses as you turn into the village? They're £275,000 — way beyond what they could afford.") "Most people think I'm Threlkeld born and bred," he said. "But I'm not." What he is, however, is a hunter born and bred. In fact, his life would be unimaginable without fox-hunting — and not just because of his name ("todd" means "fox" in Middle English).

People who consider fox-hunting to be the exclusive preserve of horse-owning toffs would do well to consider Mr Todhunter. He doesn't, for a start, own a horse. Nor is he a toff. A calm, stocky man, with a wide jaw, thoughtful eyes and a cunning grin, he spoke with a husky Cumbrian accent that tended, he said, to be much broader when he was in Cumbrian company. He earned, as he put it, "piss-poor wages — just a standard agricultural labourer's wage. I shouldn't think there's anyone in Threlkeld paid less than me."

His work involved everything from organising hunts, with all the logistical and diplomatic complications that implies, to collecting fallen stock, liaising with masters, farmers and visitors, looking after every aspect of the wellbeing of his principal work colleagues — a pack of around three dozen exuberant foxhounds who live in a kennel complex a bit further up the fellside — and, most importantly of all, managing the pack (and everything else) on hunt days. This last, in particular, is highly skilled work: the kind of craft that is passed down rather than learnt from textbooks. "It's instinct mostly. It's a gift," he said. "You've either got it or you don't: it's a dog sense — it can't be taught. You can feel the thread running between you, although you can only pull it so far before it snaps. I know what they think, they know what I think. If I'm tense, they're tense; if I'm calm, they're calm, and if I'm excited, they're excited. But if you asked me to explain how I do it, I just couldn't tell you."

Like an artist, he earns his money not just for the hours he puts in but also for the accumulated wisdom of a lifetime. If he ever lost his job, however, he would be homeless and carless as well as jobless. "Any young person thinking of starting this would have to be very brave," he said. "Especially if they had the chance to do something else instead."

His right arm was in plaster when I met him. "How'd it happen? About 200 people have asked me how'd it happen. I tell 'em: if accidents were complicated, they wouldn't happen. No, it were just a simple thing. I slipped in bracken, put my hand down to break me fall, and there were a rock down there and I managed to land with me on top of it. So now I'm trying to do everything with one hand. One or two of the farmer lads have said, how can I help, but I say there isn't really much you can do, beyond getting a bucket and washing the floor, because anything else, by the time I've explained what needs doing, it'd be quicker to have done it myself. Anything else, with hounds . . . It isn't the same as just feeding sheep. If it isn't someone they know, they just won't respond." There was, of course, no question of taking time off sick.

Perhaps this was, at some level, a life of privilege. It didn't sound very comfortable to me. But the Blencathra Foxhounds, who have been based in Threlkeld for 180 years, have always prided themselves on their democratic credentials. "You can be down and out, out of work, or the Prince of Wales — there's no distinction," said Barry. Or, as an old song has it:

The bold pack of Blencathra is free alike to all,
The poor man from his cottage and the rich man
     from the hall,
All are welcome here to follow, no thoroughbred
     you'll need,
But manly strength and daring, the mountain
     chase to lead.

— the point being that, because of the steepness and unevenness of the Lakeland fells, there is no place for horses in hunting in these parts; which, for obvious reasons, makes the sport a bit less exclusive.

"It's very much part of village life," said Barry. "Most of the village gets involved. There's probably 50 at least will be out regular [following the hounds] and then you've got the holiday meets and all the times when the families bring the kids out and things. And I think there's about 15 or so locally on the hunt committee, which includes farmers, plumbers, a gardener, an electrician, a joiner, a mechanic, a postman. Threlkeld is one of few villages in Keswick area that still has a good village life, and hunting has a lot to do with that. We'll do our fundraising within the local area, so perhaps we'll have a function at the golf club, or we'll use the village hall, or use the cricket club for a meeting, or either of our pubs for our opening meet and a singsong. So we're helping these venues keep going — we're supporting the village as well as the village supporting us.

"For the opening meet, which alternates between the Horse & Farrier and the Salutation, I'll walk the hounds from kennels here down through the village, and there'll be people out in the gardens, taking pictures and cheering us on, and we walk to the pub car park, stand outside the pub, and the roar in the car park is just tangible. And then, since I've been huntsman I've always called by the school on the way to the fell and all the kids come out and say hello to the hounds. I think at one point somebody sent a letter or something, complaining about children being shown this barbaric . . . you know . . . claptrap. Anyway, the school governors said, to hell with it — the hounds have been coming to the village school for years, and there would only be the odd kid in that school that hasn't got some connection with the hunt — you know, a mate, or their father or mother hunts."

Since February 2005, of course, no one in Threlkeld has strictly speaking hunted, in the sense of going out with hounds with the explicit purpose of hunting down and killing a fox. Instead, people and hounds have followed an artificially laid scent (American fox urine, apparently), which interests the hounds enough to give all concerned a vigorous day's exercise but not, on the whole, enough to hold their attention if a real fox is

346

foolish enough to cross their path. The hunt remains on the right side of the law as long as Barry makes a genuine effort to prevent the hounds from chasing and killing such foxes, and as far as I am aware he does. None the less, around 20 foxes a year now die at the hands of the Blencathra Foxhounds, compared with about 100 before the ban.

It is, according to Barry, "a totally different thing. We've changed from being a full-ahead fox-catching pack of fellhounds to doing hound exercise line-hunting. The hounds aren't fooled, and a lot of people following aren't happy. But we're still hanging in there, and people are doing their best to support us."

He has been prominent for more than a decade in the nationwide campaign to save fox-hunting, and although he accepts that, as things are, "at least I can still be out on the fells with my hounds", he is a very long way from being reconciled to the current legislation. "I would never have dreamt — years ago, as a farmer's boy living in Caldbeck — I would never have dreamt it would ever come to this. It's a tragedy. Communities have been destroyed by this — it's an absolute tragedy."

This struck me as an overstatement. I know a lot of people feel strongly about such issues — let's not forget that, on 22 September 2002, 407,791 people from around rural Britain demonstrated in Westminster on the Liberty & Livelihood March. But not all of those marchers can have been specifically concerned with the right to hunt foxes, or they would have called it the Save Fox-hunting March, which they pointedly didn't.

And even if most of them did feel that the right to hunt foxes was more important than the fall-out from the foot-and-mouth and BSE crises and the general neglect and mismanagement of rural affairs by central government, that doesn't mean that any close-knit rural communities have been forced to become the slightest bit less close-knit as a result of hunts having to make do with hunting artificial scents. We were warned that up to 16,000 jobs would be lost if the ban went ahead, but so far there has been little sign of this — presumably because most hunts have found ways to remain active despite the ban. And while I have seen communities destroyed by the motor-car, and by the closure of local facilities, and by the collapse of local industries, I have yet to hear of one that has been destroyed by the curtailment, however tiresome, of a popular local pastime.

But Barry, once he was in full cry on the subject of "the ban", was as hard to restrain as a pack of errant hounds. "The Act is an arse as far as I'm concerned. It's full of ridiculous loopholes. For example: you're allowed to drive a fox with a full pack of hounds to an eagle or an eagle owl, if the eagle or eagle owl will kill the fox. Well, I spoke to some chaps in the Midlands who had an eagle owl, and what it does, it'll wallop on a fox and the talons go into the neck and semi-paralyse it, and then it commences to pick and tear at it. It can take 15 or 20 minutes to kill — instead of the hounds just going 'click'. Unfortunately, no one's interested in listening to what we say. Urban people and Labour MPs look upon rural people as rich, landowning,

Conservative toffs, and so they close their minds to our arguments."

To be fair, people on both sides of this "debate" have a tendency to close their minds to arguments, which was why I had tried to steer clear of it until this point. My own views, for what they are worth, include these:

(1) It's nonsense to cite the control of foxes as a reason for continuing fox-hunting. If fox-hunters wanted to eliminate the fox threat they wouldn't have a close season, which exists solely in order that the hunted species can replenish its numbers. In the past — for example, in the late 19th century — foxes have actually been imported from mainland Europe so that hunts would have something to hunt, while hunt-supporting landowners actively maintain landscape features — from copses and coverts to, in some cases, artificial earths — that encourage foxes. (Indeed, this fact is often cited as an argument in defence of hunting.) It would be easier and cheaper, although not necessarily nicer for the fox, to reduce fox numbers by shooting or poisoning rather than by hunting. Plain Fact No. 1: people hunt foxes because they enjoy it.

(2) It's nonsense to cite the welfare of foxes as a reason for abolishing fox-hunting. If it's fox numbers you're talking about — that is, the welfare of the fox population as a whole — then hunting has a negligible effect, and, in any case, what's wrong with the fox population as it is now? I've never heard it seriously suggested by either side that it would be better for the fox population to be either significantly larger or significantly smaller than its current size. As for the

quality of fox life — that is, the welfare of individual foxes — I refer you to Plain Fact No. 2: foxes live well and die horribly, and will continue to do so until they develop their own National Health Service. Fox-hunting just means that some less healthy foxes die from being abruptly ripped to pieces rather than from starvation or disease or bullet-wounds. None of these would be a pleasant death.

(3) The only coherent argument against fox-hunting is that it is immoral. I feel some sympathy for this argument, without being certain that it is right. I have spent much of my life surrounded by people who are involved in hunting — most of whom lead far more blameless lives than I do — and I think I understand some of the sport's attractions. What could be more innocently fulfilling than purposeful, vigorous and communal activity in the countryside, or more absorbing than close involvement with the landscape and with the thought processes of other species? Yet for me there is always a lingering suspicion that there is something unsporting — something un-English — about a large, baying mob ganging up on a single wild creature. And, if we're really honest, aren't the sport's good qualities all slightly tainted by that suspicion? However — and this brings me to Plain Fact No. 3 — it is not the state's business to legislate for the morality of its citizens. That's the real, unanswerable objection to the hunting ban. If the government wants to start banning recreations because they are immoral, why haven't they banned angling, or, better still, adultery — which also has obvious attractions but is tainted by its

tendency to cause suffering to living creatures? To which the obvious answer is that, if we wanted a government like that, we should vote for the Taliban.

I could go on for pages, but I won't. The rights and wrongs of the fox-hunting issue are, in a sense, irrelevant to the indisputable social fact that the sport exists and plays a central part in many rural lives. It has done for centuries. (By the way: don't believe those who tell you that fox-hunting as we know it only started in the late 18th century; there's ample evidence to show that fox-hunting with hounds has been widespread in England for 700 years or more.)

That's not to say that the fabric of English rural life would fall apart without fox-hunting. Of course it wouldn't. There are thousands of people whose lives do revolve around fox-hunting, but there have been millions of perfectly authentic rural lives in which fox-hunting has played no part whatsoever. A countryside without fox-hunting is only marginally more unthinkable than a countryside without morris dancing.

But maybe that is the point. Would it matter if morris dancing were banned? Of course not, or not to most of us. It is only the tiniest thread in the tapestry of rural tradition, just as fox-hunting is a slightly larger thread. No thread is indispensable. Yet in another sense it would matter: because each time you remove a thread from the tapestry, the fabric that remains grows thinner and greyer.

For Barry Todhunter, meanwhile, the idea of a rural world uncoloured by the traditions of fox-hunting is all but unthinkable, and he is determined to preserve them. "It never ceases to amaze me," he said, "how something so basic as the instinct to hunt animals should have survived — in this hi-tech world of the internet and busy roads and globalisation . . . To think that that's survived this long, and that the tradition of hunting with a pack of hounds has evolved through the generations and survived . . . That's amazing in itself; and it's to do with the tenacity of rural people. And we're not going to give up now, either."

He lived in hope of seeing the ban overturned, which, again, seemed to me to be unrealistic. With each season that passes, more people will see that, whether the ban was justified or not, the world hasn't obviously come to an end as a result; and the arguments for a repeal will become less pressing. Fox-hunting has been unfairly maligned and shouldn't, in my view, have been banned. But if it didn't exist, it really wouldn't be necessary — in the 21st century — to invent it.

But I suspect that, for many, that has ceased to be the important question. What matters more is a burning sense of injustice at the way their urban rulers have treated them — and a burning desire to right that injustice. "I can't believe," said Barry, "when there's so much wrong with the world, with the war in Iraq and everything, that they carried on with this blinkered assault on rural life . . . And using the Parliament Act — it was like using an Exocet missile to break an egg.

"It's a crime that rural people will never, ever forgive this government for — never, ever."

352

# CHAPTER
# TWENTY-FIVE

# Driven off

I travelled eastwards through Gilderdale Forest in Weardale and, eventually, into County Durham — dazzled, all the way, by autumn. I had forgotten that such golden forests existed; not only existed, but coexisted with fields and hills and little settlements and old, respectable market towns. England may be overcrowded and grumpy, but there are still wide-open spaces in the far north where the air tastes fresh and the roads seem always to be leading you somewhere magical. And yet surely the fields shouldn't have been *that* empty?

The road that I was on ended up taking me to Pity Me — a grey, functional village whose quaint name is variously said to derive from the Norman French for "little lake"; from the "Miserere meis" sung by local monks when fleeing the Vikings; and from Pithead Mere, an area of boggy wasteland that used to have the outwash from nearby minehead pumping engines discharged into it. Its most notable feature today is the Arnison shopping centre, much used by the increasingly affluent populace of Durham.

On the edge of the village, in a little cottage beside a farm, I met a former agricultural labourer who had worked for most of his life on the local fields but had, he said, been "driven from the land". He was a big, strong-looking man of nearly 50, with thinning brown hair, thoughtful brown eyes and a calm, matter-of-fact way of speaking. Yet there was also a troubled air about him: a certain perplexed vulnerability, and an understated bitterness in the story he told.

"I grew up on a farm a couple of miles east of here," said John Heron quietly, gesturing through his kitchen window at the wide ploughed field outside, "in Leamside. It was just a family farm, of 50 acres. We'd been there since the 1800s. It was at the end of a cul-de-sac, and there was a row of about 20 houses below the farm. Everybody knew everybody, and childcare was just a matter of knocking on the house next door.

"It was only a tiny farm, but in the 1930s, this farm supported my grandparents, five children — who all grew up and worked on the farm — and two staff." John's father took over in the 1960s, and John, in turn, took it over in the 1980s, leasing it from his mother after his father's death. It was a much less profitable enterprise by then, with small farms struggling to compete with a new breed of semi-industrial agricultural giants (and, in many cases, being absorbed by them). None the less, it was just about viable, as long as John and his brother subsidised their meagre earnings from it by working as agricultural contractors as well.

"My brother and I worked for a lot of other farmers in the area. We worked as sheep-shearers, on a contract basis, and then in the wintertime we used to busy ourselves with forestry and fencing. Potato-riddling, too — we did a lot of that round here. It wasn't ideal, but you could make a reasonable living."

Then wheat prices began to collapse, and "the profitability of farms fell dramatically". This didn't just squeeze the family farm; it also squeezed the contract work. "As prices got reduced, farmers didn't fence so much, so there was less winter work around." They tightened their belts, but survived.

Then, in the early 1990s, came the set-aside revolution. "It had been around for a while, but the amount of set-aside that people could put out of production was vastly increased. So of course there was no need to plough it, no need to fence it. It doesn't seem to have occurred to anyone to think what the effect of set-aside would be on people who worked on the land. But it made a huge difference. I know one farm, over to the east, where there's 750 acres, and they were only growing wheat on 180 acres of it. So there was no need for any labour at all."

By that time, John was struggling. "But I had been in the Territorial Army [TA] for a few years, as a hobby, and so as the days on the land became more short, I started doing more training with them. Because you get paid for it, and so it sort of took up the slack."

In 1996 he was called up as a reservist and sent to Bosnia for six months. "So I got contractors in to do what needed to be done on the farm" — which wasn't much by then — "and it all seemed to work OK." His brother had given up by now: "He got himself a JCB and started working in the building trade, converting farm buildings and things. My good friend Jim, who used to shear with us, went into building as well, although he still takes a month off in the summer for shearing. There's an awful lot of farm-buildings being converted these days. They're redundant for modern farming use, you see — too small for the machinery — so it's either that or let them fall down. And people who would once have worked in farming are working in building instead."

It was around that time that he lost hope. "It was getting obvious that the farm wasn't really viable." In 1999, it made a net operating profit of £200; the contracting work wasn't really taking up all the slack any more. Then, in 2001, came foot-and-mouth.

"Foot-and-mouth devastated this area, and for me personally it was another nail in the coffin. You could hardly get round the farms because of the restrictions, and when you did get there, the viral restrictions — wash-down, disinfectant — it just slowed you down so much you could hardly do it." Even when it was over, the effects remained. "We used to shear upwards of 20,000, 25,000 sheep. Afterwards I'd guess we were down to 7,000 or 8,000. A few have come back, but a lot of the farmers have taken compensation and restructured.

"But us shearers — we never got a penny in compensation. It was only the livestock owners who got compensation. And of course meanwhile the other farms were all cutting back on contract labour to try and reduce their losses."

It was, in the circumstances, something of a relief to be called up for another six-month reservist's stint, this time in Afghanistan. Not that he wanted to go away, with one small child at home and another on the way. But, for the same reason, he needed to earn a living. "The TA had become my main source of income — and at least the Queen pays her bills on time."

After that, he accepted the inevitable: the world he grew up in had ended. The family farm was leased out, and John and his family moved, initially, to a housing estate in Durham. He began to earn his living in the security industry, at first abroad but now only in Britain.

"It's good work, the security industry, but it's very piecemeal — you know, we need you next week, but not for a couple of weeks after that. And it's not the same as working on the land that you know. I still might do the odd week's tractor-driving, or put up a fence for someone, but basically that's over. I've given up the Reserves now — it wasn't fair on Alison [his wife] to spend all that time away, now we've got two kids. But now Alison's back teaching, and really, from the old days when I supported her, she's now the main breadwinner."

He looked at the floor for a moment, as if embarrassed. We were in his sitting room now, with the remains of last night's fire still smouldering. It was a pleasant, tidy house, yet somehow it seemed too small for this big, fit, restless man. Still, I said, at least you're back in the countryside now. "Yes," he said, "I was glad when this place came up. The estate in the city was all right, but everyone was so busy all the time.

"Mind you," he added, "it's not the same here, either." By "here" I took him to mean not so much the village — to which his cottage was barely attached — as the countryside around Durham generally. He hardly saw anyone from his Leamside childhood. "A lot of them have gone. The houses seem to change hands very frequently. In fact, in several cases people have bought two of them and knocked them into one. But of course, if a farm worker is lucky enough to get an offer for his house then of course he's going to cash in."

He still had friends in the area, and enjoyed sharing country pursuits with them when time and money permit. "I've always loved shooting, ever since my father got me started with a .410 when I was 12. I couldn't afford to pay the full price for a day at a full commercial pheasant shoot, but there's half a dozen of us who get together and get permission to go over various bits of land for a walked-up day. It's not wholesale slaughter: just pheasants, rabbits — you use your common sense. You get some really good woodcock shoots December and January. We get a big influx of migratory woodcock come in from Scandinavia on the last full moon of November."

But the ancient rhythms of nature all too often took second place now to the mad beat of the post-rural 21st century. "Everyone seems to be that busy keeping their heads above water that they don't have time to help one another any more. People had a lot more time for each

358

other in the past." Meanwhile, many newcomers displayed a strange attitude to the messy realities of agriculture. "What's got me, and still does, is townies who complain about mud on the road, or say, 'Can you keep the smell down?' when you've been muck-spreading — as if there's some kind of volume control. Or complaining if you've had the tractor in the field late at night. Once I ploughed until 3a.m. to get the muck into the soil, to stop the smell — and they complained about that too. Or they complain about hedge-cutters, and then the next minute they complain about the hedges not being cut. Or they get the hump because there's a flock of sheep in the road — I've seen people just about driving right over the lambs."

It was, we agreed, ironic that he should have switched from farm work to soldiering. Both are crucial, difficult callings on which the rest of us ultimately depend, and which we tend — especially today — to reward with a crushing lack of appreciation. "Most people don't give soldiers the respect they deserve, for going off and risking their lives. And most people don't respect people who work on the land. Not like they did in the past."

The trouble, he believed, was that too many people "don't understand that the land is a food factory. You try asking people not to leave their cars parked in a lane one day, so that a combine can get past. They don't think it's got anything to do with them.

"But of course most people don't grow up around farming any more. When I was a kid, whenever anything was going on, on the farm, everyone wanted

**359**

to be there. Everyone wanted to sit on the tractor or the combine. Now you can't go near a tractor until you're 14. So people don't learn what farming involves. But the farms were here first — the houses came later.

"But that doesn't count for anything now: it's their countryside now. I've been driven off the land by economic forces, just like thousands of others."

It sounded melodramatic, yet I don't think it was an exaggeration. Only a few weeks earlier, I had read that the proportion of the UK workforce employed in agriculture had fallen to 1.7 per cent, compared with 5 per cent in 1951. A quarter of farms had (according to Defra) an income of "less than zero"; half had an income of less than £10,000. The average farm worker earned £12,500 a year — £10,000 less than the national average. And of course for every poorly paid farm worker there were dozens of might-have-been farm workers for whom working on the land was no longer an option.

Meanwhile, the new countryside-dwellers continued to pour in with their money. In 2007 the average rural house cost £30,000 more than the average urban house. Membership of the National Trust had grown by 500,000 — from 3 million to 3.5 million — in the five years to 2007. The heritage-building sector and the organic-farming sector were now worth £2 billion a year each, while the rural-crafts sector was likely to be bigger than agriculture within 15 years (according to the Countryside Agency). There was, in other words, no shortage of economic vigour in the countryside — or of people who valued the nice things about it. There was just a lack of space in it for ordinary labourers wanting to toil in the fields they grew up in — even in the remotest counties, which was where the rural population, and rural house prices, were now rising fastest.

"Still," he reflected, before hurrying off to pick up his daughter from her play-group, "you can't turn the clock back. And despite everything, I can't imagine ever leaving here. Not unless they build an estate out the back. No, I'll turn my toes up here — definitely."

# CHAPTER
# TWENTY-SIX

# The canny shepherd

On a thin, leaf-strewn Northumbrian lane, with wet trees leaning on both sides and a brutal wind tearing ripples in big brown puddles all along it, I almost drove into a small man on a quad bike. He wore a flat cap, a big, dripping, waxed coat and a broad grin, with two sodden sheepdogs perched behind him. A bright white smile flashed from beneath his huge, black, bristling moustache, and I formed the impression — in the split second between swerving to avoid him and swerving back to avoid a wall — that he was brimming with improbable exuberance.

He bounced off in his direction. I drove on in mine. Rain pelted relentlessly. I shivered and wondered how anyone could look so cheerful while so exposed to such weather, especially in a great cold emptiness like this? Even his dogs had looked doubtful.

I carried on and reached a village called Colwell, which isn't much to write home about, unless you have someone at home who is interested in small, sloping villages of about 20 stone houses, many of them with long front gardens, several of them for sale and nobody out and about. I drove through, slowing only to note its dilapidated village hall and its lack of a church, shop or visible human beings. Assorted lanes then took me towards Kirkharle, Capability Brown's birthplace, where the farm where Brown first worked as a gardener's boy had been converted into an upmarket crafts and retail complex; and then, via innumerable bare, deserted hills, to what used to be Colwell's neighbouring village: Thockrington. It isn't any more, owing to a mishap in 1847. A villager who had been at sea returned with cholera; everyone died, and the village was burnt down. All that remain are some bumps under the sheep-chomped, wind-dried turf; a farm; and a small 12th-century church on top of an exposed ridge, half sheltered from the wind by a big, precarious ring of dry-stone wall.

The church is still in use — every other Sunday, plus baptisms, weddings and funerals — and looks remarkably solid for its age. I wandered around outside for a while, wondering what first prompted someone to build a settlement in this bleak place; trying to imagine what the village might have looked and felt like 160 years ago; thinking how much more terrifying disease must have been in those days, especially so far from any hint of medical succour; and noting, too, that the churchyard included the grave of Lord Beveridge, inventor of the modern welfare state, who was buried there in 1963.

Then I wandered down to the farm and found that same quad bike I had seen earlier, with the same two dogs sitting and dripping on it. Their owner was near by, still grinning, in a huge pen of sheep.

He had taken off his coat — the rain had more or less stopped — and it was no surprise to find that his handshake, though firm, was ice-cold. He wore waterproof leggings, thickly stained up to mid-thigh with several varieties of muck; above the waist he wore just a woollen shirt and woollen sweater, with a tweed cap on his head. Close up, I could see a few lines of white in his crow-black hair; he was, it turned out, not quite 50. His name was Graham Dick. His voice sounded Scottish, to my ear, but he was a born-and-bred Northumbrian.

"I'm from Rothbury," he explained, "down in the Coquet Valley" — which is about 20 miles to the north-east. "I've only been here for eight years." By "here" he meant not only a little bungalow on the edge of the farm area but also a cold expanse of about 1,200 acres of fields — pretty much all that the eye could see — for which he was the sole shepherd.

Before that, he'd been a shepherd at Rothbury, as had his father before him. "It was a bit of a wrench leaving," he said. "I was born and bred in Rothbury and lived there 40 years. But you have to work. And this was a better position, and a better house." (There may, he hinted later, have been other reasons: "I'm more appreciated here. I don't like working for someone who's younger than me who don't know nothing.")

He said that I was welcome to watch him. I did so, as he sorted his way through, by my estimate, about 200 sheep, systematically shifting groups of them from sub-pen to sub-pen while he administered a distinctly 21st-century multi-vaccine — against, among other things, blackleg, tetanus, pulpy kidney and lamb dysentery — to each one and, where necessary, clipped muck-encrusted wool from their backsides. The sub-pens were formed by metal hurdles — like the crowd-control barriers you find in London — which he shifted, or asked me to shift, with a quick cunning that would have stood him in good stead with a certain kind of IQ puzzle. It certainly outwitted the sheep.

"Any one sheep only comes into the pens four or five times a year," he explained. "But there's a lot of sheep, and in the summer they get dosed every four or five weeks. And the grass is turning that wet now that I'm giving them an extra dose." He administered a variety of other medications while doing this, and he also used the process to identify which ewes were thriving and which were not. The latter would be "taken off" for slaughter, and "we'll breed off the rest".

By "we" he means . . .? "Well, it's me really. There's a local lad comes in and helps during lambing, and I've been getting a contractor to help with shearing these past two years, because I've got a bad back. But most of the time it's just me and the dogs."

Wasn't that a bit lonely? "Not really. It's what I do."

He lived with his wife in a low house of grey rain-hammered stone on the edge of the farm area. The main farm building was occupied by his employer, of whom he spoke highly. The next biggest housed some moody-looking brown cows, which glowered suspiciously at us. "We're calving at the moment, so we're a bit busy."

We? "OK, me. And the dogs."

Was he always busy? "Pretty much. I have the odd quiet day, but there's usually something. I start at 6.30a.m. every morning, except during lambing you never stop — sometimes I'll just sleep in the hayshed and kip for an hour or two. And if it's really wet and horrible, like these last two years, I'll be out right through the night. Then there's castrating and ringing, and then the dipping and clipping. There's always something — a lot of the time you're just going around with the bike and the trailer and the dogs to see if there's any problems. And if there's nothing else there'll be a fence or wall needs mending."

The dry-stone wall around the pens was surmounted by a wooden rail, about the height of my head. What was that about? "Oh, we had some wild Blackies a few years back, and they used to jump out. These ones," he added, "are Suffolk crosses — and the ones with white faces are Cheviot crosses. We've about 1,300 here in all, and about 40 cattle. These ewes are all last year's, born around April or May. Would you mind opening that gate for me? That's right, and then close it again when I say."

As the sheep filed through the gap I had just created, I mused on what it would be like to do this job without — most days — another human being to talk to from dawn to dusk. Why, I asked him, had he chosen this way of life? "I don't know. I never thought of doing anything else. My father was on the farms, too — he worked 60 years on the same farm. I'm the same. This'll do me till I retire, I hope."

Presumably shepherding had changed a bit since his father's day? "Yes and no. Some things are handed down from father to son, but other things are very different. He fenced and dry-stone-walled, same as I do, and I probably picked up that off of him. But other things are very different — all this medication we have today, for example. And of course there were still horses when my father started, before there was the tractors. But it's still the same job.

"I was fortunate with the boss I first worked with: his family had been farming for generations. He'd learnt from his father. And I learnt from him, and from my father — who had worked for the boss's father. Of course, there's lots of things you can only learn for yourself, by making your own mistakes. But I've had plenty of time to pick things up." He first helped with the lambing when he was 12.

Would his own children follow the same path? "I don't think so. My daughter wants to be a fashion designer. My son works in Hexham, in a hospital. He's doing very well — he's a clinical audit clerk — but he's in that building all day long. I couldn't stand that. Life's for living outdoors."

A violent squall, from nowhere, crashed on us like a wave. Leaves and icy raindrops sprayed crazily across the farmyard. Much of my notebook dissolved into pulp. Graham smiled, finished the sheep he was doing and then, when he was ready, pulled on his jacket. His bare hands looked red with cold. "You might want to go under that tree," he said; then continued: "Aye, it's not so bad, the outdoor life."

I told him — from under my tree — that I'd heard endless tales about hill-farmers struggling to make ends meet; many have given up in despair. Was what he did viable? "Aye, just about. It's hard for them as has rent to find — but the farmer here owns this place. We do all right, but there's no money in wool any more. A few years ago, wool used to pay the rent. Everyone used to take their own wool down to Hexham. Now it goes all the way up to Hawick, and if you're getting shearers in to do the clipping then you lose money on it. And a ewe only fetches 80p to £1. The farmer here makes a living from silage and hay, not wool.

"But everything's changing, like, all the time. You don't see many farm workers — it's all done by machine. And even farmers are moving on. Everyone's getting into tourism. Farm shops are the big thing now, and bed-and-breakfast — anything for tourists." One fellow shepherd, from Rothbury, had set up a walking business based in the retail complex at Kirkharle, offering printed "walks" and courses in the use of Global Positioning Systems.

Other landowners hoped to realise some value from their windswept acres by allowing alternative-energy companies to erect wind farms on them. Altogether, some 117 turbines were planned, by four different developers, in this very area, just south of the protected wilderness of Northumberland National Park but no less windswept or outstanding in its natural beauty. I only discovered later — from a local paper — that this very farm had provisionally featured in these plans, and might yet do so in future. Intense local opposition, principally relating to the heritage value of Thockrington Church, had persuaded the company in question to reconsider its plans, but it was still theoretically possible that a 50m meteorological mast might appear before long just a few fields south, to be replaced ultimately by a full-scale 28-megawatt, 14-turbine wind farm. Such threats — or, if you prefer, opportunities — are increasingly common in the remote corners of rural England.

Graham made no mention of this issue — perhaps because it was a delicate subject; perhaps because a wayward ewe had broken his train of thought. Instead, when he spoke again, it was of "all these conservation and stewardship schemes" on which farmers in the area, and throughout England, increasingly rely for their income. "I'm not a great believer in that," he said. "You're doing things the way they want, not the way you want."

He never paused, as he talked, in his processing of the ewes: manoeuvring, manhandling and medicating. He handled them all with a firm, confident gentleness that I suspect was wasted on them. They yielded to his manipulations with sullen resignation and occasional panic, and gazed at him afterwards with what looked like amazed awe; I saw no trace of the affection or gratitude that you can sometimes sense from a dog or horse.

Every now and then he would yank out a particular sheep from a group and put it into another sub-enclosure. These were the ones that weren't doing so well. He didn't seem to hesitate or deliberate before

**369**

selecting them — it was almost as if he had already marked them down as under-achievers. Could he recognise each individual sheep?

"Yeah, you get used to them. Not so much the lambs, like, but the mothers, like, the ewes, you do. You get certain characters you remember — you think, yeah, that bugger was a bad 'un last year, or had twins, or whatever. Certain things stick in your mind, you know?"

Presumably, I ventured, you spend more time with sheep — or at least with animals — than with people? "Maybe. I don't know. We don't see a lot of people. There's a lot of new people moved into Colwell, from the south, because they like the countryside, or because the property's cheaper and they can retire. There are a lot of commuters to Newcastle now, and two or three new houses are being built. So there's a lot we don't even know. And then the other shepherds and farmers — well, you can see, they're a long way off." He waved out across the fields. The squall had passed, as abruptly as it had begun, and the wet green grass shone brilliantly in the sun. A couple of grey farms were just visible towards the horizon. "We get on all right, but we don't see much of each other from day to day. We'll help each other out if someone's got a problem, but normally we're out in our fields. That's one reason why I do my music."

Music?

"Shepherds' songs. Old Northumbrian music. I sing them. They're songs of Northumberland and the Borders, handed down over the generations. Some of the things are in dialect — it's closer to Scottish than to Geordie. They're mostly shepherds' songs, although to tell you the truth one of the ones I sing was written by a draper. But he must have been interested in the shepherd's life."

He sang me a snatch; later on, he gave me a tape. It was a curious, unsettling sound: a rich, confident baritone, banging out long, unaccompanied ballads about the lives and loves of shepherds. The tuneful but austerely relentless style made me think of Middle Eastern music, but the words were plainly local:

Oh, the shepherds of the Coquet and the Alwin
    and the Reed,
O the Bowmont an the Breamish, they are aal
    the same breed;
Wi his collie dog aside him and his stick with
    horned heed,
That's the canny shepherd laddie o the hills.

They clim oot amang the heather ere it's torned
    the break o day,
Cross the peat, the bent, the moss-haggs an the
    bogs they'll wend their way;
Quick te catch a yowe that's maaky or a tup
    that's strayed away;
That's the canny shepherd laddie of the hills.

A listener accustomed to jolly pop songs might pronounce them dour, but I think that might be to miss the point — which is that, when Graham sings, the sound you hear has been handed down orally from singer to singer for generations. It is, if you like, the voice of the Northumbrian past.

"They're from the time when shepherds used to come down from the hills for a local show, and maybe stop down for the night before they went back up to the hills the next day. So that was when they all saw each other, so you can imagine it was quite a big thing for them. It still is, in a way. They've been passed down from generation to generation."

There was a time when each part of rural England had its own distinctive tradition of such songs, and most ordinary people knew at least some. Labourers would sing together in the fields; a man who knew many — such as John Clare's father, a flail-thresher who knew more than 100 ballads by heart — would find himself much in demand at fairs.

But traditional balladeers could hardly be described as much in demand today: the competing attractions of the global entertainment industry are just too strong. But there's a bit of life yet in what Graham does. "I do them whenever I'm asked," he said. "Sometimes two or three times a week. Sometimes a pub will have a Northumbrian night, and I'll do some there. Or I'll do a few for Burns Night. And then we have shepherds' suppers — maybe half a dozen a year, mainly in the winter months, when all the shepherds get together. I'll get paid but it's only pocket money. It's really just that I'd like to try and keep it going."

He was the first such singer in his family, but was very conscious of picking up a tradition that previous generations have guarded before him. "I always sang at school, and then there were some older people asked me to try that kind of music, and I just happened to take to it. There weren't that many doing it then. There aren't that many today. I've tried to get one or two of the younger ones into it, but they're not interested. But it needs to be handed down before it passes away. Some of it's written down but a lot of it isn't. I think it's important to keep it going.

"It's a good social life. But it's mainly the elder ones, although some people are trying to learn some of the youngsters at school, like, to get them interested. I hope they do, because if no one takes it up they're going to die out sooner or later."

He finished dosing the last sheep, and invited me back to his house, where he gave me a cup of tea and insisted on sharing his lunch — a ham sandwich — with me. This was all the more appreciated because I had begun to shiver with cold. His plan was to rest for about 20 minutes and then go out again. It was growing dark — not because it was late but because huge rain clouds were now gathering over us. Did he never feel tempted just to stay in and watch the telly?

He laughed. "No. I like getting out into the fresh air." Didn't the cold get to him? Didn't the damp make his bones ache? "No. I don't know. I have had a bit of back trouble the past couple of years, that's quite painful, and sciatica and all, down the back of my leg. I'm meant to be having an X-ray on Friday. They think it might be a spot of arthritis, but I don't think anyone can say what causes it." I think I could.

The house was small but comfortable; above all, it was windproof. His wife was out, which apparently happens less often than she would like. "She doesn't drive, so it can get a bit lonely for her. But she's a country lass — from Harbottle, further up the Coquet Valley — so she knows what the country's like."

Nightlife in Thockrington is, clearly, on the quiet side. "We don't go out much: maybe one or two music nights, but that's about all. I'm not much of a night person. I'd rather get an early start in the morning. That's when you see things. I like to see the birds — you get all kinds of birds here, birds of prey; my wife had a woodpecker in the garden for two winters. And deer, badgers, foxes, rabbits. It's pretty wild.

"I don't watch TV much. I might do a bit of work with the dogs in the evening, training them. Or I might dress a stick for a while." He showed me a tub full of wooden walking sticks: seasoned, carved and polished and, in some cases, intricately shaped. Some had horn handles, some wood; of the latter, a few were all one continuous piece of wood. It was impossible not to marvel at the patience and craftsmanship that must have gone into them — but of course this, too, was something that shepherds have done for generations.

"I get obsessed with the stick I'm dressing, sometimes. Look at that one — that was a hazel branch. It's cut from the back end. Took me three weeks, off and on. I learnt myself, but there's better stick dressers than me. George Smith was the daddy of them all."

One day, he said, he hoped to retire. "I used to wish I had a farm of my own, but now I'm not sure. Maybe if I won a lot of money I would. But otherwise, I just hope that by the time I retire I'll be able to buy a little house with a wood-burner and maybe a little bit of land, and I'll train dogs for people. I've always trained dogs. I just worked it out as I went along. I had my first dog when I was 15. Next year I bred off it and kept one back — you always hope the young ones will get a little bit of the idea from the older ones. A bit like people really."

And who would he pass all his knowledge on to? "A lot of farmers worry about that. There's not that many sons take over any more. Once upon a time you expected the son to take over, but nowadays they're encouraged to do other things, and who can blame them? But who knows? You can miss generations — my grandchildren might take it on. Or someone else's might. I like to think one or two might carry on, after I'm gone."

He glanced at the clock and hurried back into the rain. I left him climbing back on to his quad bike — where the dogs, as far as I could tell, had been waiting all that time — and headed back south in search of somewhere to stay. As I drove, I watched the huge green fields sweeping past, empty apart from a few walls and sheep, and tried to imagine honestly how it might feel to be always here, rooted in the land and the past to the exclusion of almost everything else, while the rest of the world hurtled into its hi-tech, globalised, overcrowded future. I wasn't sure that I fancied it. It could be lovely or lonely, depending on how you looked at it: it would depend who you were. But that, I realised, was Graham's secret: he knew who he was.

# CHAPTER
# TWENTY-SEVEN

# Exile

"Stop here for a moment," said Dale Daniel, with a catch in his already husky voice.

We walked over to a gap in the hedge.

"Look," he said, reverently. "There's Paradise. That green bit down there."

I peered through at a pleasant Durham valley. To our right was the ancient village of Escomb, with a famous Saxon church at its quiet heart. Ahead, the richly vegetated river Wear curved along the valley floor, with gilt-leafed woods on the far side. To our left, a street of squat stone houses — part of a small, nondescript settlement called Witton Park — clung to the hillside. Dale, balding and gap-toothed, was pointing to a patch of brighter green just beyond the street's end, looking, from here, a little like a football pitch.

"That's where the iron works used to be," said Keith Belton, a local historian and, like Dale, a native of the village.

"Aye," said Dale, his old sweatshirt flapping in the breeze. "All gone." And we stood in silence for a minute, thinking about what had passed.

Then we got back into the car and drove down into the village.

"Look," said Dale, "that's Black Road. They call it Meadow Road now, but it was Black Road then. That was where we all wanted to go. We moved streets as they were coming in, to try to get away. If you got to Black Road, you were safe. We never got there."

So what happened?

"We left. It was 1969. A terrible day, a heartbreaking day for my mother and father. They'd lived there all their lives. I just cried. I don't think they ever got over it."

"We left earlier," said Keith. "In 1960. My dad couldn't make a living. Well, he couldn't after what they'd done."

He drove on through the narrow streets. "Look," said Dale, "that's where the ice-cream shop used to be. And, look, I was born in that street there. And that's High Thompson Street, where Keith's grandfather used to live."

"Oldest place in village," said Keith, who was now a grandfather himself.

"It's changed a lot," said Dale, who at 60 was seven years younger than Keith. "All the streets were in here, and the iron works is through this bridge. There were pubs here, and all the kids would run out and buy the beer for the men, because it was so hot, and the pubs were open about 20 hours a day. This was called the station yard, and they've built houses. And that's one original street, Viaduct Terrace, only they've changed it to the Green now. But the actual nucleus of the village is gone — they bulldozed it and moved us on. I think there's only seven of the people I was at school with that are left."

"Where we are now," said Keith, a little later, "we'd really be sitting on top of the blast furnaces. The smoke would have been terrible, belching out all over the village 24 hours a day. You can't imagine it."

I think it was around this point that it struck me how odd all this was. Not only was I being shown round the village by two bred-and-born villagers who hadn't lived there for decades. Not only were they pointing out landmarks to me that weren't, in many cases, physically there. But the implied moral of their nostalgic presentation ran directly counter to some widely held rural assumptions.

According to the conventional ruralist's way of looking at things, the real golden age of this corner of the English countryside ended centuries ago — some time between the mid-18th century and the mid-19th century. Until then, all around was green and pleasant. Assorted landowners — based at nearby Witton Castle, or in the Prince Bishops Palace in Durham — enjoyed the hunting and the views; assorted countrymen bred sheep and cattle and enjoyed the simple pleasures of agrarian life. Then, in loud, clumsy steps, came industry. Small-scale coal-mining operations were begun in 1756. The Stockton & Darlington Railway arrived in 1825. Even then, it must have been a charming spot, for the field in the valley was known locally as "Paradise" when, in 1846, the industrialist Henry Pease formally opened the Witton Park Iron

Works on behalf of the fast-growing company of Bolckow & Vaughan. "He said: 'It'll be a lot more of a paradise when it has my chimneys belching smoke into it,'" said Keith. And belch they did.

That, from an arcadian countryside-lover's point of view, was the end of the idyll. It was also the beginning of something else: a village. And for Dale and Keith that was a far more beautiful thing.

"Bolckow & Vaughan wanted the best workers," said Keith, who as well as being the older was the more historically inclined of the pair, "so they offered the best money. Two or three pound a week. People came from everywhere — the Welsh, the Scottish, the Irish, men from every county in England. They all came here to make their fortunes. My ancestor came up from Brighton in the 1860s. And all these houses — threw them up as they came."

"The money was unbelievable," said Dale, a retired school caretaker who had also spent much of his working life as a bookie. "Two or three pound a week — that's like £1,000 a week now, maybe more. It was like the California gold rush. My ancestors came up from Wales in 1872 — the whole family, brothers, sisters, the lot."

What they came to was a chaotic, multicultural community that by 1874 would have 4,400 people, 630 houses, 57 different small traders, 12 alternative places of worship and 31 public houses. The workmen received their pay fortnightly, whereupon — in the understated words of one contemporary observer —

"the place becomes a scene of drunkenness and disorder".

"It was," said Keith, "unbelievably rough. It really was the wild west. The Irish and the Welsh were fighting, the English and the Scots were fighting, the Irish and the Irish were fighting. There was no law." Some incidents made the local newspapers — such as the notorious "Battle of John Street" in 1862. "But," said Dale, "there was many a murder that there were never anything done about."

That was the first boom. The first bust came in 1884. Bolckow & Vaughan, realising that there was much less ironstone in the area than they had imagined, and that the future in any case was in steel rather than wrought iron, closed the iron works. "The devastation was unbelievable," said Keith. "It was closed overnight. No one had anything. I've known people weep just reading the newspaper cuttings on microfiche, when they read about the suffering and the children starving."

There were tales of men tramping so far in search of work that they returned with their feet "wringing with wet and blood". The Witton Park Distress Committee served 32,347 emergency meals to children in the first three months. Soup was distributed at a rate of 40 gallons a day. The local workhouse was extended.

Some starved; some begged; many left. The population fell by 1,000 in 20 years. But some hung on. Perhaps it was then that a sense of community began to form. Meanwhile, hope returned. Coal mines sprang up around the county; by 1900, most villagers were working again. In World War I, the village became famous for the large number of Belgian refugees it took in. "I think there were 172 in the end," said Keith. "They couldn't believe the welcome they were given." Meanwhile, some 400 villagers went off to fight; 67 did not return. A village hall — the Witton Park Memorial Institute — was built in their memory, surrounded by poplars: one for each of the fallen.

A decade of peace ushered in the next catastrophe: the Great Depression. The village was all but crushed. Unemployment reached 98 per cent; the free soup flowed again. The Prince of Wales visited, and declared that the houses were hovels. "Which," said Dale, "they were."

World War II brought new respite, with plenty of work in the services and the munitions factories. Then came peace, demobilisation and the broad, sunlit uplands of post-war recovery. Or so everyone imagined. But they reckoned without Durham County Council — and, specifically, its ambition "to create a more modern, efficient and compact settlement pattern appropriate to the needs of the 20th century".

"They wanted us wiped off the map," said Dale. "Simple as that."

From the planners' point of view, it made sense. There were about 370 pit-related settlements in County Durham, and most of the pits were close to exhaustion, which implied the bleakest of futures for the settlements. Solution: get rid of them. In the 1951 County Development Plan, each settlement was classified as A, B, C, or D. In the 122 "category D" villages, no further development would be allowed. And that meant that, sooner or later, the village would die.

It took a while for the ruling to bite, but bite it did, especially at Witton Park, which was the biggest and most decrepit of the affected villages. Houses there could be condemned as unfit for human habitation as soon as the council had earmarked somewhere else for the inhabitants to be moved to. A series of soulless estates in Bishop Auckland was developed for the purpose and the clearances began. House by house, street by street, the old village was razed and the old villagers were moved on. Many went to an estate that was officially called Woodhouse Close but was known to its new residents as "The Reservation".

"They shipped out about 3,000 people," said Dale. "At one point the population was below 500 — I think it's about 700 now."

The more they moved, the less viable the community became. "There was nowt wrong with employment when they started," says Keith. "But it all had a knock-on effect. My father had a shop that was doing great, but all his customers went, so he had to go too. He never got one penny piece for losing his business." In 1967, the local pit was finally closed, which didn't help.

Similar stories were unfolding all over the county, but nowhere so grotesquely as in Witton Park: partly because so much of it was so ripe for demolition, and partly because the villagers were so reluctant to leave. Contemporary reports carry quotation after quotation from desperate villagers, begging to be allowed to stay.

"I've lived in Witton Park all my life and never took no hurt in it," protested one bewildered 74-year-old. "My mother didn't take to it at all," said a younger woman tearfully of life on The Reservation, "and within a year she died."

"People died of broken hearts," said Dale. "The old vicar, he said it murdered people. He said, not only have you butchered a village, you've murdered a people."

"It started in the mid-1950s and went on for 10 years and more," said Keith. "They were making it so bad for people that they hoped they'd just move away. If they'd got rid of it all at once, that's one thing, but to piecemeal away — you wouldn't treat a dog like that. But the worse they treated us, the more we stuck together."

"The spirit of the village was unbelievable then," said Dale. "It was always the same: Witton Park against the world. Everybody else was against it, so the villagers stuck together through thick and thin."

By the late 1960s, their protests were being heard. "The village that wouldn't die" was featured in the national press, radio and television. In fact, only one category D settlement disappeared entirely: the tiny village of Hamsteels, a dozen miles to the north. The villagers there protested bitterly too, but they were too few to be heard. You can see where it isn't today: an unspoilt patch of green where once there were streets. In the Home Counties, such an exchange would be considered a triumph.

The struggle dragged on for decades, from a failed appeal in 1957 to a public inquiry in 1971 to the final withdrawal of the A, B, C and D categorisations in 1979. Even then, it would be another 16 years before the first new development began at Witton Park.

By then, most of the original villagers had put down roots — and in many cases died — elsewhere. Yet for some reason the spirit of the place lived on in their hearts, which seemed odd, looking at the place today. It struck me as just a normal 21st-century village going about its business, with cars rolling back and forth, "For Sale" signs sprouting outside neat front gardens, two boys kicking a ball around on a patch of grass and a drill screaming from a hillside house that was being extended. At one point I saw two pedestrians pass one another in the street without the slightest sign of acknowledgement, as Londoners do. "It must sound weird," said Dale, "us going on about how brilliant it was. But I've never known a place like it. Everyone would always look out for you. Everyone was a good neighbour. You never locked your doors — there was nothing to pinch, anyway."

"Mind you," said Keith, "the place was knackered. Most of the houses were unfit. We all knew that. It was unbelievable how people lived. There was rats running around. I'm 67 now, and I was 14 before I saw my first toilet. All you had was earth closets and a tin bath that you'd fill with water from a cold-water tap. But it was a community second to none."

"And they could easily have rebuilt in the village, instead of moving us," said Dale. "That's all people wanted, to be allowed decent affordable housing and to be left where they were. But they wouldn't listen. They couldn't understand that a village could mean so much to people. But it did, and it still does.

"Do you know what we did in the year 2000? We did it on the internet, didn't we, Keith? We had the Gathering — a get-together of people who used to live at Witton Park. People came from all over the world — people from Canada, New Zealand, Australia — you mention a country, there were people came from there. There was over 2,000 people — people who hadn't seen each other for 30, 40 years, but still thought of Witton Park as home. Unbelievable." For a moment I thought he was going to be overcome with emotion, but his boyish face composed itself again. "I never known a day like it. Unbelievable."

"Aye," said Keith, bitterly. "It was a village like no other. But the council said we had to be moved on to housing estates. They thought: we know better than you — you're just nobody."

"But look at it now," added Dale, gesturing at the clean, sunlit streets. "It's a picture village."

Would he move back there? "I couldn't afford it." If he won the Lottery? "Even then — it wouldn't be the same. No, I don't think it would ever be the same."

Keith stopped the car by a particularly expensive-looking new development. "Look," he said. "You see those houses? That triangular piece of ground they're on, that used to be empty. And the villagers said, 'Why don't you build on there, and we'll move in there and you can knock these houses down.' And the council said, 'Oh, no, don't be silly. What do you know about it?' And there's houses just gone up there now that are £200,000, £300,000 houses."

"And meanwhile," said Dale, "some of the estates where they put people from Witton Park and all these places, they're pulling them down now."

It sounded absurd; yet, from a strictly abstract point of view, you could see the logic in the planners' thinking. What use is a village if its villagers cannot support themselves — or can only support themselves by travelling somewhere else in order to work? Surely it is more desirable, from everyone's point of view, if people live as close as possible to where they work? But logic plays only a limited role in English country life, which is just as well, because three-quarters of the villages in England are surplus to logical requirements these days. People live in them, not because it is sensible for them to do so, but because they want to. The tragedy for Witton Park was that the planners didn't grasp this until one population had been moved on and another had rushed in to fill the vacuum.

The old vicar, interviewed on the radio 40 years earlier, had his own theory as to why Witton Park had been treated so high-handedly: "If it had been a little village," he declaimed, in a crabbed, lopsided voice whose anger rang out across the ages when I listened to the recording in my car on my journey south, "if it had been a beautiful little rustic place, that had never contributed anything to the nation's welfare, entirely undisturbed by industry, entirely unspoilt by industry, there'd be no question of whether it would have survived. But because Witton Park is an industrial village, it's shabby, it's dirty, it's worker-worn, it's worn-out. And it seems to me strange that the villages that contribute to the nation's wealth get least consideration from the government when the question of rebuilding is concerned . . .

"We are now scattering communities," he continued, "and planners cannot build communities. They can only build bricks and mortar. It takes people to make communities."

# CHAPTER
# TWENTY-EIGHT

# The end of the road

There are, depending on what definition you use, between 8,000 and 16,500 villages in England. They include: Catherine-de-Barnes, Crackpot, Edith Weston, Enham-Alamein, Filkins and Broughton Poggs, Friday Street, Germansweek, Great Fryup, Hanging Houghton, Helions Bumpstead, Hopton Wafers, Ireland, Iwerne Courtney or Shroton, Leinthall Starkes, Lilliput, Lydiard Millicent, Nempnett Thrubwell, Nether Thong, Nomansland, No Place, Nox, Ocle Pychard, Painter's Forstal, Pease Pottage, Praze-an-Beeble, Ramsey Forty Foot, Ryme Intrinseca, Saul, Sinfin, Spittal-in-the-Street, Twice Brewed, West Quantoxhead (St Audries), Wetwang, Wham, Whitcott Keysett, White Ladies Aston, Wyke Champflower, Wyre Piddle, Yelling and Zeal Monachorum. Even I could see that it might be unwise to attempt to visit all of these. Yet how tempting they seemed . . .

And what about all those other villages I kept hearing about? What about Cobham, for example, in Surrey, where an invasion of Chelsea football stars was said to have brought unimagined prosperity to the local bookmaker but put many other village noses out of joint? Or Chobham, also in Surrey but 10 miles west of its near namesake, which was once equally awash with wealth but mislaid much of it in the early 1990s, when 19 villagers lost more than £17 million among them as Lloyd's Names? Or Norton Fitzwarren, in Somerset, where the landlord of the Ring of Bells pub was made to take down his award-winning hanging baskets and window-boxes on health-and-safety grounds? Or Ditherington, in Shropshire, where a barmaid had just been prosecuted for bigamy after being found to be married to both a man and a woman? Or Witham Friary, in Somerset, which was facing catastrophic drought after the Duke of Somerset decided to cut off its water supply?

And what, for that matter, about all those *other* villages that still called out to me from the history books: from Bosham, in West Sussex, where King Harold prayed the night before Hastings, to Eyam, in Derbyshire, whose 17th-century inhabitants resigned themselves to death rather than risk passing on the plague to neighbouring settlements?

I wanted to visit them all.

"But *why?*" said Clare, with uncharacteristic exasperation, during one break between journeys. "Why do you have to *go* to them?"

It was hard to answer. I knew that I was growing as sick as she was of my incessant travels. Why couldn't I just stop at home, in my own village?

"You could," she added, "spend the rest of your life doing this."

She was, if anything, understating the matter, given that any one of the 9.5 million people who live in rural England (4.4 million in small rural towns, 3.5 million in villages and 1.6 million in scattered dwellings) might, for all I knew, have some important story about the countryside to tell; as, now I thought about it, might millions of others who used to live in rural areas but could no longer afford to do so.

It was, I agreed, ridiculous to keep making these expeditions. In one two-week period alone I had, among other things:

... listened to (and later had a drink with) a traditional story-teller, born and bred in Ascot, who earned her living by travelling from village hall to village hall in Oxfordshire and Gloucestershire, telling some remarkably vivid old "tales of the Cotswolds" to any villagers daring enough to listen;

... spent a cold Tuesday evening on a moor above Blubberhouses, in North Yorkshire, talking to a 65-year-old vicar's wife who had spent every Tuesday evening for years — except those she had spent in jail as a result of such evenings — protesting against the US military base at Menwith Hill. (I shared her company with a policeman who used to live in the next village to mine who now spent many of his Tuesday nights sharing mugs of hot tea with her and trying to discourage her from taking her protests too far.);

... spent a morning in an ancient, rattling Rutland windmill whose messianic keeper, lonely as a lighthouse-keeper, had devoted more than a decade to restoring his once-ruined tower to productive glory;

. . . spoken to a 95-year-old blacksmith's son from Sandon, Essex, who remembered carrying water from the village pump to his father's forge in the years before World War I;

. . . and spent an afternoon in Scartho, in Lincolnshire, with a part-time bus-driver who claimed to be a colonel in a 104-year-old private army called the Legion of Frontiersmen, whose *raison-d'être* was to protect the British state in times of crisis using outdoor skills more commonly associated with Scouts (although for reasons of age and bickering his force was down to just three men, two of whom were "not in the best of health").

I was delighted to have done so, and would have been delighted to spend many more such fortnights, exploring the inexhaustible variety and eccentricity of that portion of the modern English population that happens to inhabit the countryside. But where would it all end? I could spend several lifetimes doing this.

Meanwhile, a new, more powerful argument had arisen for calling it a day: I had begun to hate my car.

Actually, I had begun to hate all cars. The loathing had been building for months. Every time I came to a new village, the first thing I'd notice would be that it was half choked by the same unnatural infestation of metallic motorware as everywhere else: brash, bright and brutal, like a swaggering army of conquering aliens. The second thing I'd notice would be the lack of children outdoors — a direct result of these giant mechanical cuckoos having taken over our collective nests.

I began to feel uncomfortable being in one — especially as my hostility started to alert me to the automobile's other shortcomings. For example: I realised that, in the countryside, cars deaden their drivers' relationships with the land outside, insulating us from the cold and the mud and the smells and thus enabling us to remain, in our bones, town-dwellers rather than deep-down country-dwellers. We are creatures, most of us, of the tame, mechanised, indoor present rather than the wild, outdoor past. Our cars allow us to remain so, and the land seems paler and less interesting as a result.

Cars suck the life out of communities too, insulating people from their neighbours as well as their environment. I mentioned much earlier that, before all this started, we had spent a year living in a village in France, where life had seemed much more communal than in an English village. There were two obvious reasons why. One was that lots of people still worked with their hands on the surrounding land (making unprofitable wine with the aid of state and EU subsidies). The other — for us — was that we spent almost all our time in the village. We had a car but, not having a network of family and friends to visit around the country, we hardly used it. So we lived in the village instead, and were immediately happier for it.

We weren't surprised. We all know that — to paraphrase Pascal — most rural ills result from villagers' inability to stay quietly in their own village. But in England — for us — that knowledge made no difference. Much as we liked our village, we drove all

393

the time — even before my gratuitous questing. There were simply too many competing attractions pulling us away. It's the same for most people. The average person in the UK lives (according to a BBC study in 2007) 80 miles from their parents. So that, straight away, is a good reason for anyone with a car to make extensive use of it. Throw in a few in-laws, siblings, cousins, aunts and friends made at other stages in life — not to mention shifting employment opportunities, and shops, amenities and recreations that are more to one's taste than those on one's doorstep — and it is easy to see why many modern villagers spend infinitely more time driving than chatting in the street. No doubt we end up with lives that are more precisely tailored to our individual tastes than would otherwise be the case, but our villages suffer as a result, not just because their inhabitants are often physically absent, or because their public transport networks wither from lack of use, but also because of a more corrosive kind of absence: the spiritual absence of the modern Briton who sees things from a global rather than a local perspective; who wants to have it all — work, leisure, beauty, culture, education, entertainment, shops, friends, excitement, novelty, influence — irrespective of where those things are to be found and how many miles must be travelled in order to have them. It's hard for something whose essence is local — as a village's by definition is — to thrive in the face of that kind of absence.

And that, of course, wasn't all. Cars also do terrible things to the atmosphere. By way of a reminder, the summer of 2007 saw the worst floods in the UK in living memory; in many cases those of us lucky enough to escape them got our own reminders in the winters before or after. One freak downpour caused extensive damage to our own house. Such downpours have, I discovered, become a fact of life in much of central England. The Association of British Insurers says that winter rainfall has increased by 30 per cent in the past 40 years. You would need a thick skin not to wonder if this might not be at least partly attributable to our environmentally reckless use of fossil fuels.

Inevitably, as I racked up the miles, the shadow of climate change began to loom more darkly in my mind. Later, the air began to fill with other anxieties: about foot-and-mouth, bluetongue, bird flu and worse. It started to feel rather antisocial to keep roaring up and down the countryside, pumping out fumes and potentially spreading germs.

Even then, I repressed my worries for a while. But when my car started making an alarming grinding sound each time the road bent to the left, I accepted the obvious. It was time to bring all this to an end.

Only not quite yet.

# CHAPTER
# TWENTY-NINE

# Open society

"The trouble with round here," muttered a cross, hunched lady on the grubby double-decker bus that occasionally goes to Peterborough from the nearby village of Helpston, "is there's too many foreigners. You're not allowed to say it, but it's not England any more."

For something that's not allowed to be said, it gets said a lot, especially in this part of England. The population of the Peterborough Unitary Authority (which includes Helpston) is reported to have grown by 10 per cent in the past three years, swollen by the arrival of more than 16,000 migrant workers. Those who object claim that they place an undue strain on local services; local employers claim that the migrants do jobs that English workers simply don't want to do any more.

It's not for me to judge who is right. It did strike me, though, that Helpston, Glinton and Northborough — the cluster of villages just above Peterborough where John Clare spent those periods of his life when not in a lunatic asylum — hardly seemed to be feeling the economic pinch. Glistening with new housing estates, fast roads and fierce railways, they looked as prosperous and urbanised as anywhere I had visited, flaunting their "best kept village" and "best rural retailer" signs to passing commuters while fussing about plans to urbanise them even further. (Apparently another 2,500 houses were on the way soon.) There were John Clare memorabilia on sale in the Helpston village shop, and I was told that Clare enthusiasts had just been awarded a £1.27-million grant from the Heritage Lottery Fund to buy, restore and turn into a "tourist and education centre" the thatched cottage in which he was born in 1793. But Clare — who "was never easy but when I was in the fields" — would have found today's crowded version of his "happy Eden" unrecognisable and, I suspect, intolerable.

On the outskirts of Peterborough, I spoke to a farm-worker whose experiences of rural life might have been more recognisable to the great peasant poet than those of many of today's well-to-do villagers. He was 29 years old and, like John Clare, was small, pale and thin, with big, angry-looking eyes. His clothes looked worn-out, and he had the hunched posture of someone who is often cold. He had grown up in a remote village where pretty much every family had its own smallholding — "we had wheat, potatoes, hay, four pigs, two cows, chickens" — and could remember watching his grandfather and his contemporaries harvesting with scythes: "They would get you watching and then you would be helping to gather it up."

He had done farm-work for as long as he could remember — before school, after school, even during school — and vividly remembered the great harvest festivals that had continued unchanged in his village for generations. But the holding was too small to support a family of six without supplementary income from elsewhere, and when additional work as a warehouseman began to pall he came to eastern England to seek his fortune.

"That was two years ago," explained Jakub Zawistowski, eking out a soft drink in a noisy pub. "I work in several strawberry farms. Essex first, near Manningtree. Then Norfolk. They pay minimum wage — nearly five times what we get in Poland. We live in caravans, like a camp, with other workers, mostly from Eastern Europe. It was hard work: they want quick pickers. But we like it there." Then the employer went into liquidation, leaving many workers with big backlogs of unpaid wages. Jakub came to Peterborough, where his girlfriend, Katya, found a job at an electrical goods shop. They rented a room in a crowded house, and one of the city's many employment agencies for migrant workers found Jakub a job: on a potato production-line in Grantham, turning potatoes into chips. He was now getting up at 4.30a.m. to be bussed there with lots of other Peterborough-based Poles, and was working 12 hours a day for, again, the minimum wage.

"I like England," he told me. "I like to see how different people live. But it's totally boring work now, and Peterborough is a disgusting town. I don't like to do this much longer. It is exploitation. We want to go back to Poland soon and farm with pigs. Make a profit this time. Is more beautiful in Poland. We can see mountains in the village. Here is too flat."

I wished him well, as I had the many foreigners I had come across on my rural travels. What generally struck me about such people — a Turkish man running a roadside snack-bar in Oxfordshire; a Polish chainsaw operator near Newton Abbot whose hobbies included Orthodox church singing, life-saving and boxing; a young Azerbaijani who professed himself "very, very happy" with his job washing cars in the rain in Gloucestershire; a Hungarian working at a "dog hotel" near Cambridge; a Latvian near Manningtree who had done ten farming jobs in as many years in Essex and Suffolk — was how cheerful and positive they usually seemed. How hard life must be in their own countries, I thought.

Now I thought: as landless people who work on the land, moving uncomplainingly from farm to farm to be exploited, perhaps these migrants have more in common with the "real" people of the English countryside than I do.

I headed back northwards into Lincolnshire, where I caught myself bemoaning the absence of hedgerows. I had been thinking about the vanishing of the fabric of the countryside generally, and why it is that this bothers us so little. Since 1945 Britain has lost 97 per cent of its flower-rich meadows, 94 per cent of its lowland raised bogs, 70 per cent of its lowland heathland, up to 50 per cent of its fens and coastal marshes, between 30 and 50 per cent of its ancient woodland, 93 per cent of its tree sparrows, 70 per cent of its song thrushes, more than 60 per cent of its lapwings and farmland skylarks, a third of its butterflies, a quarter of its lakes and ponds, and, as you may remember, 99 per cent of its eels. How, I wondered, can anyone sleep in the shadow of such figures?

Presumably, I decided, we do so because most of us think about the things in question only on the occasions when they are actually present. Unless you are on a particular patch of land that you know very well, you don't see what isn't there. You don't see an absence of skylark. You just don't see a skylark.

In Lincolnshire, however, you see an absence of hedge. Mile after mile of huge, low, black field stretches bleakly towards the North Sea, interrupted only by the occasional ditch or lonely farmhouse. Driving through it, I felt vividly and miserably aware not just of the 200,000 miles of hedgerow that Britain had lost since 1945 (mainly in the name of large-scale, high-yield, mechanised agriculture) but also of all those other lost creatures and habitats. How could we have lost so much? Who would have imagined, returning gladly from war, that the rural tapestry of wildflowers, birdsong and tangled lanes that so many soldiers — my father among them — had imagined and yearned for in their darkest hours would simply disappear within a generation through greed and neglect?

Perhaps it's lucky, I thought, that my father's life ended when it did; lucky, too, that John Clare — who was traumatised by the loss of a single Helpston elm —

isn't around to see this. Then I thought: hang on — John Clare hated hedgerows.

Maybe that's putting it too simply. What he hated — and what inspired great poems of rage such as "To a Fallen Elm" — was enclosure: the systematic process of land privatisation that most of our "traditional" hedgerows were created to enforce. There would have been older hedgerows that Clare would have known and loved, but he grew up in a landscape whose "only bondage was the circling sky"; where a child could wander all day across the furze heath behind his home until the village was below the horizon and his parents were frantic with worry and "the very sun seemed to be a new one and shining in a different quarter of the sky". I'm sure he would have been horrified by the quasi-industrial processes that had created this particular hedgeless desert; yet it was, in some respects, nearer to the England that he knew than the "unspoilt" countryside I grew up in.

And it struck me, as I considered this, that a great deal of the "unspoilt" countryside of our imagination is a direct physical symbol of the triumph of the powerful over the powerless. The latter may have raged against their disenfranchisement from time to time — notably in the wave of riots, rick-burning and machine-smashing that swept across southern England in 1830 — but the powerful — the enclosers — got away with it. Not until the 1870s — under the leadership of Joseph Arch and George Mitchell — would the labourers of rural England develop enough collective muscle to achieve a lifestyle readily distinguishable from slavery; even then, they remained largely impotent in the face of the landowners' stranglehold on power. By 1873, two-thirds of the land in the UK was owned by fewer than 11,000 people. The golden age of rural England — regretted not just by me but by countless nostalgic films and picture postcards as well — was, in effect, the age of the grand estates, when a handful of newly enriched fat cats lived elegant lives of field sports and stately homes with the badly paid assistance and deference of a vast servant and labouring class whose ancestors had once had their own stake in the land they worked on, but had somehow lost it through legislative sleight of hand.

I emerged from this reverie in Nottinghamshire, where I veered westwards towards Sherwood Forest and, before long, became lost in the ragged uplands between Mansfield and Lincoln. I finally stopped in Laxton: the first village I had seen in months that might conceivably merit the description "sleepy". (Did you know, by the way, that in 2007 the phrase "sleepy village" appeared in 270 different articles in UK national newspapers?)

It was small; still; made mainly of old red brick; and, by the feel of it, empty. Perhaps a third of the buildings were vaguely modern; the rest seemed to be from the 19th or, in some cases, the 18th century. Many were farms — which was odd, because I had grown used to seeing farms only in isolation, usually on village fringes. But I knew they were farms, because they looked exactly like the toy farms I remembered from childhood, with a farmhouse in one corner of a square walled yard and barns and shelters coming off the other walls.

One of them, a neat, rose-hung affair near the top of the village, contained a farmer's widow called Margaret Rose, who entertained me in her oak-beamed parlour for the best part of an hour with stories of Laxton's past. An intelligent, lively widow in her early eighties, she was particularly eloquent on the subject of World War II, which began when she was 14. "They used to come over here to bomb Sheffield and come back again, and there was all these ammunition dumps in the Sherwood Forest, and Newark used to get plastered regularly too, because of the ball-bearing factory. This village actually had the first civilian casualty of the war — Miss Willis, who lived in the schoolhouse. She managed to get back in the house, but they dropped these bombs and it killed her at the back of the door.

"We had the Horse Guards here," she continued, "and the horses, they commandeered so many stables: and I don't know how many soldiers was billeted. They took over the parish room; the air-raid wardens were at vicarage; there was a Land Army hostel at Tuxford; and the Americans were down here too at one time — even black Americans. Yes, the war had quite an impression on village life. There were some prisoners of war, too, Italians, up at the common. They lived in that cottage and looked after themselves and worked on the farm — because we were short of labour then, you see. And I don't think they were in a rush to be off anywhere else."

There were several near misses from the bombing. "This plane dropped bombs all the way up the village street and then it dropped this big bomb in the top field and you could've put this house in the crater it made. If it had dropped that one in the village it would have killed half of Laxton." On one occasion she and her family were saved from a shower of glass and shrapnel by "me dad's coat hanging on the back of the door". Every bit of glass had been blown out of the window, and "shrapnel had gone through the beams in the house". Another time, her parents were in the garden when her father suddenly said, "This is a wrong 'un, Mary," and flung them both to the ground — just in time. "There was shrapnel and bricks flying everywhere."

Then there was the bomb at the school — "We couldn't go to school for I don't know how long because it blew all the windows out." And "just over here they dropped one in the cattle-yard there and blew it all to pieces and killed the cattle".

Despite this, she didn't remember worrying much. "I think now about these 14- and 15-year-old girls, worrying about going out at night . . . I mean, we used to go on our bikes to dances, and we were only about 14 and 15, and there were all these soldiers and prisoners, but we were never frightened, not really." She remembered once being followed by some Italian prisoners coming back from a dance in Edwinstowe — "but they were just laughing really. It was," she added, "a happy childhood."

Margaret supplemented her pension by doing bed-and-breakfast and enjoyed sharing her memories of the village with anyone who had time to listen. She was born a Frecknell — an old Laxton name — and had rarely left the village. "We would go on these trips out to the coast, probably once or twice a year, when we were children, but that was all. We were mostly here. My father was running the Dovecote [the pub] when I was a girl. But it was a farm then as well as a pub — he had about 40 acres of land with it, and he used to keep bees as well."

She left school at 14 and worked for a while in the village shop. Then came war and then, afterwards, she married a local boy — Reg Rose — and moved down to Bottom Farm. "We were there 40 years"; then her son took over — continuing a tradition that goes back for centuries on both sides of the family. It was hard to imagine anyone having deeper village roots.

"I was actually born at the end cottage of Beech House. A lot of these farm cottages was two if not three homes in them days: just sort of one up, one down, with a sitting room and a hole in the ceiling and a ladder. Then we came to the Dovecote. I suppose it was a close-knit community, but they didn't all come to the pub. You used to get half the village come at Christmas, because my mother used to make mince pies and sausage rolls and that sort of thing. But they'd never come all year. But there were some beech trees outside, where a lot of chaps used to hang around, and then there were football and cricket teams as well. There used to be whist drives, too: we used to have 12 hands of whist and then a dance after. And there was the parish room, as well, that used to be like a reading room, and there was a lot of farm chaps went there, and we used to go in there and all get together.

405

"But we didn't really get that much free time then. When I first got married, it was a full-time job just keeping the house going. I didn't have washing machine — we had this washing copper in the corner, and we used to build a fire beneath it, and keep fire going all day long. Then you used to have to get down on your hands and knees and scrub floor, because they were most of them either flagstones or old red quarry tiles, weren't they?

"Then we'd be baking, or making butter. We used to take eggs, apples, parsley, mint, to market; we used to grow a few taters, too. Nearly everyone used to grow 5 or 6 acres, for our own consumption and also to sell.

"And then when it was harvest and hay time we used to take the cooked dinners in a basket out to the men, and used to have it in the fields, because it was such a long way for them to come home, from the extreme field. I remember once sending a cooked dinner, meat and vegetables and gravy and that and pudding and custard, and I didn't send them no knives and forks . . . But they managed."

She smiled, and the light from the windows flashed on her spectacles. "Of course most people worked on the farming then. Nearly all the farmers had farm chaps living in. Some came from large families in other villages. Some of them came from homes [i.e., institutions] as well. That old chap that work for Dick Clark — he was a home boy. I don't know what the correct political term is now — but there was places for that sort of people in rural communities then. Because, if you've only got to do a bit of hedge-cutting or chop sticks or pick taters or pick sugar beet . . .

"That old chap that my grandad had for years, old Sam Pickering: he used to go and sit out in stick shed at night. There was no television, no wireless, no nothing like that, so he'd sit there chopping sticks. He used to have to go and feed horses at night as well, and then he'd come in and go to sleep."

But there is more to Laxton than some vividly preserved personal memories. It is also of great historical significance — as Margaret's son, Stuart, explained when he gave me a guided tour of the place. "There were 30-odd farmers with holdings in the village when my father started farming here," he told me. "Now there's 14. If it gets any fewer than that, it'll be hard to keep this going. But it's still going for now."

The "this" he was referring to was Britain's last surviving "open-field" system of farming — the cooperative form of agriculture by which most English villages supported themselves in the centuries before enclosure. It survived in Laxton by accident. While the rest of England was being enclosed, Laxton's two principal landowners, Earl Manvers and the Earl of Scarborough, managed to sustain a quarrel for much of the 19th century that prevented them from agreeing a mutually satisfactory way of enclosing the local farmland. Then came an agricultural depression that made enclosure seem hardly worth the trouble and expense — especially to Earl Manvers, who was creating a stately home at the time. By the early 20th century, Laxton's medieval farming system was beginning to be seen as historically important, while two world wars created other priorities. When the Manvers family put their lands up for sale in the 1950s, the Ministry of Agriculture was persuaded to buy it. It was sold again in 1981 ("when Mrs Thatcher decided that everything like the railway and the water and all those sort of things should go into private"), this time to the Crown Estate, which made an undertaking to Parliament to preserve the open-field system. And so, more or less, it continues today.

"It is," said Stuart, "a struggle. The Crown Estate isn't a registered charity, so they have to make it economic, and that creates a lot of pressures. All of these farms are worth more for their rental value as houses — you know, just a nice country house with a pony paddock — than they can charge people for 120-acre, 140-acre farm holdings. But we've only had one barn conversion so far, and we've got enough pressure at the moment to keep them at bay. But how long that'll last I don't know."

He was 50 years old and had a certain solid, roast-beef-of-England quality to him, with a stocky frame, a wide, pink face under his fair hair and big arms bulging from his rolled-up shirt-sleeves and fleece waistcoat. As we drove along muddy tracks in his Land-Rover, he scarcely seemed to glance at the big, hedgeless fields as he pointed out significant features — as if the memory of the local geography, and of the traditions by which the land is farmed, had been imprinted on his mind since birth.

The gist of the system is that, instead of each farm having its own fields, enclosed by hedges or fences, all 14 farmers have a share in the village's three big, open fields. These aren't as big as they used to be — since 1635, Laxton's acreage of unenclosed land has shrunk from 1,894 to 483, partly as a result of four outlying farms to the south and west of the village, for which land was enclosed in the 1720s and 1730s. And each of the farms in the open-field system has some enclosed land of its own as well. But what remains has to be farmed cooperatively. That's not the same as farming communally: wooden pegs indicate the limits of each farmer's share of each field. But it does require constant collaboration.

With so many people involved this can be complicated. The system evolved piecemeal over the centuries as the area of land under cultivation gradually expanded and rights to different bits of it were passed down (and divided) through the generations. There are 164 different strips within the three big, open fields. ("A strip," explained Stuart, "was what you could plough in a day.") If people disagree about what to plant where, or what to harvest when, then the system can become very inefficient. But that is, in a sense, the beauty of it: the village is forced to talk.

"That," said Stuart, accelerating up a waterlogged track towards a wind-whipped headland, "is why we have the Court Leet." This is the kind of manorial system of local government that most villages would have had 500 years ago, and the only one in the country that still has legal authority. "I'm the Leet clerk," said Stuart. "And there's a bailiff, Robert Aigue. The court meets once a year, in November, but Robert and I sort of keep our heads together over the day-to-day running. But there's also, for each of the open fields, what's called a foreman. So if there's an issue in one of the fields or something, then me and Robert and one of the foremen will sort it out." There are also 12 jurors — elected annually — who inspect the fields at the end of the year, on Jury Day, and present their report to the court. Farmers who have let the side down in some way — by straying over strip boundaries, for example — can be fined. "It's normally not much — just a few quid — and if someone thinks they've been hard done by they'll appeal, but it serves its purpose. We fined one bloke £25 for something he'd done for two or three years in a row. He eventually got it reduced to £15, but I'm sure he'll not do it again."

The system is much studied by academics, and the barn next to the Dovecote Inn has been converted into a visitor centre. But for Laxton's farmers it remains primarily a system for earning a living and — no less important — for preserving Laxton's own special character as a village.

"There's been talk of amalgamating two or three of the big farms, to make them more efficient," said Stuart, "and leave the others with just two or three strips. But we've all said that we need to stay equal, because one of the things that Laxton's all about is treating everybody equal."

Does that mean that everyone is equal? "Not at all. Some people are making a better living than others. But it's not competitive. It's the opposite — it's more community. If my neighbour's combine breaks down, a couple of us will dig in and help him out, and then later on he'll probably come back and do me 5 acre of ploughing or something like that. But everybody's surviving one way or another.

"Of course, a lot of us have a secondary income as well, whether it's bed-and-breakfast or going out to work somewhere else. And not everyone does much farming: some of the older ones might rely on contractors for the farm work, or enter into an arrangement with a younger person and share equipment. I do agricultural repairs as well as this, as well as a bit of outside catering — you know, hog roasts. But I'm also farming a couple of strips for somebody else this year, because I'm growing spring beans and he wants spring beans too.

"Look," he said suddenly, "there's one." We were, I think, on the edge of the Mill Field at the time, and there, where the field met the path, was a boundary peg: a pale wooden post hammered deep into the ground like an old-fashioned tent-peg. It was quite hard to make sense of it all, from where I sat. The field stretched as far as the eye could see, and if Stuart hadn't pointed out the lumps at the end where centuries of ploughing with a mouldboard-plough (which always pushes the earth to the right) had created a series of grassy knolls, I would have found it hard to spot the difference between this and one of the arable prairies I had seen earlier. "That's what we call the spring-crop field," he explained, gesturing as far as the eye could see. "So that will be spring barley, or beans, or something like that." Another of the big fields would be given over to a summer crop, while the third would, up to a point, lie fallow. (In practice it grows grass for forage.) "Where you can see the bits that are ploughed," Stuart added a bit later, "that may be several different strips." The fact that a blustering wind was lashing us relentlessly from the west — sharpened from time to time with squalls of cold rain — made it even harder to focus; even, sometimes, to hear.

"The chap who lives down there has Limousins," I thought he said at one point. What, the cows? "No, no: limousines. He's got a stretch limo, a Bentley, a Mercedes people carrier. Takes people to airports and things."

A bit later, he gestured at a wide strip of grassland at the bottom of the hill and said, "Look, there's one of the sykes." These — pronounced "sukes" — are pieces of grassland for grazing that are auctioned off each year at the Court Leet. "We take a £2 levy on every bid, which we spend on beer. It all helps to keep us all talking to each other." The main value of the grassland these days is as Sites of Special Scientific Interest (SSSIs). "There's 80 acres of sykes here have never had spray or fertiliser on them — ever." There wasn't a grazing beast to be seen.

"Of course," said Stuart, "the other thing that's changed is that 50 years ago all the farms in Laxton would have been mixed farms. On their own holdings they'd all have had eight or 10 cows, they'd have a few pigs, sheep, a few chickens . . . All these places used to have a pigsty, and there always used to be a pig-killing going on somewhere during winter months. Everyone used to come — there was such a lot of meat that had got to be sorted and minced and made into pies and such, and hams trimmed up and salted, and cleaning all intestines out for sausage skins . . . You was never short of a job when you killed a pig. But now nobody has their own pig any more. It's almost all arable."

I looked round at the empty fields and realised that we had driven halfway around Laxton without seeing another living creature. Where, I asked, were all the other farmers?

"Oh, they'll all be indoors doing their VAT receipts. There is," he added, "a hell of a lot of paperwork these days."

Much of it, in Laxton, is done by Stuart Rose. The village receives something in the region of £50,000 a year from Defra's Countryside Stewardship Scheme, as well as assorted environmental grants "to do with the sykes and the SSSIs and the fallow field". The Leet clerk is responsible for sharing it out fairly.

In an odd sort of way, the mention of grants and subsidies seemed to make Laxton's system of agriculture feel more authentic — more like real farming and less like some quaint re-enactment. As Stuart said, "We've got to make a living — it's not just for the heritage." Yet I remained not wholly convinced. Laxton's farming system survives because it is considered worth conserving: without the protection of the Crown Estate it would be exposed to the same irresistible market forces as everywhere else. I wonder how long it would last then.

As the rain grew wilder, we went back to Stuart's home, Bottom Farm. With its clutter of family photographs, "Happy Birthday Daddy" cards and "I love my dad" socks drying on the radiator, it felt like the kind of typical modern home that you might find anywhere in England. But the life of the Rose family is inextricable from the life of Laxton: there were, by my count, four different Rose households in the village today. I had missed that year's Court Leet session, so Stuart showed me some old film of two previous ones: one from 1935 and one from 1975. You could see why the Crown Estate likes it, with the bailiff still summoning people to court with the same archaic formula ("Oh, yes, oh, yes, oh, yes, all manner of persons who owe suitor service to the Court Leet of the Queen's most excellent majesty, all who have been summoned to attend at this place, draw near and give your attendance"), the jurors still signifying their willingness to serve by kissing the Bible — and those same jurors still wearing cloth caps and sitting on straw bales when they set off in a trailer for their annual tour of inspection. Stuart's commentary on the wrinkled, black-and-white faces ("He's dead . . . He's still here . . . That's my uncle, he's gone . . . That was Pa, he's dead . . . He's dead . . . He's gone too . . .") reminded me that the line between the idea of "village" and the idea of "extended family" is still, in some places, a thin one.

**414**

But families change too, and Laxton was only partially insulated against the social revolution in the wider countryside. "It's still a good place to live," said Stuart. "But it's changed, and it's going to carry on changing. There's no school, for a start. We all went to the same school when I was young — except when the potatoes had got to be got in, and then nobody went to school. But now all the children go to different schools. Then there's the church. We used to go twice a day on Sundays, and we all sang in the choir — even if you couldn't sing, you still used to get your cassock and surplice on and go through the motions. But now the church has all been amalgamated with about five other parishes, and the vicar has got that many villages to look after that he hasn't got time to come round visiting and doing all the social side. We still get a good turnout on Plough Sunday, and you might get 50 or 60 for the family service once a month, but for a normal communion service it's probably just eight or 10. So that's two important changes, because the vicar and the schoolmaster used to be important figures in the community: if anyone was in trouble, they had got the craft to sort it out.

"We've still got the pub, so that's something, although of course they rely mainly on the tourist trade now." (When I went there, it was bursting at the seams with agricultural machinery buyers from Wales, who had come for a trade fair in Newark.) "And our post-office-and-shop has survived — you can recognise it by all the Andrex in the window. But you've heard all the GPO [General Post Office] announcements on the radio, and I don't think anybody will take it on when the current lady stops. We do try and help her: we do daft things like go and buy our tax disc stamps from her and then go down to Ollerton to get our tax discs, just to put some business through. But she's in her seventies and she can't keep doing it for ever.

"But the main change is that you're really not getting so many young people in the village. We've got a tremendous reservoir of retired people, but their children have not managed to get employment or afford to live in the village. There's not many who were brought up in the village actually stayed: of my year at school, there's only one other lad that I know of — and he's a Retford man." (Retford is about a mile down the lane.)

"Most of the farmers have roots in the village — maybe they've inherited, or there's some link down the line. But of course 50 years ago it wasn't just the farmers, it was the labourers who used to work for them, and the village professions who did business with them — you know, Willie Moreton was the wheelwright, and the blacksmith's shop was at the top of the village. But none of them are needed any more, and so all their homes are now lived in by people who earn their livings in other ways.

"The problem for young people is that if they've got a decent qualification and a decent job, they don't stop in Laxton, and if they're in a low-paid job they can't afford to live in Laxton."

So what did people do? "Well, it is still basically a farming community, which you can't say of many

**416**

places. Say the population's about 200,250, somewhere around there — then I'd say about 50 of those are living on working farms. That has to be worth something. Apart from that, well, there's quite a lot of retired people ... There's a retired schoolteacher. There's a chap who used to work for a local agricultural supplier. There's a builder. There's a chap who's got a textile business. Someone who works for the land and drainage board. A lady who's an ex-teacher. Someone who has a little haulage business. A couple of schoolteachers. Don't know ... Retired ... A retired chemist ... A lorry-driver ... A woman who's got a catering business ... Another builder — there are three in the village ... An electrician ... A plant operator ... Another retired person ... There's quite a few secretaries and clerical type of people in the council houses — you know, working for the local council, or for businesses in Mansfield or Newark ... Then there's a brickworks down the road that used to employ quite a few people in the village, a couple are still employed there ... There's an agricultural engineer ... A couple work at the Thorsby estate [the Manvers seat] — one on the woods and one on the gamekeeping side ... There's Janet, the post-lady — she's semi-retired ... But I don't know what the chap opposite the pub does. In fact, there's a couple of others I don't know what they do. When I was at school I could have told you everyone in the village.

"Of course," he added, "we get quite a lot of tourists come here now, so a lot of people do bed-and-breakfast as well. I suppose they're all developments on making a living. But there's not much call for blacksmiths or wheelwrights, and the fewer people you have involved in the farming, the more separate and self-contained everyone gets."

He thought for a moment. "I suppose you never really know who's about any more, do you? That's the other thing. Because people can come in by car from anywhere, tourists or whatever, so you start to lose that sense of it being our streets. My daughter is 17, she works at the pub, and my wife won't let her walk down from the pub on her own, when she's finished a shift. We always come and fetch her."

# CHAPTER
# THIRTY

# The unarmed struggle

I stood among wide fields of scrappy stubble on a cold Yorkshire plateau above Towton. Crows and clouds swirled chaotically in a troubled sky, as if in the mind of Van Gogh. A line of power stations smoked furtively on the horizon. An east wind whipped bleakly across everything. No hedgerows survived to give shelter from it, apart from one small cube of box on a bend in the road, about 3m in height, width and depth. This concealed — perhaps on purpose — a worn stone cross.

According to an inscription at its base, the cross marked the site of the battle of Towton, which took place on Palm Sunday, 1461. This was the bloodiest battle in English history. Up to 28,000 men are reported to have died that day; considerably more than the 19,200 killed by machine-gun fire on the first day of the Somme in 1916 — and these ones were mostly hand-carved by their fellow Englishmen (in many cases, by their own sons, brothers or fathers). I can never remember whether it was the Yorkists or the Lancastrians who won — only that the slaughter made little difference to the ultimate outcome of the Wars of the Roses — and that scarcely anyone these days has heard of it.

A bare, unfenced track led between two fields to a sagging wooden gate, tied shut with baler twine. A grubby white sign leant against it: "Private. No access. No horses". I gazed past some grey sheep down the steep, balding meadow behind it. It was on this slope that the worst of the massacre took place; those who escaped mostly drowned in the stream at the bottom. It was hard to imagine so many people crowding this empty place, yet I thought I could still feel the fear in the air.

Back at the road, a tall pensioner with a bushy white moustache, turned-up anorak collar and tightly jammed-down cloth cap was studying the stone cross, which had four withered bouquets tied to it: two of white roses, one of red and one of rotting yellow chrysanthemums. He came from Leeds and made a hobby of visiting battlefield sites; he was hoping to get to Stamford Bridge later. An old woman sat in his car, obscured by a "disabled passenger" sticker, and ate a sandwich.

"The thing about Towton," he said as he was leaving, "is the scale of it. When you take into account what the size of the population was back then, 28,000 was one adult Englishman in 50. It's unimaginable."

Even if contemporary chroniclers hugely exaggerated the numbers — even if the true figure were, say, just 7,000 — that still represents a massacre of dizzying proportions. To get a sense of what it would have felt like, you would need to imagine 100,000 Englishmen being killed in a single day today — by other Englishmen. I tried to do so. All I could think was that, in much of the land, they must have felt as though their world had ended.

"Many men were utterly destroyed," wrote Polydore Vergil in his *Anglicae Historiae*, "and the whole realm brought to ruine and decay." Shakespeare, a century and a half later, dwelt on the bloodbath in *Henry VI Part 3* ("O piteous spectacle! O bloody times!" cries the king). Yet today, for at least 99 modern Englishmen in 100, that battle might as well never have taken place. The echoes of the screams have died; the horror has slipped from our collective memory. Perhaps five centuries is longer than any story can survive.

Or perhaps it is simply that, from time to time, worlds really do come to an end.

Some time later, on a wet Saturday, I found myself in the dreary region known by some as the Isle of Axholme. My spirits sank. I imagine they often must for strangers entering the area.

For most of its history, this unglamorous triangle of north Lincolnshire was scarcely habitable: a patch of highish fenland among the pestilential triangle of marshes enclosed by the rivers Trent, Idle and Don. Its inhabitants were a race apart, dredging obscure livings from various forms of fishing, hunting and small-scale agricultural activities such as reed-harvesting. They had little contact with folk beyond the fens. Abraham de la Pryme, the 17th-century antiquary and diarist, dismissed them as "little better than heathen". Sir

William Dugdale, his contemporary, called them "a rude and almost barbarous sort of lazy and beggarly people".

Modern civilisation came knocking in the 1620s but wasn't welcomed. Charles I engaged Cornelius Vermuyden, the Dutch engineer and speculator, to drain the area; he gave Vermuyden a third of it as a reward and claimed another third for himself. The locals, who had been living off the waterlogged land for centuries and had been under the impression that they owned it all, were outraged. They had no desire to see it either expropriated or drained. Decades of bitter attrition ensued, in which Vermuyden's works and workers were regularly attacked, and settlers from the Low Countries were brought in to keep the work going, adding to the bitterness. "Progress" won, in the sense that the drainage was mostly completed by 1649 (using the forced labour of Scottish prisoners of war), and the land has been heavily exploited by conventional agriculture ever since. But the losers' resentment festered for many long years.

Today, those troubles are as distant a half-memory as the once endemic marsh-sickness. Yet the drained land retains that damp, unwelcoming air that outsiders have often sensed in fen country. A miserable rain was gusting across it when I drove through, pelting intermittently on to wide, low-lying fields of matted leaf vegetables; earth, sky and everything in between felt damp. I stopped for petrol east of Doncaster and, queuing to pay, was chilled by the charmlessness of my fellow customers: not a single please or thank you in any of the four transactions that preceded me, just slack-jawed scowls from pasty, pierced faces, with mounds of semi-clothed belly and buttock bulging truculently beneath them.

I drove on, feeling cold and alienated, weaving on minor roads through flat fields. What houses I passed were scattered, low, square and closed; every window was locked against the cold. It didn't take much imagination to think myself back into the days when a traveller could cross the marshes only with the help of a skilled (but probably treacherous) local guide.

From time to time a converted windmill, sailless and neatly painted, rose from behind a hedge to remind me of the area's Dutch connection. (They were once used to power pumps.) But my overall impression was of a damp, prosaic English winter. Lincolnshire, I thought: what a dump — famous for nothing apart from its poachers and its agri-industrial wilderness and (according to one recent report) the UK's biggest obesity problem. No wonder the Pilgrim Fathers got out (from Scrooby, just to the south). And no wonder Grayson Perry, the transvestite, Turner Prize-winning London potter, had just given his latest fashionable show (in which he condemned "the biscuit-tin idyll of cosy village Britain" as a "candlelit, back-breaking, sexist, tubercular, child-death hell") the ironic title "The Charms of Lincolnshire". Time to be getting home, I muttered, and flicked the windscreen-wipers on to full.

Then I passed through a village called Westwoodside, and wondered why there were suddenly so many people out walking. They were all heading eastwards, trudging through the drizzle in purposeful twos and threes, out of the village and over a low hill with a curiously shaped water-tower near the top.

Before I knew it, I had passed the hill and was driving down into Haxey. And then I stopped.

It's not the kind of place you would expect a tourist to stop in. It's big, functional and mostly modern, right at the "town" end of the village spectrum — not so much biscuit-tin as family-size crisp packet. On this occasion, however, I had no choice. The main street was packed solid with people.

I parked some way off and walked back to explore.

"It's the Hood," said an old lady with a woolly hat and no visible teeth. "Sixth of January."

I looked at her blankly.

"They'll be along soon."

An eddy of moving people forced us apart, and I found myself heading deeper into the village, mesmerised by the size and variety of the swirling crowd: old, young, big, small, smart, scruffy, white and non-white. I'm no expert in crowd-counting, but I'd be amazed if there were fewer than 2,000 people out and about. All milled happily, with that air of talkative expectation that you get in a crowd heading for a football match. Many carried beer, in cans and plastic glasses; much, clearly, had been drunk already. Some teenage girls were giggling outside a hairdresser's; hoodied youths with beer-cans slouched past them in gangs. "Oi," yelled one of the latter, menacingly, to a similar-looking youth in another group, "you ain't left

Gran by herself?" "She'll be all right," said the other. "Just gonna see the start." "No," protested the first, "she's gotta have someone with her." "Going for a piss in the forecourt," confided a voice near by, interrupting my train of eavesdropping. "Mustn't break years of tradition."

I asked a serious-looking man in a flat cap to explain what was going on. He drew in a long, patient breath, as if wondering where to begin. "There's the Fool, the Boggins and the Lords," he pronounced, eventually. "Sorry, the Lord, the Fool and the Boggins. The Fool has the marked face. The Lord has the wand — no, hang on, the Chief Boggin . . ." He petered out, as if he had perplexed himself, then added brightly: "They'll be in a pub now. You'll catch them if you can get in."

Two pubs were in view: the Duke William and the Loco, nearly next door to one another. The crowd clustered densely in and around each. After 10 minutes of patient squeezing, shoving, apologising and weaving, I made it as far as the doorway of the Loco, from where I could see a large room packed as tightly as a rush-hour railway carriage, with a patch of bright red in the middle. This turned out to be a group of about 13 burly men, most dressed in red sweatshirts but two wearing long red jackets — hunting-pink, I suppose — and one wearing a longer, bluer number flapping with bright ribbons. These last three all wore bowler hats with pheasant feathers sticking out of them and, in two cases, extravagant flower arrangements on top. One carried a long, multi-ended staff; another held what looked like a giant leather sausage.

They were swilling back beer and chatting boisterously, as men in pubs do. Several swayed a bit, and at least some of the collective impression of redness they exuded seemed to glow from their cheeks. But what struck me most was how solid most of them looked: big, broad-shouldered and bull-necked, as English countrymen are traditionally supposed to look.

Without warning, they began to sing.

It was an ordinary folksong: the hearty, bouncing, reasonably well-known ballad called "A Farmer's Boy". But its beauty was startling: a dozen or more strong bass voices, not bellowing like rugby players but booming like well-played tubas, in perfect unison. The words filled the room with a power and resonance that made my neck tingle:

> The sun had set behind yon hill across the
>   dreary moor,
> When, weary and lame, a poor boy came up to a
>   farmer's door:
> "Can you tell me where'er I'll be, and of one
>   who'll me employ
> To plough and sow, to reap and mow
> And be a farmer's boy, and be a farmer's boy."

A hundred or more drinkers listened and looked, rapt. Some younger ones stood on chairs to watch. The roar of trade at the bar paused. One or two joined in with the singing.

By the middle of the next song, "Drink Old England Dry", lots of people were joining in. A small old lady near by — wedged against the wall opposite — seemed to have tears in her eyes as she swayed gently, mouthing the words ("Come drink me brave boys and we'll boldly call for more. /For the French they invade us and they say that they will try/ They say that they shall come and drink old England dry").

By the end of the third, "John Barleycorn", most of the pub was singing, although the power and sweetness all came from the group in red. It's a familiar but unsettling song: a grotesque symbolic yarn on the themes of fertility, harvest, sacrifice, mutilation, resurrection and drunkenness whose roots, some say, lie in pre-Christian times. Yet here it was, holding spellbound a boisterous 21st-century audience of internet-users and satellite TV-watchers. It can't have been the beer, because I had yet to reach the bar, but I felt an overpowering sense that a living rural past was in the room, holding the present in its grip as I watched.

I wasn't far wrong. As the scene unfolded, dreamlike, it gradually revealed its mysteries. Over the next hour or so, the men in red wrestled their way to the door, paused for a round of what looked like port but someone said was rum, battled their way through the crowd to the Duke William, squeezed their way in, repeated the entire ritual, staggered out, and continued their way up the street towards the church. They could have been celebrities mobbed by autograph-hunters: everyone seemed to want to exchange a word, or shake hands, or clap hands on a back; there were even several journalists, from local television and radio, quizzing the men in the fancy coats as they tried to make headway.

At one point, the man in the ribboned coat — whose face, I should have mentioned, was smeared with dark paint — seemed to try to run away. He was caught by the men in red sweatshirts, who carried him to a stone mounting block outside the church. He climbed on to it and began to address the crowd. They greeted him with a twitching forest of raised cameras and phones. "My lords and ladies and gentlemen," he shouted, swaying alarmingly. "We are gathered here today to play the ancient game of Haxey Hood. I welcome you all from near and far. I trust you all will enjoy our ancient tradition . . ." He paused to wobble. A tattooed man to my right belched deafeningly. "Up on yon hill the game will commence. Tonight there'll be a feast —" The next bit was drowned by a minor domestic argument just in front of me. ("Pick her up," snapped a plump woman to a wiry man, indicating a short, plump child. "She can't see a thing from there." The man made a half-hearted attempt to do so. "Can't," he said sulkily.) Then smoke and flames began to billow around the speaker's ankles. "As you can see," he continued, "things are starting to warm up."

All of this, I gradually learnt (from various not always consistent or even coherent informants), was part of a local tradition going back 650 years or more. It's called the Haxey Hood and takes place on 6 January — Old Christmas Day. Its centrepiece is a sporting contest in which drinkers from four pubs, three in Haxey and one in Westwoodside, wrestle for possession of a symbolic "hood" (actually the leather sausage-like object I had just seen in the pub). The winners — the first to get the Hood back to their pub — are allowed to keep it there for the next year. This contest is supposed to be a mutated re-enactment of a 14th-century incident in which the local landowner's wife, Lady Mowbray, dropped her hood while riding on the hill that separates the two villages. The 13 farm labourers who were working there at the time chased the hood as the wind blew it around the field. One finally caught it but was too shy to return it to its owner, so one of his companions did so. The grateful lady thanked him for acting like a Lord and added that the shy one was a Fool. As a mark of gratitude, she gave the men 13 acres of land to hold in perpetuity, as long as they re-enacted the chase every year. So they did.

There may well be some truth in this tale: tenants of Lord Mowbray were granted some land around Haxey in perpetuity in 1359. But documentary evidence of an annual Hood re-enactment goes back only a couple of centuries (which is also the approximate age of "Drink Old England Dry" and "A Farmer's Boy"), so one cannot be certain. What one can say is that, whenever it began, the tradition has since acquired a life of its own. The principal actors in it are now the Fool (representing the shy labourer), the Lord (representing the bold one), and 11 Boggins — including a Chief Boggin — who represent the other labourers. The high officials are appointed when a vacancy arises and remain in office until they have had enough. Dale Smith, a lorry driver, was playing the Fool for the 12th year in succession; Phil Coggan, an engineer, was in his 18th year as Lord. Both are former Boggins, from families whose Hood connections go back generations; both have been involved with the event since they were children; both hope that their own offspring may continue the tradition.

Each year they go through the same routine. On New Year's Eve they collect the Hood from the pub that won it last year; for the next five days they tour the surrounding villages and pubs, in costume, singing their songs and collecting money for charity; on the 6th itself they work their way through the four participating pubs in Haxey and Westwoodside, singing and drinking. ("You need a liver of iron for this," said one villager.) The Fool then makes a speech outside the church and is "smoked" by a burning bale of wet straw. The smoking was probably more severe in years gone by.

Then the Fool signifies the approach of the main event by declaiming the words that most Haxey-dwellers have known by heart from childhood:

> 'oose agen 'oose.
> Toon agen toon.
> If a man meets a man,
> knock 'im doon;
> but doan 'urt 'im.

You can probably work out what this means. (If not: it's "House against house" — that is, public house against public house; "town against town" — that is, village against village; "knock down any man you meet — but don't hurt him". Some say that this last clause is a modern interpolation.) The crowd in the street certainly seemed to have no difficulty with the concept, roaring along with the Fool as he chanted the words from his smoke-cloud. Then, as if a tide had changed, they surged out of the village, up the hill and on to a muddy field sown with winter wheat.

It was, I think, about 3.30p.m. when the Chief Boggin — I think it was the Chief Boggin — threw the first of 12 rough hessian "hoods" to be chased and wrestled for by children and teenagers. This was just a prelude, but you wouldn't have guessed that from the intensity with which the youngsters chased and fought for them. It was like rugby, with fewer rules, played on an uneven pitch on which well over a thousand spectators were hanging around as drinking, smoking, chatting obstacles. At one point a pushchair was knocked over, and several girls were flattened by large boys. No one seemed bothered, picking themselves up with smiles on muddy faces.

Finally, at getting on for 4p.m., the main event began. You could tell it was about to do so from the frisson of nervous anticipation that rippled round the field. "If you're going in there, for God's sake be careful," said a father (I presume) to a lad of about 19. "Yes, yes," said the lad, licking his lips. "Seriously," said the father, and gripped his arm.

Some 50 or 60 of the heftiest men present gathered round. The Lord repeated the ritual shout ("'oose agen 'oose . . .") and launched the leather sausage into the air. A dozen brawny arms grabbed at it, and the Sway began.

My jaw dropped. Everything up to this point had been colourful and peculiar but essentially recognisable as part of the modern world: ordinary people having a boozy day out, teenagers getting boisterous, tradition-buffs indulging in a bit of quaint ritual — no more threatening than a display of morris dancing on a bank holiday. The Sway was something else: irresistible, mad and distinctly frightening.

Imagine a rugby maul, which typically contains around 16 men and rarely lasts longer than a couple of minutes. Even that is considered by some to be an imprudently intense focusing of brute physical power and weight. Now multiply that in size by four, remove the rulebook and the carefully practised teamwork, and transfer it all to a muddy, sloping wheatfield — and you might begin to have a faint sense of what the Sway is like.

Then factor in that there are not two teams but four, and that there is no obvious way of telling their members apart, or what any of them are doing, or whereabouts in the *mêlée* any of them are. Bear in mind, too, that most of those involved have been drinking beer for half the day. And then note the crucial fact that that initial brawl of 50 or 60 is just the beginning. Once the Sway has a visible presence, other people begin to bind on to it, pushing or pulling as they see fit. Before long there must have been nearly 150 people involved, all heaving and leaning and wrestling in a fearsome embodiment of the idea of raw manpower.

432

In rugby, the great fear is that a maul or scrum will collapse and cause serious injury. The Sway is less stable and more dangerous. If the average participant weighs, say, 80 kg, then the Sway as a whole must weigh about 12 metric tonnes. Every few minutes, it collapsed.

You couldn't always see it, because the rows of pushers became steadily more upright the further you got from the point of collapse. But you could feel the earth shake, and the air instantly boomed with urgent cries of "Back off". Minutes would then be spent hauling off bodies until the unfortunates at the bottom of it all could be rescued. The bottom-most emerged caked from head to foot with black mud. Remarkably, none had been crushed to death.

There was a time, apparently, when participation in the Sway was more or less compulsory for anyone who presumed to be considered a man. The Boggins — whose main concern today was to prevent injury in collapses — were once largely employed in the rounding-up and conscription of non-contestants. One tale relates that, in the 1940s, a travelling salesman tried to drive through Haxey on Hood day. His car-keys were snatched and thrown into the middle of the Sway, from which he was invited to fetch them. Even today, although there were plenty of able-bodied men spectating, I felt vaguely ashamed to be on the sidelines. "You big jessie," said a young woman to a traumatised, mud-caked youth who limped out of the heap towards her.

OK, I said to myself. I may not be a true sturdy oak of English rural manhood, but even we rootless media-types have our pride. I flung myself into what seemed to be the Haxey side and started heaving.

For the first few minutes nothing happened. I heaved. Another part of the Sway collapsed and we were called off. We started again. It collapsed again. Then, on about the third or fourth attempt, I found that my outer layer had become an inner layer, and I began to experience something of the almost mystical power of the Sway. Not everything — only the local strong men know what really goes on in the centre — but definitely something. No matter how vigorously I struggled, I had no power over my movements, which were entirely determined by a force greater than me. It was like trying to stand in the sea while a huge wave withdrew: this was power on a completely different scale to my own strength. I was swept off my feet.

"What do we do if it collapses on us?" I asked my neighbour — whose face I couldn't see properly but whose beery armpit I was sure I would recognise if my head were ever wedged in it again. "Lie still and wait for the Boggins," came the reply. "I've been stuck at the bottom for ages once, waiting for everyone to get off. There was this Boggin holding my head up with his hand. Stopped me drowning in mud."

It was shortly after this that I decided I had done my bit. There is a limit to what you can observe from the middle of a mass embrace. And there was a limit to the enthusiasm I could summon for health-endangering but apparently ineffectual heaving when I had no real

434

sense of what, if anything, my efforts were achieving. I'm reasonably muddy now, I reasoned — why risk injury or worse to no good purpose?

I think this was wise. Back at a safe distance, I saw first one and then another body carried out — still living, in each case, but clearly in pain. The ambulance waiting on the far side of the field flashed quietly into life. Others limped away in obvious distress. "It's cracked ribs mainly," Phil Coggan, the Lord, told me later. "Or else people get hurt where it's their own fault because they've got too full of ale." It seemed to me that a lot of people were having problems with feet and ankles. Every five minutes or so, someone would throw out a mud-caked shoe or boot from the centre of the Sway while it was reforming after a collapse. I saw at least a dozen retrieved in this way, at different times — along with a hat, two socks and a belt. "There'll be a pair of trousers along in a minute," said a woman.

To some eyes, I suppose the violence might have seemed shocking, but the dominant note was of *bonhomie*. "What's good about this," said a bearded Haxonian with a video-camera, "is that every single person in the village will be out here. It's part of living in Haxey. If they don't like it, they don't come and live here."

The communal nature of the event was startling. According to research published in 2006 by (for some reason) the Royal Society of Arts, two-thirds of Britons take part in no community activities at all, and most adults suffer from "community-detachment syndrome". More than half wouldn't chat with a stranger in the village shop (although 24 per cent — according to another survey around the same time for Direct Line Home Insurance — have found the time to quarrel with their neighbours over issues relating to their gardens); 82 per cent would not strike up a conversation at the school gates. Such figures are not surprising, but they are depressing. And it was therefore both humbling and uplifting to realise that here — in this ostensibly barbaric spectacle of muddied, drunken oafs making fools of themselves in a field — was a rural(-ish) community genuinely and intimately in touch with itself. Perhaps other communities should take note.

A hundred years ago, one might have interpreted the Hood as a distinctly rural tradition, but there didn't seem to be many genuine farmers' boys involved. A farmer or two, certainly, but actual agricultural labourers are as rare in Haxey as anywhere else; in any case, a lot of those present came from Doncaster. As far as I could work out (and systematic research was difficult in the chaos) the most popular employment among the hard-core wrestling in the centre was building, in one form or another. Dale Smith, the Fool, used to be a farm worker but switched to lorry driving "when that went". Phil Coggan, the Lord, works as an engineer in an oil refinery in Immingham, 40 miles away on the coast. Yet he's no white-collar commuter-incomer: there have been Coggans in the area since time immemorial. (A Robert Coggan was shot and killed in 1628 in a confrontation between Haxey-dwellers and Vermuyden's workers.)

"This is our big day," Phil Coggan told me. "It's bigger than Christmas or New Year. A lot of people come back to Haxey for the Hood — people who you haven't seen their face all year, but they come back."

I could see their point. It might have been cold, and muddy, and a little wild for some tastes, but there was a genuine carnival atmosphere.

A huge, swaying Boggin with arms the size of sides of pork was weaving through the crowd, slapping backs in a warm-hearted kind of way. "I'm Maxi," he said, slapping mine. "That's a nice name," I nearly said, but didn't, because he had just knocked all the air from my lungs. He repeated the information twice, grinning broadly, and then — just as I worked out that he was actually saying "I'm Haxey" — moved on to share it with the woman on my left.

"Moving fast today, isn't it?" said a leather-jacketed Westwoodsidian in his mid-forties, jumping excitedly from foot to foot. I wasn't sure what he meant: by my estimate the Sway had moved about 10ft in half an hour, and had collapsed at least 20 times in the process. After 45 minutes it seemed to be pretty much back where it started. But there must have been subtleties that escaped my inexpert eye. "I think we're getting there," he continued. "Yes, yes, look at that." All I could see was a groaning mass of men, swaying from side to side, but he seemed convinced.

"Seventeen years I done it," he added, "but I can't now. Done my back in. Fell off the back of a lorry. COME ON, WESTWOOD!" he yelled suddenly, and

437

his voice was joined by scores of others, full of passion and urgency.

Others seemed more relaxed. "Come on, let's get another pint down," said one muddied youth to another, as they peeled off. Others came and went too, taking breathers or pub-breaks, or hovering on the fringes drinking and getting stuck in when the need or mood arose. "I couldn't handle all-day drinking at all," a multi-earringed, skinheaded young man explained earnestly, "until I went to university." At one point a young, drunk-looking blonde went tottering, glass in hand, into the reforming Sway, in search of some manfriend. Shrieking friends dragged her out in the nick of time.

And so it continued until darkness had truly fallen. The imperceptible drifting away of spectators accelerated, and the rate of return from pub-breaks slowed. But the Sway struggled on, edging from side to side like a vast, grunting prehistoric beast. From time to time a camera flashed near by, and you could briefly see clouds of steam rising from the centre of the beast. On the sidelines, the night had grown chilly. Those who emerged from the heart of the beast all agreed on one thing: "God, it's hot in there."

Beyond them, I could just make out the silhouette of the water-tower against the cloud-dark sky, sinister as a sorcerer's castle. It was a desolate scene, far from the comforting light and warmth of civilisation. Just men fighting in the dark on a cold hill whose once green crop had been trampled into a uniform brown sponginess, with an ambulance's blue light once again flashing in the distance. I found myself thinking of Matthew Arnold's famous lines of existential despair (from "Dover Beach") in which human existence is compared to "a darkling plain, /Swept with confused alarms of struggle and flight, /Where ignorant armies clash by night".

But then, as the mass of humanity inched its way a little faster uphill towards Westwoodside, more optimistic thoughts returned. Who would have imagined that so much energy, recklessness and sheer mad exuberance — so much hardiness, stamina and selfless physical courage — could survive anywhere in modern England, let alone in one village field? And what a miracle that it had been allowed to survive!

Elsewhere in England, children's pancake races are cancelled because the organisers can't get insurance, contact sports are discouraged for fear of litigation, even WI cake stalls are considered too risky for the sensitive British public to be exposed to them. Wasn't there a danger, I asked Phil Coggan, that someone might get hurt and sue the organisers? "The fact is, it doesn't have any organisers," he told me. "We don't organise it: we just go round collecting money for charity beforehand and sing our songs, and that's about it. It would happen whether I turned up or not. We don't invite anybody. There aren't any posters. We don't even contact the police — they just show up anyway. If people do it, it's at their own risk. It just happens."

Perhaps that is what makes the spectacle so inspiring. Hood-players cheerfully embrace all sorts of things that sensible, civilised people abhor: risk of physical injury, risk of damage to property, binge-drinking, mud, wrecked clothing, fighting. You can imagine any number of health-and-safety professionals and public-order enthusiasts clucking disapprovingly and declaring that it just won't do. But what can they do about it? How do you control something whose essence is to be ungovernable?

I understand that the Hood was banned once, during World War I, but the young men then had other ways of letting off steam in the mud. A wise vicar ensured that it was reinstated in 1919. There was also a controversial period in the early 1980s, when a house-proud landlady banned it from the Duke William for a few years — she didn't want mud on her new carpet. She lost a lot of regulars that way. Today, however, the Hood is as firmly established as it has ever been, and it is hard to see how anyone could ever stop it.

Soon after 6p.m., the Sway crossed the brow of the hill and began to move relatively quickly towards Westwoodside. The semi-riot had been going on for more than two hours; it often continues for five or six. But the later stages tend to be quick, as morale rises on one side and sinks on the others. Some of the more half-hearted Haxonians peeled away. The Sway accelerated: off the field, on to the road, into the main street. Walls and hedges have been flattened in the past when the Sway has entered a village; parked cars have been shoved amazing distances. It's not vandalism — just that the Sway has a life of its own. I didn't see any major damage this time, but it was hard to tell in the dark and chaos. Finally, at about 6.30p.m., regulars at

**440**

the Carpenter's Arms held their landlord, Bill Howden, above their heads, feet still within his threshold, to grab the Hood that his supporters in the Sway — after a brief flurry of final resistance from their opponents — passed to him.

And then, to cut a long story short, most people involved repaired to a pub, either to celebrate or to drown their sorrows, and drank until they could drink no more. It's curious to think that John Wesley, founder of Methodism, spent much of his life in the neighbouring village of Epworth and often preached at Haxey. What did Wesley make of it all, in his day? I have no idea. I'm not even sure that I want to know.

That's part of the joy of the Hood: the fact that so much of it remains a mystery. Why do people do it? There are as many answers as participants. What does it mean? Who knows? How did it begin? No one can say for certain. Some believe that the Hood as we know it has its main roots in the troubles of the 17th century. ("Fen football" was certainly used as a cover for anti-drainage violence in other parts of the fens, although most other such games died out in the 19th century.) Others have suggested a connection to prehistoric marsh-burial rituals. Locals generally prefer the "official" explanation, about Lady Mowbray's hood. It's pretty clear that something happened in Haxey in the 14th century — something significant involving land ownership; it's clear, too, that something hugely traumatic happened there in the 17th century. I assume that the current ritual reflects elements of both. The real mystery is why it has survived into the 21st

**441**

century. And the only answer I can think of is an encouraging one: that it has been preserved by successive generations of a small number of local families, because they — as individuals, as families and as villagers — chose to preserve it, believing it to be important. Even if they no longer remember quite why.

# CHAPTER
# THIRTY-ONE

# Home

My village was bathed in winter sunlight. Slate roofs shone, brown stones glowed and damp grass reflected silver slices of brightness from the fields beyond, even as the afternoon began to fade into evening. I looked out from the end of our garden. A dozen cows munched in the big, undulating pasture, their long shadows probing towards me among withered thistle-clumps. To my right, I could see through the bare trees the heavy beige stone of the church. Far away, the sun itself was sinking towards an old, indistinct wood.

Somewhere behind the trees to my left, I could hear children playing: "Forty-seven, forty-eight, forty-nine, fifty, ready or not," shouted one, as children have always shouted. "Wait! Wait!" screamed another. I had, I realised, no idea who or whose they were.

The day had grown cold, but it was a relief to be outside, after spending much of the afternoon indoors ploughing through a depressing backlog of newspapers. (You know the kind of thing: "Supermarkets admit fleecing farmers in £270m price-fixing scandal"; "Smoking ban sounds death knell for village pubs"; "Farmland bird numbers have halved since the 1970s";

"Twice as many people die on rural roads as on urban ones"; "Severn fishermen fear new regulations will wash away three centuries of tradition"; "Action urged on migrant tensions in rural communities"; "Kissing-gates and stiles under threat from disability laws". The detail varies, but the general tenor — of unravelling rural fabric — is the same most weekends.)

Out here, at least, I could see a different countryside. Mile after mile of landscape curved away, indifferent to human fads and follies, its great contours unchanged for millennia. How vast it all seemed — how old — how solid; like an enormous land-beast, asleep but warm with a life of its own.

In the big field, three hitherto unnoticed rabbits darted suddenly for the hedgerow, their fur glowing reddish in the strange light. I looked to see what had scared them and noticed the dark shapes of two adults, two children and a dog walking slowly along the far edge of the field, towards the church. As they drew closer, I realised I had no idea who they were, either. Perhaps they were outsiders: day-trippers. Or perhaps I had become an outsider.

The memory of all those months on the road (now firmly over) suddenly appalled me: all those months when I could have been here. Most of my friends thought I was dead by now; several neighbours were convinced that we had left the village. (One flatly refused to believe my denials, assuring me that she had heard on good authority that we were living permanently in France.) The obvious irony — which several people had pointed out — was that the more time I had spent searching for authentic rural life in other parts of England, the more detached I had become from my own little corner of it. While I had been chasing ghosts, my fellow villagers had been quietly getting on with being an imperfect but essentially benign 21st-century rural community — earning livings as best they could, sharing hobbies, having occasional parties, driving because they had to, chatting when the chance arose, working on various committees, charities and societies. If I had left any gap by my absence, the community had long since closed over it.

And all for what? What had my travels taught me? I knew, as I had known for years, that rural England was changing: that traditional agriculture was dying; that market forces were repopulating the countryside with a new kind of people (people like me); that the old, quiet spaces were becoming every day more crowded, polluted and urbanised. I knew, too, that, by the time my children were my age, there would — according to official projections — be an extra 10 million people living in England, and at least 3 million more rural homes and (according to a 2007 study for the RAC by Imperial College London) 43 per cent more traffic; that the climate would almost certainly have warmed significantly further; that any farmers who survived would be more likely to be growing biofuels or managing wind farms or bed-and-breakfasts than tending livestock; and, in short, that all this — the time-worn villages, the ancient fields and woods, the old men and women with deep ancestral memories of the land, the sleepy churchyards and the beasts grazing peacefully in the fields — wasn't going to last.

But I had known all that before.

I also knew, no less firmly, that all *that* wasn't going to last either: the endless economic growth, the endless travelling, the endless ripping up and rebuilding of a countryside that had, for all its faults, sustained the English for most of their history. Sooner or later, the oil would run out; sooner or later, the borrowed money would run out. Sooner or later, a rural economy based on aromatherapists, pet-groomers and life coaches would burst from lack of substance. Sooner or later, the effects of climate change would force us to rethink our relationship with, among other things, the motor-car. Sooner or later, we would need to learn anew how to feed ourselves from our own farming.

But I had suspected that before too.

And the net result? My conclusions? I knew that most of the 5.4 million people who worked in rural England were increasingly dependent for their living on their own enterprise and initiative and were proving, on the whole, astonishingly adaptable. (Who could have imagined even 20 years ago that they would be farming water buffalo in Warwickshire and llamas in Lincolnshire and ostriches in Oxfordshire and crocodiles in Cambridgeshire; and in other parts of the country, harvesting olives, grapes — in 400 different vineyards — and elephant-grass, camomile, indigo, sunflowers and much else besides, including the wind and the tide?)

446

I also knew — as I hadn't really appreciated before — that England is full of people who care passionately about various aspects of the rural past and who work hard and imaginatively to preserve them. Country traditions aren't dying because people don't care about them — they're dying by accident. Like the millions who lost out to enclosure, modern country people are seeing their rural heritage slip from their grasp as a result of economic forces they can't quite get a grip on. ("Accursed wealth!" wrote John Clare. "Thou art the cause that levels every tree, / And woods bow down to clear a way for thee.") No doubt many good things will survive. But it still seemed a shame that so little of the England my parents raised me to love would survive for my grandchildren.

I shivered. A dove flapped past in the silence. Some leafless branches stirred in a faint breeze. And then, to my surprise, the mysterious creaking rattle of a woodpecker echoed from the top of a high fir tree in our neighbours' garden. I'm no bird expert, but I'd always thought of woodpecker noises as a morning thing. I squinted upwards to look for him, but all I could see were the tree's upper branches, spotlit golden by the sinking sun. I wondered how many decades that tree had spent overlooking this spot, with the same tiny dramas being lived out on its branches by countless generations of birds and bugs. There was, I reflected, probably more continuity on that sunlit bark — more of an ongoing local story — than there is ever likely to be again among the human villagers below.

Then I thought: what of it? Is continuity really that important? Aren't there some things that matter more? One thing that I had forgotten during my travels, and that I had repeatedly rediscovered since giving them up, was how fond I was of Moreton Pinkney and, specifically, its people. I might not have missed them consciously while I was away, but each time I bumped into someone and stopped for a chat I would remark to myself afterwards how much I liked that person, and how nice it was to catch up with them.

Our villagers may not — with a handful of exceptions — be country people in any meaningful sense. They may not be *local* locals, as the Polperro fisherman put it. But they are worth no less for that: they are just ordinary, easygoing, friendly people getting by as best they can, who happen to live in the country and consider themselves lucky to do so. Some take no interest in the village's past; others are experts on it. They include — or have included since I've lived there — rich people, poor people, old people, young people, married people, single people, divorced people, widowed people, gay people, white people, non-white people, northerners, southerners, Londoners, westerners, people born in other countries and, still, a few true local people. Except in a friendly, curious way, no one cares where anyone comes from: we are a mixed bunch — as the English have traditionally been. This seems to me a healthy and stimulating state of affairs. And if that means that we are modern and metropolitan in our attitudes, well, good for us. I would be worried if — in that sense — we weren't.

448

It's true — and sad — that villagers here have a disconcerting tendency to stay for a few years and then move on, whether because of work or for family reasons or because of the strange economic imperatives of the property market. (Why flog yourself to death trying to earn a living in a post-agricultural countryside, when you could cash in your chips and start again 200 miles further from London as a rich person?) Perhaps if they had deeper roots in the soil they might move away less lightly. Then again — thinking back to my bout of newspaper-reading — there are many parts of the world, from the Balkans to the Middle East, that would be a lot happier if people valued their roots in the land a little less and their connections with the rest of the human race a little more. Which reminded me of something else.

A few days earlier, I had got chatting at the bus-stop to a lady who had recently moved into the village. Not having met before, we talked — as one does — about the twists and turns in life's journey that had brought her here. At some point she revealed that she had grown up in a village in Devon.

"Ah," I said, "like my wife."

Then she said, with some vehemence: "I hated every minute of it."

Why?

"My mum and dad were from Liverpool. So we talked funny, didn't we? We were outsiders. And they never, ever let us in."

The more I thought about this, the more echoes it struck. Hostility to outsiders is the great English rural vice. It can be found at a national and racial level (think of those right-wing ruralists of the 1930s) and at a regional level (think of those Westmorland and Cornish "nationalists") and, all too often, at village level. (I had read only that day about a hate campaign against a new female priest in the Cornish village of Paul.) It would be hard to think of a more poignant encapsulation of how pathetic and shameful such attitudes are than that single sad image: of a whole childhood blighted by a clique of local locals too small-minded to accept a family of outsiders.

I can't speak for my fellow villagers' political views, or even for their views on such issues as immigration, but it does seem to me that one good thing about us — and about new countryside-dwellers generally — is that we are less afraid of the unknown than those who came before. We may have many faults, and we may have forgotten many truths about the countryside, but we have also forgotten — I hope — the pernicious habit of hating and fearing the unfamiliar.

I wandered out of the back gate in vague search of my children. I knew they were playing in the village somewhere but wasn't sure where.

I tried the little field opposite, where a frayed and precarious rope swing has hung for as long as I can remember from a high oak branch, to the inexhaustible delight of village children. There was no sign of them, so I walked on, thinking to go round via the fields and then work my way back through the village from the far side. The light was fading now, and I could see a few twinklings of electric light where cottages poked through the trees. I picked my way through the muddy copse and emerged into the next big field. A damp mist was beginning to rise from the ditches, and there was an elusive whiff of recently vanished wild animal in the air.

How lucky I am to live here, I thought, as I plodded across the rough turf. How lucky I am that all this feels so familiar — right down to the broken branch that still hangs tantalisingly from the oak tree in the hedgerow, as it has done for years. (Below, I noticed, there was still that odd little ditch-level hole in the trunk from which I had sometimes seen little owls emerge.)

As I crossed the next stile, I saw a pale fox, fluffy and strong, drift noiselessly across the field's far edge, pause at the corner to peer through the hedgerow, and then vanish. Perhaps its ancestors, centuries ago, had performed the same routine, identical in every detail.

Still on the stile, I paused to gaze round the familiar patchwork of landscape beyond the village: fresh plough, old stubble, worn pasture, rough, boot-brush hedges, all growing vague in the twilight. A last shaft of sunlight flamed briefly on the great tower of Canons Ashby church (where Cromwell's soldiers were once besieged by Royalists), and for a moment I felt one of those instinctive pangs of loss that had prompted my travels in the first place: a sense that the countryside's past was slipping away.

But then, as I walked down towards the village, I began to feel the opposite. England was still there. All was well. The land still had its memories. And how

451

lucky I was — immeasurably, undeservedly lucky — to have encountered so many of them: to have met so many people, in so many parts of the country, who were prepared to share them with me.

At the same moment, I became aware of something curious: I could sense my village's soul more vividly here than among its cottages. This mud, this vivid spattering of blood-red hawthorn berries, that overgrown green lane up on the right, these soft, sheep-punctured pastures — these had been here for centuries. Previous generations had known these sights, these smells, these rustlings, almost exactly as I knew them now. This grazed turf had yielded beneath their feet just as it did beneath mine. Any number of shepherds, cowmen, ploughmen, horsemen, poachers, vagabonds, labourers and cottagers — and, more recently, accountants, estate agents, teachers, doctors, entrepreneurs, tourists, pensioners, teenagers and dog-walkers — must have heard church bells on the wind at this point, as I did now; glanced, as I did now, through the ragged hedgerow; caught a glimpse of old roofs sunk in vegetation; and thought (perhaps at the end of a long day's work): ah, yes, that's my village there; that's home.

An unexpected realisation warmed my blood, like a parent's hand on a young shoulder. This was my village, after all. It hadn't vanished — not yet. It wasn't perfect, but there was life in the old creature yet, and I could, if I chose, have a share in it.

The children came home dripping and covered in slime. Light interrogation revealed that it came from the stream at the bottom of Brook Street, where they had been playing with two other village children. They hadn't planned to get wet, or dirty, but one thing had led to another and somehow everyone had ended up soaked from head to foot.

Packing them off to shower and rounding up yet another load of washing, Clare scolded them, but not fiercely. Later, when they weren't listening, we agreed how lucky we were: to have children who had both the will and the opportunity to become cold and dirty getting to know the nooks and crannies of their village, when they could have been playing on their computer.

Is that weird? Is it running away from the modern world — and sentimentalising the rural past — to think in such a way? Some would say so.

But it isn't. It is just to recognise that, in an urban century, rural ways of living have value too. Without its countryside, its country people and its country traditions, England would be a quite different nation. We should embrace the future, by all means, just as we enjoy the benefits of the present; but we should also recognise the richness of our rural past and — while we still have them — celebrate those who remember it.

**Also available in ISIS Large Print:**

# The Dream

## Harry Bernstein

On a narrow cobbled street in a northern mill town, young Harry Bernstein and his family face a daily struggle to make ends meet. Amidst the hardship and suffering, Harry's devoted mother clings to a dream — that one day they might escape this grinding poverty for the paradise of America. But the regular pleas to relatives in Chicago yield nothing, until one day, when Harry is 12 years old, the family looks on astonished as he opens a letter which contains the longed-for steamship tickets.

But the better life of which they'd dreamed proves elusive. Deprivation follows them to Chicago — and for Harry, life becomes more difficult still as he finds himself torn between his responsibilities to his mother and his first love . . .

**ISBN 978-0-7531-9512-3 (hb)**
**ISBN 978-0-7531-9513-0 (pb)**

# To Hell and Back

## Susanna de Vries & Jake de Vries

As a young soldier on the battlefields of Gallipoli, Sydney Loch witnessed the horrors of war firsthand. On his return to Australia, he wrote an account of all he saw, describing his work as fiction to evade censorship. As the war ground on abroad, Sydney's book, *The Straits Impregnable*, garnered widespread acclaim. But when the publisher revealed that it was a work of non-fiction, Australian military censors swiftly ordered it to be withdrawn from sale, and the book vanished.

Now, historians Susanna and Jake de Vries have unearthed Sydney's book for a new generation. To accompany it, they have written a biography of the remarkable life of Sydney Loch: from his early years in England and Australia to the war that shaped him and led to his work in Greece and Palestine helping refugees during World War II.

ISBN 978-0-7531-5689-6 (hb)
ISBN 978-0-7531-5690-2 (pb)

# Fire & Steam

## Christian Wolmar

The opening of the pioneering Liverpool & Manchester Railway in 1830 marked the beginning of the railway network's vital role in changing the face of Britain. Fire & Steam celebrates the vision of the ambitious Victorian pioneers who developed this revolutionary transport system and the navvies who cut through the land to enable a countrywide railway to emerge.

The rise of the steam train allowed goods and people to circulate around Britain as never before, stimulating the growth of towns and industrialisation. Workers and day-trippers flocked to the stations as railway mania grew and businessmen clamoured to invest in this expanding industry.

From the early days of steam to electrification, via the railways' magnificent contribution in two world wars, the chequered history of British Rail and the buoyant future of the train, Fire & Steam examines the importance of the railway and how it helped to form the Britain of today.

ISBN 978-0-7531-5683-4 (hb)
ISBN 978-0-7531-5684-1 (pb)

# Menagerie Manor

## Gerald Durrell

"Most children at the tender age of six or so are generally full of the most impractical schemes for becoming policemen, firemen or engine drivers when they grow up . . . I knew exactly what I was going to do: I was going to have my own zoo."

This is the hugely entertaining account of how the much-loved conservationist and author, Gerald Durrell, fulfilled his lifelong ambition by founding his own private sanctuary for endangered species in Jersey, with the help of an enduring wife, a selfless staff and a reluctant bank manager.

This book about the trials and wonders of living in the middle of a zoo is a classic that will bring pleasure to those who grew up reading Durrell and to a whole new readership.

**ISBN 978-0-7531-5677-3 (hb)**
**ISBN 978-0-7531-5678-0 (pb)**

# A Handful of Earth

## Barney Bardsley

When Barney Bardsley's husband was diagnosed with cancer he was just 36. When he died, ten trying years later, Barney felt alone and exhausted. Their savings had all gone and now she must support their child single-handedly. She would just have to take life one day at a time.

She took to tending her small allotment. Fresh air, wildlife, nature's cycles of growth and decay — she found solace in it all. This is the diary of her year in the garden, beginning with January's brisk walks, nourishing soups and dreams of spring. In May comes a messy abundance of bluebells and honeybees. And in autumn a harvest of blackberries, beans and squash. Above all, she charts how her own life is slowly restored, under the garden's healing influence.

**ISBN 978-0-7531-9480-5 (hb)**
**ISBN 978-0-7531-9481-2 (pb)**

**ISIS** publish a wide range of books in large print, from fiction to biography. Any suggestions for books you would like to see in large print or audio are always welcome. Please send to the Editorial Department at:

**ISIS Publishing Limited**
7 Centremead
Osney Mead
Oxford OX2 0ES

A full list of titles is available free of charge from:

**Ulverscroft Large Print Books Limited**

**(UK)**
The Green
Bradgate Road, Anstey
Leicester LE7 7FU
Tel: (0116) 236 4325

**(Australia)**
P.O. Box 314
St Leonards
NSW 1590
Tel: (02) 9436 2622

**(USA)**
P.O. Box 1230
West Seneca
N.Y. 14224-1230
Tel: (716) 674 4270

**(Canada)**
P.O. Box 80038
Burlington
Ontario L7L 6B1
Tel: (905) 637 8734

**(New Zealand)**
P.O. Box 456
Feilding
Tel: (06) 323 6828

Details of **ISIS** complete and unabridged audio books are also available from these offices. Alternatively, contact your local library for details of their collection of **ISIS** large print and unabridged audio books.